Literary Criticism from Plato to Postmodernism
The Humanistic Alternative

This book offers a history of literary criticism from Plato to the present, arguing that this history can usefully be seen as a dialogue among three traditions – the Platonic, Neoplatonic, and the humanistic, whose first practitioner was Aristotle. There are many histories of literary criticism, but this is the first to clarify our understanding of the many seemingly incommensurable approaches employed over the centuries by reference to the three traditions. Making its case by careful analyses of individual critics, the book argues for the relevance of the humanistic tradition in the twenty-first century and beyond.

James Seaton is a professor in the Department of English at Michigan State University, where he teaches courses on the history of literary criticism, American literature and culture, and literature and law. His previous books include *Cultural Conservatism, Political Liberalism: From Criticism to Cultural Studies* (1996) and *A Reading of Vergil's Georgics* (1983). He is the editor of *The Genteel Tradition and Character and Opinion in the United States* by George Santayana (2009) and co-editor with William K. Buckley of *Beyond Cheering and Bashing: New Perspectives on The Closing of the American Mind* (1992). Seaton's articles and reviews have appeared in such publications as *The Wall Street Journal, The Weekly Standard, The Claremont Review of Books, The American Scholar, The Hudson Review, The University Bookman, Modern Age, Journal of the History of Ideas, Society, The Review of Metaphysics, Yale Journal of Law and the Humanities, Legal Studies Forum, Cardozo Studies in Law and Literature,* and *Michigan State Law Review.* He has been a frequent guest speaker at the Kirk Center for Cultural Renewal in Mecosta, Michigan.

Literary Criticism from Plato to Postmodernism

The Humanistic Alternative

JAMES SEATON
Michigan State University

CAMBRIDGE
UNIVERSITY PRESS

CAMBRIDGE
UNIVERSITY PRESS

32 Avenue of the Americas, New York NY 10013-2473, USA

Cambridge University Press is part of the University of Cambridge.

It furthers the University's mission by disseminating knowledge in the pursuit of education, learning and research at the highest international levels of excellence.

www.cambridge.org
Information on this title: www.cambridge.org/9781107514935

© James Seaton 2014

First published 2014
First paperback edition 2015

A catalogue record for this publication is available from the British Library

Library of Congress Cataloguing in Publication data
Seaton, James, 1944– author.
Literary criticism from Plato to postmodernism : the humanistic alternative / James Seaton, Michigan State University.
    pages   cm
Includes bibliographical references.
ISBN 978-1-107-02610-0 (hardback)
1. Criticism – History.   2. Literature – Philosophy.   I. Title.
PN86.S44   2014
801'.95–dc23   2013048026

ISBN 978-1-107-02610-0 Hardback
ISBN 978-1-107-51493-5 Paperback

This Book Is Dedicated to the Memory
of Roger Hornsby (1926–2009)
Professor of Classics at the University of Iowa
Exemplar of the Humanistic Tradition

Contents

Acknowledgments

I wish to thank Edward Ericson and Keith Condon for their advice and encouragement at an early stage of this project. I am grateful for the readings of chapter drafts by colleagues Stephen Arch, Sheila Teahan, and A. C. Goodson. I am especially thankful for former colleague Donald Gochberg's painstaking reading of the fourth chapter. Catherine Fox did the index quickly and expertly. The thoughtful comments of the anonymous reviewers chosen by Cambridge University Press were most helpful. Lewis Bateman of Cambridge University Press gave me the opportunity to develop my ideas into a book. I am grateful to him and his assistant Shaun T. Vigil for their good offices throughout the process from proposal to book. For their work in the final stages of that process, I wish to thank the anonymous copy editor for meticulous editing and Devasena Vedamurthi for her efficient, careful work overseeing the production of the book from the manuscript to the final print-ready files. My grown children, Ann, James Jr., Amanda, and Jeremy, encouraged and inspired me. As always, my greatest debt is to my wife, Sandra Seaton.

I am grateful to the journals listed below for permission to include material from the following essays and reviews: *Academic Questions*, "Theory with a Capital T: Cultural Studies' Assault on Popular Art," 23.4 (Winter 2010): 469–80; *Explorations*, "Lionel Trilling and Edmund Wilson: Criticism and Responsibility," XI (2009): 161–74; *The Good Society*, "Defending the Humanities," 17.2 (2008): 76–80, copyright 2008 by The Pennsylvania State University Press, used with permission; *The Hudson Review*, "Ellison the Essayist," 49.3 (Autumn, 1996): 497–502; and *The University Bookman*, "A Stirring Defense of the Conversation," Web site Exclusive (2007–2008), June 22, 2008. Special thanks are due to Philip Terzian, editor of the "Books & Arts" section of *The Weekly Standard*, for allowing me to work out my ideas in the following reviews and for permission to include revised excerpts from them in this book: "America's Critic: Edmund Wilson, Mandarin in Chief," 11.14 (December 19, 2005): 33–6; "His Master's Voice: Edmund Wilson in the Library of America," 13.36 (June 2, 2008): 35–7; "The Liberal Paradox: Why Lionel Trilling's 1950 Classic Remains Essential Reading in 2009," 14.46 (August 31, 2009): 34–5; "Heilman of Letters: Teacher First, Critic Second, Guardian of Values," 15.24 (March 8, 2010): 37–9; "The Critical Trio: Adorno, Horkheimer, Marcuse and the World They Unmade," 15.34 (May 24, 2010): 34–6; "Sticks, Stones, Words: The Academic Study of Literature Is Theoretical," 15.46 (August 23, 2010): 34–7; and "Go South, Young Man: A Critical Vision of American Life and Letters," 16.1 (December 20, 2010): 30–3.

Introduction

The Three Traditions

Literary criticism is surely not a science. Unlike practitioners of the natural sciences, literary critics so far have been unable to agree about standards of proof and methods of inquiry. The doubts Plato raised in his dialogue *Ion* persist today; not only is literary criticism not a science, it is not certain that it deserves to be considered an art or craft either (what the ancient Greeks called a *techne*), like cookery, fishing, or carpentry, where the criteria for evaluation are relatively clear and the methods for procedure, even if rule-of-thumb, can be explained and taught. In the twenty-first century, roughly 2,500 years since Plato wrote his dialogues, there are more schools of criticism than ever, although in some of the most influential academic centers literary criticism has been replaced by cultural studies. How can one make sense of the history of this would-be discipline from Plato through the twenty-first century?

A survey of literary criticism from Plato and Aristotle through the cultural studies of the twenty-first century suggests that the history of literary criticism should not be seen either as a long progress toward a culmination in which literary criticism eventually becomes a science or as a mere chaos of opinions whose only ordering principle is chronology. Literary criticism may be seen as a continuing conversation among three traditions, two of them originating with Plato – the Platonic and the Neoplatonic – and the third, founded by Plato's student Aristotle, which may be called the Aristotelian or humanistic tradition. In his *Republic*, Plato condemned poetry not only because it told lies about the gods but also because it expressed and reinforced ideas and attitudes that he considered irrational, although accepted by most of his fellow citizens. Critical schools suspicious of poems, plays, and fiction because they reinforce the prejudices and false consciousness of the unenlightened majority are Platonic in their literary criticism even if they have nothing else in common with Plato. Neoplatonists like Plotinus have agreed that ordinary people were hopelessly mired in illusion, but these critics believe that art and literature properly understood can lead adepts to spiritual heights from which the concerns of everyday life would be revealed as mere trivialities. Critical schools that are Neoplatonic in their tendency value great literature, especially poetry, as a vehicle for moral and/or spiritual transcendence of conventional common sense. The humanistic tradition, in contrast, follows Aristotle in paying due respect (although not unquestioning allegiance) to common sense while turning to literature for insight into human life rather than for knowledge about the gods or for access to a higher spiritual realm.

notion of tradition

The notion of "tradition" is loose and capacious; membership in a tradition is a matter of affinity and tendency rather than explicit philosophy or theory. A Marxist critic, for example, would belong to the Platonic tradition if he or she judges literary works primarily or entirely by the degree to which they affirm Marxist ideas. On the other hand, a critic could be influenced by Marxism and yet insist, like Edmund Wilson even during the height of his Marxism, on judging literary works by literary criteria. Believers in Christianity, Judaism, Islam, or any other religion may be Platonic or humanistic in their literary criticism. The techniques of the New Criticism, for example, have been used on occasion by some critics to claim in Neoplatonic fashion that modernist literature provides a vehicle for moral and spiritual transcendence of modern civilization. Other New Critics – or the same critics on other occasions – have used similar techniques to reaffirm the humanistic tradition's contention that literature provides valuable insight into human life in all its variety. In the United States, versions of the Platonic tradition have been dominant in the academy since the 1960s, whereas, in the earlier part of the twentieth century, partisans of modernism offered a secular version of the Neoplatonic tradition in defending the modern masterpieces. This book makes a case for the continuing relevance of the third tradition, the humanistic.

The humanistic view of literature may be seen as a middle way between the Platonic condemnation of art and literature and the Neoplatonic elevation. The humanistic tradition begins with Aristotle, was revived in the Renaissance, and includes such figures as Alexander Pope ("An Essay on Criticism") and Samuel Johnson in the eighteenth century, Matthew Arnold and Henry James in the nineteenth, and Edmund Wilson, Lionel Trilling, and Ralph Ellison in the twentieth. Although scarcely recognized in the academy, it continues in the twenty-first century in the essays and reviews of journals of opinion both left and right. The case for the humanistic alternative does not require that one agree with all the opinions of all the critics who might be considered participants in the tradition. That would be impossible in any case, since humanistic critics have disagreed among themselves about particular writers and literary works, as well as about politics, economics, social questions, and religion. They do share, however, some common ideas about literature and its relation to human life. Critics in the humanistic tradition do not share the disdain of both Platonists and Neoplatonists for the attitudes and beliefs of most human beings. Humanistic critics turn to literature for insight into human life, not knowledge about or access to ultimate reality; nor do they make extreme claims for the good or ill effects of literature's moral impact. From Aristotle on, critics in the humanistic tradition have held that literary works may arouse strong emotions but, if they are well-made, also allow for the resolution of those emotions. They contend that the influence of literature, especially in the best works, is indeed real and valuable, but usually indirect, difficult if not impossible to prove, and always subject to debate. Humanistic critics share Horace's belief that literature at its best both teaches and delights and, furthermore, that the teaching and the delighting are intertwined, so much so that one cannot be separated from the other.

The first chapter discusses the two rival traditions originating with Aristotle's great teacher Plato. The first, which received its classic formulation in Plato's *Republic*, looks at literature with suspicion, certain that almost all literary works misinform about the nature of the universe, promote false views about human life, and inflame antisocial emotions. Those who may be considered part of the Platonist tradition in literary criticism (including those who disagree entirely with Plato's metaphysics) acknowledge literature's power to influence emotions but hold that even the best-known literary works have nothing worthwhile to teach about either the universe or human life. Critics in this tradition have embraced many different theories, philosophies, and religions; their literary criticism is "Platonic" not so much because of the specific metaphysical or political doctrine they profess but because they use adherence to that doctrine as a basis for judging literary works. Participants in this tradition may share little with Plato beyond the certainty that works of literature have nothing to teach them. The second tradition, derived from the Neoplatonic interpretation of dialogues like the *Ion* and the *Symposium*, argues for the spiritual value of art and literature. Neoplatonists, beginning with Plotinus, argue that beautiful things, including beautiful works of literature, can induce a love of beauty for its own sake that leads one to lose interest in earthly desires and instead move to a contemplation of beauty in the abstract and finally to a contemplation and love of the source of all beauty, the divine. Although the two traditions originating with Plato disagree in their judgment about literature, they agree that the key issues about literature are whether it induces moral or immoral emotions and whether it teaches truths or falsehoods about the nature of the universe. Both Platonists and Neoplatonists share a tendency to believe that most human beings are ignorant, foolish, and selfish, whereas they themselves possess the moral and intellectual high ground, possessing as they do truths beyond the capacity of the rest of mankind to attain and unselfishly concerned as they are with the good of all.

The second chapter argues that many of the most influential Romantic and modernist critics, reacting to apparently widespread indifference and even hostility to literature, went too far in the claims they made for literature and especially for poetry. The Romantics and also some modernists followed the Neoplatonists in arguing that literary merit derived from, and was an expression of, the ascent of the writer to a realm of the spirit far above the everyday world bounded by common sense. Romantics such as William Wordsworth, Samuel Coleridge, Percy Bysshe Shelley, and Ralph Waldo Emerson made grandiose claims for poetry and for poets as explorers of a spiritual realm unknown to common sense. Their claims were endorsed by Victorians like John Stuart Mill and Matthew Arnold, even as the latter rejected the philosophical idealism that seemed to provide a theoretical basis for Romantic intuitions about ultimate reality. Proponents of modernism, such as F. R. Leavis, Herbert Read, Allen Tate, and Philip Rahv were not philosophical Neoplatonists, but they all felt that literature, especially modernist literature, affirmed a view of life entirely at odds with ordinary (bourgeois) attitudes. Leavis, Read, Tate, and Rahv differed from each other in many respects, but the criticism of all four intimated that one could not be thought to really grasp the modernist masterpieces unless one was ready to condemn bourgeois values and customs – that is, the way of life of almost all one's fellow citizens – with something of the same thorough-going intensity the works themselves were held to express. Literature alone affirmed truly humane values, values hopelessly compromised and betrayed by business, politics, and middle-class family life. Literary intellectuals could thus at least congratulate themselves, amid the general catastrophe, on their moral and even spiritual superiority to the bourgeoisie that surrounded them.

Now that modernism has given way to postmodernism in departments of English, middle-class morality is still disdained, but it is no longer the modernist masterpieces or, for that matter, any literary works at all, that authorize the wholesale rejection of attitudes and ways of life embraced by the unenlightened. English departments once had a specific subject matter that could be broadly defined as fiction, poetry, and drama written in English, but under postmodernism the conception of a specific subject matter for a discipline no longer applies. In the new superdiscipline of "cultural studies" there are no boundaries at all about areas of study. It is theory rather than subject matter that determines whether one is doing "cultural studies" or not. The third chapter takes account of the role of the Frankfurt School's "critical theory" in preparing the way for contemporary postmodernism both by its advocacy of the Platonist supremacy of "Theory" and by its assumption that "late capitalism" in the United States and the other liberal democracies deserved to be overthrown. Although revolution does not seem to be on the horizon for the United States so far in the twenty-first century, English studies have certainly undergone a transformation.

One illustration is the version of literary study encouraged by the "casebooks" designed for classroom study of novels like *Emma* and *The House of Mirth*. These casebooks are designed to introduce students to a variety of contemporary critical approaches, but whether the school of the critic is feminist, Marxist, New Historical, or something else, the tradition of literary criticism it exemplifies is likely to be Platonist, if the essays in the volume on Jane Austen's *Emma* in the Bedford/St. Martin's series of "Case Studies in Contemporary Criticism" are representative. The notion that theories might be judged by the extent to which they make room for the insights and perspectives Jane Austen makes available in her great novel is left for critics belonging to no school recognized in the casebooks, such as Lionel Trilling and Marilyn Butler (whose fine essay is happily included in the *Emma* casebook despite not being identified with any school), to develop.

The humanistic tradition in literary criticism surveyed in the fourth chapter begins with Aristotle and survives today in journals of opinion from a variety of political viewpoints that address readers on and off the campus who are assumed to be interested in both culture and politics, literature as well as foreign policy, ideas as well as elections – journals such as *The New York Review of Books*, *The New Republic*, *The Weekly Standard*, *The Claremont Review of Books*, *National Review*, and *The Nation*. From the viewpoint, however, of influential English graduate programs, prestigious academic journals, authoritative anthologies of criticism, and the most prominent academic theorists, the humanistic tradition in literary criticism seems to be invisible. The *Poetics* has not been a major factor in critical debates since the ill-fated attempt of the "Chicago School" to re-establish the authority of Aristotle in the middle years of the twentieth century. Alexander Pope and Samuel Johnson are all too easily classified as neoclassical figures whose criticism has only a historical interest. Matthew Arnold's attempt to connect literary criticism with cultural criticism might seem to make him an early exponent of cultural studies, but today Arnold usually appears as a spokesman for a kind of genteel humanism whose irrelevance to contemporary discussions is taken for granted. Although the critical attention devoted to Henry James's fiction has, if anything, increased in recent years, James's criticism has not been given its due, perhaps because of its conversational style and partly, one suspects, because James was unwilling to link the cause of art to a denunciation of bourgeois values. New Critics like Allen Tate, John Crowe Ransom, and Cleanth Brooks, so influential only a few decades ago, are scarcely mentioned, unless on occasion they are summoned up to condemn the New Criticism as the product of hopeless reactionaries and racists. Yet it is possible to take full account of the individual flaws and limitations of these critics and still recognize the continuing relevance of the tradition extending from Aristotle through the essays and reviews in contemporary journals of opinion that, in different ways and to different degrees, they all exemplify.

The literary and cultural criticism of such prominent twentieth-century figures as Edmund Wilson and Lionel Trilling, discussed in the fifth chapter, is virtually unknown to twenty-first century graduate students in departments of English literature and either unknown or disregarded by most of their professors. The criticism of Wilson and his peers, like that of Matthew Arnold, was driven by two seemingly contradictory notions, that "nothing was quite so important as literature and that literature was never to be treated as an end in itself," as Joseph Epstein puts it ("Matthew Arnold and the Resistance" 22). This dual commitment has been one of the defining qualities of humanistic literary criticism at least since Horace wrote that the best works both delight and instruct. The tension between the two perhaps accounts for the unsystematic quality of most humanistic criticism, whereas the ability to remain true to both commitments may be one reason why the essays of the best humanistic critics remain compelling even though the critic's specific opinions on metaphysical, political, or other issues possess only a historical interest. Edmund Wilson and Lionel Trilling were both deeply influenced by Marx and Freud, but it is not their Marxism or Freudianism that draws readers to their essays. Wilson and Trilling were undoubtedly wrong about many things, but they had enough intellectual modesty to believe that they had something to learn from literature, and it is their repeated willingness to discover new insights and appreciate newly dramatized old truths that give continuing life to their essays.

One of the strengths of cultural studies over the traditional humanities is supposed to be its willingness to treat works of popular culture with the seriousness demanded by their social and cultural importance. The sixth chapter acknowledges the limitations of makeshift classifications like "highbrow" and "lowbrow" but observes that thoughtful, unpatronizing criticism of popular songs, films, and other artifacts of popular culture began long before cultural studies and continues today. Conversely, the theory guiding cultural studies precludes treating the best works of popular culture with the seriousness they deserve because it insists on treating them only as sociological data, to be judged only in terms of their political effect, rather than as works of art in their own right. The refusal to consider works of popular culture as works of art is justified on the grounds that aesthetic judgments are inherently antidemocratic and because artistic assessments are, it is argued, inevitably subjective, apparently unlike political opinions. The essays of Ralph Ellison, however, make a convincing case that democracy does not call for the renunciation of standards but instead for a willingness to seek out excellence wherever it may be found. Cultural democracy, Ellison suggests persuasively, insists that excellence may be discerned in works outside the traditional "highbrow" genres and should be insisted on in the most unlikely places, including a small train station near Tuskegee, Alabama.

The seventh chapter takes up the ideas of Irving Babbitt and John Dewey, as well as of contemporaries like Anthony Kronman and Stanley Fish, about the proper role of the humanities, among whose disciplines humanistic literary studies is, as this book argues, central but not supreme. The case for literary study is ultimately weakened rather than strengthened by suggesting, like many of the partisans of Romanticism, that literary critics, because of their understanding of the works of Blake or Wordsworth or Shelley, can provide authoritative answers to questions about the nature of the universe, or, like many of the partisans of modernism, that literary critics, because of their knowledge of the works of Eliot, Flaubert, and Joyce, can provide authoritative answers to political and social questions. Scholars in the humanities should always be prepared to challenge natural scientists who feel qualified because of their knowledge about physics or biology to make authoritative judgments about moral, cultural, and political questions. Although the evidence for evolution through natural selection is a scientific question to be settled through scientific inquiry, the question of the implications of "Darwinism" for human life is not, nor can it be resolved by the methods of natural science. In "Literature and Science" Matthew Arnold wisely made no attempt to debate Thomas Huxley – "Darwin's bulldog" – on the scientific evidence for evolution through natural selection even as he firmly rejected Huxley's notion that "training in natural science" should replace the humanities as "the main part of education, for the great majority of mankind" (61). One way in which cultural studies differs from traditional humanistic inquiry is that the former recognizes no boundaries to the reach of its guiding theories, just as dialectical materialism once claimed the right to oversee and correct both the physical sciences and the humanistic disciplines. The humanities, as traditionally understood, make no claim to special knowledge about the physical universe, but they do assert the ability to illuminate human life in ways that the physical and even the social sciences cannot.

The humanistic tradition from Aristotle on has turned to literature to clarify, deepen, and question without entirely rejecting
the confused but capacious set of ideas and attitudes that make up
the common sense of an era or a society. Humanistic criticism,
even when considering the most ambitious works of the imagination, avoids the jargon of the schools. Some have contended that a
specialized vocabulary is necessary to transcend the categories
and attitudes associated with ordinary common sense. The willingness of humanistic critics to use the language of public discourse suggests that they see no need for such "transcendence."
Although few humanistic critics could be considered disciples of
George Santayana, their implicit appeal to the common reader
over the would-be theorist betrays the same respect for common
sense over the theories of the schools that Santayana affirmed
explicitly in the introduction to *Scepticism and Animal Faith*: "I
think that common sense, in a rough dogged way, is technically
sounder than the special schools of philosophy, each of which
squints and overlooks half the facts and half the difficulties in its
eagerness to find in some detail the key to the whole" (3). The
obligation of literary criticism to make the great works of literature more consequentially available not only to academics but to
general readers without any special intellectual equipment beyond
the educated good sense of their time has been shirked in recent
decades by some of the most acclaimed academic critics. It is an
obligation that the humanistic tradition, from Aristotle to
Alexander Pope and Samuel Johnson through Matthew Arnold
and Henry James, to Edmund Wilson, Lionel Trilling, Ralph
Ellison, and beyond, has repeatedly recognized and met.

I

Plato and Neoplatonism

Plato famously condemns almost all poetry in his *Republic*. His critique of the "imitation" practiced by the poets is part of Plato's exposition through his spokesman Socrates of the theory of the Forms or Ideas, the ultimate realities of which objects in the everyday world are but imitations, leaving the works of painters or writers mere imitations of imitations. Socrates congratulates himself at the beginning of Book X on the decision to keep virtually all poets and poetry out of the ideal city: "I also recognize in many other aspects of this city that we were entirely right in the way we founded it, but I say this particularly when reflecting on poetry." He feels "a certain friendship for Homer, and shame before him, which has possessed me since childhood," but nevertheless "a man must not be honored before the truth" (277). In other dialogues, however, Plato's view of poetry is not nearly so adverse. In the *Ion* and the *Apology*, the possibility that poetry is a product of divine inspiration is left open, and in the *Symposium*, poetry seems to be regarded as uncontroversially good.

The short dialogue *Ion* is in some ways even more important for the history of literary criticism than is the *Republic* or any other platonic dialogue, for it is only in the *Ion* that Plato focuses on literary criticism rather than on literature itself. Ion is a rhapsode, one who declaims Homer's epics in front of large crowds, gaining wealth and celebrity from his ability to entertain and thrill

hot so much in Ion

#

 # key

audiences. But Socrates does not seem interested in the devices Ion may use to entertain an audience but rather in his ability to know "what the poet means." This, Socrates contends, is the necessary basis for Ion's skill as a declaimer: "since a man can never be a good rhapsode without understanding what the poet says. For the rhapsode ought to make himself an interpreter of the poet's thought to his audience; and to do this without knowing what the poet means is impossible." Ion eagerly agrees: "What you say is true, Socrates: I at any rate have found this the most laborious part of my art; and I consider I speak about Homer better than anybody" (409). So Ion claims not only to be expert in reciting Homer, about which there is no doubt, but he also claims expertise in speaking "about Homer."

Ion is enthusiastic about Homer, and he communicates his enthusiasm to his audiences, thereby achieving success as a rhapsode. Socrates suggests, however, that neither poets like Homer nor rhapsodes like Ion owe their success to knowledge of an art or craft but instead to divine inspiration. In the dialogue's longest speech, Socrates suggests that poets make poems not by skill but through the inspiration of the Muse, whereas interpreters of poetry like Ion simply transmit to others the inspiration that was transmitted to them from the poems: "the Muse inspires men herself, and then by means of these inspired persons the inspiration spreads to others, and holds them in a connected chain" (421). Ion, like his hero Homer, is inspired but lacks knowledge of any specific art or craft. Under Socrates's questioning, Ion is unable to point out any aspects of Homer's work about which his insight is superior to those who do know particular arts or crafts, such as chariot racing, cooking, or medicine. Furthermore, the famous rhapsode cannot explain why he prefers Homer over Hesiod and all other poets. Indeed, Ion asks Socrates to explain his inability to him:

Then what can be the reason, Socrates, why I pay no attention when somebody discusses any other poet, and am unable to offer any remark at all of any value, but simply drop into a doze, whereas if anyone mentions something connected with Homer I wake up at once and attend and have plenty to say? (415)

Literary criticism as practiced by Ion seems to be simply the ability to communicate one's enthusiasm by conveying emotion to others. Literary criticism, it appears, is not an art or a craft that can be explained and taught but is instead an inexplicable phenomenon, just like poetry itself.

The dialogue thus raises the question of what it is that literary critics know that experts in other fields do not know better. More than two thousand years later, there is still no generally agreed-on answer to this question. The exponential increase in not only the quantity but also the ambitions of literary criticism since it has become an academic enterprise has made the question more pertinent but perhaps even more difficult to answer. Many critics are members of schools whose claims to expertise are derived from knowledge of fields and theories that claim to provide systematic knowledge about human life in general (e.g., Marxism or psychoanalysis) or of others that affirm viewpoints about political and social issues related only indirectly to literary criticism (e.g., feminism or postcolonial studies). Just as in the *Ion* the fisherman or the cook is better qualified than Ion the rhapsode to judge passages from Homer dealing with fishing or cooking, likewise knowledge derived from, for example, Marxist or Freudian theory supposedly enables the Marxist or the Freudian to better interpret and judge those parts of literary works dealing with aspects of human life covered by his or her favored theory. (One obvious difference is that the claims to expertise of the Marxist or the Freudian extend much further than the comparatively limited claims of the fisherman or the cook.) Similarly, the person with the correct political and social views about human sexuality, for example, would presumably be better qualified to judge passages to which questions about sexuality might be relevant than would critics who do not hold such views.

Ion concedes that he does not have the special knowledge that a cook or a fisherman would possess, but he does claim that he could be a good military general if he chose. Socrates is willing to assume for the sake of the argument that Ion is "good at generalship," but he wants Ion to tell him "when you judge of military matters, do you judge as having skill in generalship, or as a good rhapsode?" In other words, is Ion a good judge, as he claims, because he just happens to have special expertise in "generalship," or is his supposed expertise in military affairs the result of insight acquired from his understanding of Homer? Ion tries to avoid the issue by claiming that, to him, the arts of the rhapsode and the general are really the same: "To my mind, there is no difference." Ion, it turns out, is nevertheless not willing to grant that "anyone who happens to be a good general is also a good rhapsode," but he is sure that "anyone who is a good rhapsode is also, in fact, a good general" (443). Socrates politely asks Ion why, if he is indeed "the best general," he has not led any armies in battle: "Then how, in heaven's name, can it be, Ion, that you, who are both the best general and the best rhapsode in Greece, go about performing as a rhapsode to the Greeks, but not as a general?" (445). Ion's reply is unconvincing, and Socrates decides that one of two conclusions is possible: either Ion is a dishonest man who refuses to reveal what sort of art or knowledge he possesses as a result of studying Homer, or Ion simply does not, in fact, possess any special art or knowledge at all. If the latter is the case, then Ion's ability to speak well about Homer must be the result of inspiration rather than knowledge. Ion himself would rather be thought inspired than dishonest, and the dialogue ends with Socrates good-naturedly agreeing to consider him divinely inspired.

Like many of the early dialogues, *Ion* ends inconclusively. Ion, it seems clear enough, makes no attempt to deceive Socrates about his special knowledge – he simply has none. Socrates succeeds in demonstrating that Ion's supposed ability to "speak about Homer better than anybody" does not derive from any discipline or art that could be explained and justified, but the dialogue leaves open the question as to whether poetry itself and interpretations of poetry offered by putative experts like Ion should be regarded as sources of divine wisdom or as mere outpourings of strong but irrational emotion. On the side of the former option, there is the fact that it is Socrates himself, employing all his eloquence, who makes the case that poetry comes from the gods. He describes a magnetic chain of inspiration that begins with a god, moves through poets to their interpreters or declaimers (such as Ion), and finally reaches the audience. On the other hand, if Plato had wanted to offer this explanation of the power of poetry and of speakers like Ion as a conclusion, the dialogue would have ended with Socrates's eloquent speech. Socrates, however, seems more interested in the kind of knowledge that human arts or crafts can supply, leaving the implication that poets and their interpreters are untrustworthy at best, even though possibly inspired. Socrates demonstrates that Ion has not learned anything from his study of Homer that is not better understood by specialists in particular arts and crafts. Poetry itself, it appears, is not an art or craft that can be learned but rather a product of inspiration, which in turn inspires rhapsodes like Ion. Whether the products of such inspiration should be valued or discounted is left unclear, although Socrates's irony suggests the latter.

The *Apology* presents a somewhat different view of poetry and literary criticism. According to Socrates, his most prominent accuser, Meletus, spoke "on account of the poets"(91), although the accusation, as Socrates paraphrases it, says nothing about poets or poetry. Other accusers, Anytus and Lycon, represent other groups: "Anytus on account of the artisans and the public men, and Lycon on account of the orators." All three accuse Socrates of being "a wrongdoer because he corrupts the youth and does not believe in the gods the state believes in, but in other new spiritual beings" (91). Socrates suggests that he aroused the anger of these groups by questioning members of each about their claims to wisdom and concluding that those claims were vastly inflated. It is worth noting, however, that although Socrates discovers that the poets do not know all they claim to know, his inquiry does not impugn their poetry. The craftsmen, it appears, know more than the poets, in line with Socrates's observations that "those who had the most reputation seemed to me to be almost the most deficient" (83), whereas "others who were of less repute seemed to be superior men in the matter of being sensible" (85). The artisans at least understand how to make specific goods, whereas the poets are unable to explain how they come to write their works or what their poems might mean. Not that poems are necessarily hard to understand – Socrates comments that "there was hardly a man present, one might say, who would not speak better than they [the poets] about the poems they themselves had composed" (85). Nor does Socrates mean to say that poems are worthless; on the contrary, poems include "many fine things"; it is just that poets themselves possess no special knowledge but instead create "because they were inspired":

> So again in the case of the poets also I presently recognised this, that what they composed they composed not by wisdom, but by nature and because they were inspired, like the prophets and givers of oracles; for these also say many fine things, but know none of the things they say; it was evident to me that the poets too had experienced something of this same sort. (85)

Plato's *Apology*, then, accords with his *Ion* in leaving open the possibility that poems are inspired and valuable, saying "many fine things," even though poets themselves, according to the *Apology*, and interpreters of poems, according to the *Ion*, have no particular wisdom or expertise. The *Apology* does, in addition, suggest a possibility not found in the *Ion*: that literary works may be interpreted without the benefit of any special knowledge by almost anybody who happens to be acquainted with the poems in question. One suspects that the interpretations supplied by non-poets would make no claims to the sort of deep wisdom that Ion claims to possess but instead offer commonsensical plot summaries and "meanings" that merely restate proverbial observations about life.

If Plato leaves room in the *Ion* and in his *Apology* for the possibility that poetry is valuable because poets can, through divine inspiration, "say many fine things" not otherwise likely to get said, the *Republic* rejects that possibility clearly and repeatedly. In the *Republic*, Plato's Socrates does not merely question others but instead presents his own ideas about morality and about the nature of reality. These ideas contradict traditional notions about the good life and about the gods, but in the *Republic* it is Socrates's ideas about the soul, justice, and the gods that prevail. After Thrasymachus gives up at the end of the first book, no one makes a serious attempt to debate Socrates again. Glaucon takes up Thrasymachus's argument in Book II that "the life of the unjust man is, after all, far better than that of the just man" but he quickly explains that "that's not at all my own opinion" (36). Glaucon wants Socrates to explain why it is really better to be a just man rather than an unjust man who has a reputation for justice. Glaucon's brother Adeimantus, pointing out the need for Socrates to defend justice in itself, observes that when poets like Homer and Hesiod "extol justice" (41) they do so for the benefits reputation brings rather than for justice in itself. According to Adeimantus, none of the poets nor anybody else "has ever blamed injustice or praised justice other than for the reputations, honors, and gifts that come from them" (43). If the Platonic Socrates wants to persuade his listeners that he is right and "the opinion of the many" (36) is wrong, he must convince them that the poets have no special insight into human life or about the gods, since it is the poets who affirm "the opinion of the many" in the most convincing and powerful ways.

Socrates in the *Republic* is a very different character from the Socrates of the *Ion* or the *Apology*. In the *Apology*, he says that he is wiser than another only because "he thinks he knows something when he does not, whereas when I do not know, neither do I think I know, so I am likely to be wiser than he to this small extent, that I do not think I know what I do not know" (25). The Socrates of the *Republic*, on the other hand, knows a great deal. The Socrates of the *Republic* has nothing to learn from the poets. He knows, for example, that gods or god are entirely good and thus the cause of only good things and not "the cause of everything, as the many say." Homer is simply wrong to portray Zeus as "the dispenser to us 'Of good and evil alike'" (57). Socrates furthermore knows – and has no trouble persuading Glaucon and Adeimantus to agree – that "the god is altogether simple and true in deed and speech, and he doesn't himself change or deceive others by illusions, speeches, or the sending of signs either in waking or dreaming" (61), in pointed contrast to the Zeus of the *Iliad*, who does all these things, and who is himself deceived on occasion (e.g., by his wife Hera in Book XIV).

The Socrates of the *Republic* has worked out a theory about the nature of reality: Plato's famous theory of the Forms or Ideas.

Although Plato's ideas were not widely accepted in his own time and have been much disputed, although immeasurably influential, since, in the *Republic*, the theory of the Forms is accepted with little debate, as though the conclusions Socrates draws are intuitively obvious to any reasonable person of good will. In the context of the discussion in the *Republic*, the willingness of Athenians or anybody else to accept the stories of the gods told by Homer and Hesiod seems willfully foolish. Socrates scarcely has to offer any arguments at all to convince Glaucon and Adeimantus that Homer and the other poets have no special authority or wisdom, once the two brothers stop pursuing Thrasymachus's notion that injustice is better than justice and begin to listen to Socrates expound the structure of an ideal city (45). Even in Books II and III, before Socrates advances the theory of the Forms, he has no trouble getting his interlocutors to agree that poetry should be subjected to heavy censorship in the ideal city. The notion, plausible enough in *Ion* and the *Apology*, that well-known poems are worthy of respect even if their meaning is debatable, is left behind.

Poets and painters are not only imitators, but they are imitators of imitations. Ultimate reality is found in the Forms, of which everything in the world of the senses is an imitation. Painters and poets, then, are at a third remove from reality. The couch in a painting is not as much a real couch as the one made by a craftsman, which itself is an imitation of the Form of a couch. A painter can copy the look of a couch without knowing anything about the way couches are made. Similarly, Homer can depict generals and rulers of cities without having any particular insight into either generalship or the governing of cities. Socrates concludes that "the imitator knows nothing worth mentioning about what he imitates; imitation is a kind of play and not serious; and those who take up tragic poetry in iambics and in epics are all imitators in the highest possible degree" (285). Worse yet, almost all poetry imitates bad or weak people because it is much easier to imitate characters driven by their emotions than those who are guided by reason and thus possess a "prudent and quiet character":

Now then, the irritable disposition affords much and varied imitation, while the prudent and quiet character, which is always nearly equal to itself, is neither easily imitated nor, when imitated, easily understood, especially by a festive assembly where all sorts of human beings are gathered in a theater. For the imitation is of a condition that is surely alien to them. ... Then plainly the imitative poet isn't naturally directed toward any such part of the soul, and his wisdom isn't framed for satisfying it – if he's going to get a good reputation among the many – but rather toward the irritable and various disposition, because it is easily imitated. (288)

Plato's refusal to allow Homer in his ideal city seems more reasonable because the alternative, according to Socrates in the tenth book of the *Republic*, is the view that poets like Homer "know all arts and all things human that have to do with virtue and vice, and the divine things too" (281). The champions of poetry, it appears, think of the *Iliad* and the *Odyssey* as sources of infallible, all-sufficient wisdom rather than as sources of pleasure and of valuable but limited and certainly far from all-sufficient insights about human life. If lovers of Homer feel no need to inquire about either human life or the nature of reality because they believe they already possess authoritative knowledge about "all arts and all things human that have to do with virtue and vice, and the divine things too," then it is easy to understand why there is, as Socrates says, "an old quarrel between philosophy and poetry" (290).

In the postmodernist era, the notion that poetry in particular and literature in general can teach all one needs to know about human life finds few takers; but many critics and theorists, most of whom vehemently reject what they consider Plato's "logocentrism," share the view of literature affirmed in Plato's *Republic*: the great majority of literary works, including many generally considered classics, encourage antisocial emotions and attitudes (patriarchal, racist, homophobic, etc.) while providing no reliable knowledge about human life. The philosophy of the *Republic* leaves no room for judging poetry according to literary excellence; all that counts is its political and social impact. Such judgments cannot be reduced to the kind of certain knowledge that is alone valuable, and, in any case, they do not matter. In contrast, for

Aristotle and the humanistic tradition he founded, judgments of
literary quality are central to literary criticism. Contemporary
cultural studies follows Plato in considering art and literature
only "insofar as such works connect with broader social factors"
while discounting consideration of "aesthetic value." *The Norton
Anthology of Theory and Criticism* explains that, in cultural
studies

> Literary texts, like other artworks, are neither more nor less important
> than any other cultural artifact or practice. Keeping the emphasis on how
> cultural meanings are produced, circulated and consumed, the investiga-
> tor will focus on art or literature insofar as such works connect with
> broader social factors, not because they possess some intrinsic interest or
> special aesthetic value. The subsumption of literature into the broader
> cultural field explains the widespread perception that cultural studies
> poses a threat to literary criticism. (2478)

If Plato is the originator of a powerful critique of literature still
influential in the twenty-first century, he is also the source of a very
different tradition, the Neoplatonic, which argues that great art,
including literature, brings one closer to the divine. Plato's
Symposium is one of the founding documents of this tradition.
The *Symposium* is a surprising dialogue for one who comes to it
after reading Plato's critique of poetry in the *Republic*. Poets have
no place in the ideal city of the *Republic*, but the *Symposium* is
set in the home of a poet, the dramatist Agathon, who is celebrating winning a prize for his first tragedy. One of the guests
is Aristophanes, the comic poet whom Socrates blames in the
Apology for creating the false portrait of him that makes the
accusations brought against him by Meletus and the others seem
plausible. In the *Symposium*, however, Aristophanes and Socrates
do not seem to be at odds with each other at all. When Socrates
speaks, he claims to be merely repeating "the discourse upon Love
which I heard one day from a Mantinean woman named Diotima"
(173), and he offers no reservations in accepting her as a voice of
wisdom. When Diotima identifies poets with craftsmen and
describes poems as the products of an art or *techne*, a description
at odds with Socrates's views in other dialogues, he makes no
objections but simply accepts without qualification Diotima's

view that "of anything whatever that passes from not being into being the whole cause is composing or poetry; so that the productions of all arts are kinds of poetry, and their craftsmen are all poets" (187). At the very end of the *Symposium*, after everybody else has either gone to sleep or gone home, Socrates argues with Aristophanes and Agathon, but he does not take the occasion to object to Aristophanes's portrait of him in *The Clouds*. The Socrates of the *Symposium* does not raise the objections to poetry presented in the *Republic* nor does he claim that poetry is the result of madness or inspiration, as he suggests in the *Ion* and the *Apology*. Instead, seeming to take it for granted that poetry is a craft whose techniques may be understood and debated, Socrates is busy "driving" the writer of comedies and the writer of tragedies "to the admission that the same man could have the knowledge required for writing comedy and tragedy – that the fully skilled tragedian could be a comedian as well" (245). The notion that there could be any sort of "knowledge" associated with writing poetry of any kind or that there could be such a person as "the fully skilled tragedian" seems at odds with Socrates's views on poetry and poets in the *Ion*, *Apology*, and *Republic*.

In the context of the *Symposium*, the notions that poets cannot be trusted or that poetry is fundamentally irrational would seem as implausible as the same ideas seem reasonable and almost obvious in the *Republic*. Similarly, although almost all emotions seem dangerous in the *Republic*, in the *Symposium*, the speakers agree with the suggestion of Eryximachus to spend the evening making speeches in praise of Love, a proposal with which Socrates immediately concurs, saying "I do not see how I could myself decline, when I set up to understand nothing but love-matters" (99). If the Socrates of the *Republic* seems quite different from the Socrates of the *Ion* or the *Apology*, the Socrates of the *Symposium* seems a different character again.

Socrates prefaces his own speech (the last of four), however, by questioning Agathon in the style of other dialogues. After getting Agathon to agree that "Love" must always " be only love of beauty, and not of ugliness" (171), Socrates asks Agathon a question whose implications point in the opposite direction from the conclusions

reached in the *Republic* about art and philosophy. Having established that "Love" is necessarily the "love of beauty," Socrates asks
Agathon "you hold, do you not, that good things are beautiful?"
(173), to which Agathon can only assent. In the *Republic*, the good
is the ultimate reality, which can be attained, if at all, only after
disciplined intellectual effort requiring the strict subordination of
emotions to reason. In contrast, in the *Symposium*, it appears that
Love by its very nature is always in search of good things.

It is true that the "love" that may lead to a knowledge of the
Form of the good is quite different from the sort of love that
involves sexual desire or even the kind of love that focuses on a
particular individual. Those men whose love is purely physical
turn to sexual intercourse with women (199) and stop there. On
the other hand, if one is attracted to beautiful bodies, one can first
forgo an attraction to one beautiful body in particular and then
"his next advance will be to set a higher value on the beauty of
souls than on that of the body" (203). Ultimately, the seeker is led
to love no earthly thing at all but only what Socrates in the
Republic would call the form of the Beautiful, "existing ever in
singularity of form independent by itself, while all the multitude of
beautiful things partake of it in such wise that, though all of them
are coming to be and perishing, it grows neither greater nor less,
and is affected by nothing" (205). Socrates closes his speech by
repeating his belief in the ideas of Diotima and emphasizing his
own belief in the power of love rightly understood:

> This, Phaedrus and you others, is what Diotima told me, and I am
> persuaded of it; in which persuasion I pursue my neighbours, to persuade
> them in turn towards this acquisition the best helper our human nature
> can hope to find is Love. Wherefore I tell you now that every man should
> honour Love, as I myself do honour all love-matters with especial devo-
> tion, and exhort all other men to do the same; both now and always do I
> glorify Love's power and valour so far as I am able. (209)

Diotima herself has not said anything about poetry or poets,
and the kind of beauty she considers the starting point for spiritual
growth – the love of a beautiful body – seems related to sculpture
and painting in a straightforward way but to literature only by
analogy. In the *Phaedrus*, where the treatment of love and beauty

is similar to their treatment in the *Symposium*, Socrates points out that "sight is the sharpest of the physical senses," and it is "beauty alone" among all the "lovely realities . . . that may be experienced through sight" (485). But in criticizing Homer's epics, tragedies, and all poems as mere imitation of imitations in the *Republic*, Socrates assumes that poetry and painting are analogous arts. The Socrates of the *Republic* first asserts that paintings are merely imitations of imitations and then immediately extends his critique to poetry: "Therefore this will also apply to the maker of tragedy, if he is an imitator; he is naturally as it were third from a king and the truth, as are all the other imitators" (280). If Plato can classify both painting and poetry as imitative arts when pointing to their limitations, it would seem reasonable for even the most faithful Platonist to assume that the analogy between painting and other arts such as sculpture would hold when emphasizing their possibilities – specifically, the possibility that a love of beautiful things may lead to a love of Beauty itself and finally to an apprehension of the Form of the Good.

Plotinus (ca. 204/5–270), the most important and influential Neoplatonist, uses sculpture as his example in making the case that works of art should not be considered as material objects imitating other material objects but instead as the products of mind:

Now it must be seen that the stone thus brought under the artist's hand to the beauty of the form is beautiful not as stone – for so the crude block would be as pleasant – but in virtue of the Form or Idea introduced by the art. This form is not in the material; it is in the designer before ever it enters the stone; and the artificer holds it not by his equipment of eyes and hands but by his participation in his art. (73)

Plotinus rejects the argument of the Socrates of the *Republic* that the imitative nature of the arts means that works of art are thereby inferior to what they imitate:

Plotinus / REJECT

Still the arts are not to be slighted on the ground that they create by imitation of natural objects . . . we must recognize that they give no bare reproduction of the thing seen but go back to the Reason-Principles from which Nature itself derives, and, furthermore, that much of their work is all their own; they are holders of beauty and add where nature is lacking. Thus Pheidias wrought the Zeus upon no model among things of sense but by apprehending what form Zeus must take if he chose to become manifest to sight. (74)

In the Neoplatonic conception of the universe, here entirely in accord with the Plato of the Republic for whom the Form of the Good is the source of all being, Spirit or Mind is the ultimate reality, of which everything material is a lesser emanation. The principle that the source is more real than its embodiment holds true throughout the Neoplatonic universe, so that the superiority of the artistic conception in the mind of the artist to the painting or sculpture that is actually produced is merely an illustration of a universal principle, as Plotinus explains:

Art, then, creating in the image of its own nature and content, and working by the Idea or Reason-Principle of the beautiful object it is to produce, must itself be beautiful in a far higher and purer degree since it is the seat and source of that beauty, indwelling in the art, which must naturally be more complete than any comeliness of the external. In the degree in which that beauty is diffused by entering into matter, it is so much the weaker than that concentrated in unity; everything that reaches outwards is the less for it, strength less strong, heat less hot, every power less potent, and so beauty less beautiful. (73–4)

Although Plotinus uses sculpture as his example, his lastingly influential thesis that an artwork is the product of mind and therefore not inferior but superior to the material objects it may represent could be applied just as directly to literary works. In *The Defence of Poetry*, Sir Philip Sidney (1554–86), looking for any argument he could find to affirm poetry, offered a variation on the Neoplatonic notion that works of art are superior to what they imitate or represent, both in regard to the natural world and to human life:

Nature never set forth the earth in so rich tapestry as divers poets have done, neither with pleasant rivers, fruitful trees, sweet smelling flowers, nor whatsoever else may make the too much loved earth more lovely. Her world is brazen, the poets only deliver a golden.

But let those things alone and go to man, for whom as the other things are, so it seemeth in him her uttermost cunning is employed, and know whether she have brought forth so true a lover as Theagenes, so constant a friend as Pylades, so valiant a man as Orlando, so right a prince as Xenophon's Cyrus, so excellent a man every way as Virgil's Aeneas. (9)

Sidney also echoes but does not develop the Neoplatonist claim that the artwork, although superior to what it represents, is itself inferior to the conception of the work in the mind of the artist: "any understanding knoweth the skill of the artificer standeth in that *Idea* or fore-conceit of the work, and not in the work itself." Sidney immediately adds "that the poet hath that Idea is manifest by delivering them forth in such excellence as he hath imagined them" (9), an admission that would seem to nullify the original point that the skill of the artist "standeth in that *Idea* or fore-conceit of the work, and not in the work itself." But then Sidney made no claim to be a consistent follower of any doctrine, certainly not the Platonism of the *Republic* or of Plotinus. For both Platonists and Neoplatonists, virtue and knowledge coincide, whereas Sidney praises poetry because it serves "the end of well doing and not of well knowing only" (13). Defending poetry against the authority of Plato, Sidney is not above asking "whether any poet do authorize abominable filthiness," as Plato does, according to Sidney, in the *Symposium* and the *Phaedrus*. As for the banning of poets from the Republic, Sidney suggests "a man might ask out of what commonwealth Plato did banish them. In sooth, thence where he himself alloweth community of women" (39).

Unlike both Plato and Neoplatonists like Plotinus, Sidney is not willing to reject the way of life of his time and place in favor of a putatively higher spiritual ideal. When Sidney declares that "the poet is indeed the right popular philosopher" (18), "popular" is just as important as "philosopher." Poetry is not better than philosophy because it has access to knowledge philosophy cannot attain but because poetry successfully encourages human beings to do what they already know is right. For Sidney "moving is of a higher degree than teaching" (22). Poetry, because it gives pleasure to all, is able to move even "hard-hearted evil men" to virtue:

For even those hard-hearted evil men who think virtue a school name . . . and therefore despise the austere admonitions of the philosopher, and feel not the inward reason they stand upon, yet will be content to be delighted,

which is all the good fellow poet seemeth to promise, and so steal to see
the form of goodness (which seen they cannot but love) ere themselves be
aware, as if they took a medicine of cherries. (24)

Nor does he, like Socrates in the *Republic*, object to poetry that
stirs up martial emotions on behalf of a cause that is less than
entirely virtuous. Sidney considers it to the credit of poetry that it
is "the companion of [military] camps," so much so that "even
Turks and Tartars are delighted with poets" (37). And if some
who are moved by poetry remain unregenerate, the fault lies with
their hard-heartedness rather than with poetry. Sidney cites the
example of

[T]he abominable tyrant Alexander Pheraeus, from whose eyes a tragedy well made and represented drew abundance of tears. ... And if it
wrought no further good in him, it was that he, in despite of himself,
withdrew himself from hearkening to that which might mollify his
hardened heart. (28)

Although Sidney makes use of some Neoplatonic ideas in making
his case for poetry, he does not share the Neoplatonic (and
Platonic) disdain for emotions and attitudes not lending themselves to spiritual elevation. One of the most eloquent passages
in *The Defence of Poetry* occurs when he testifies to the intensity
of emotion he feels when he hears an "old song" that to Sidney
himself seems the opposite of elevated: "I must confess to my own
barbarousness, I never heard the old song of Percy and Douglas
that I found not my heart moved more than with a trumpet; and
yet is it sung but by some blind crowder with no rougher voice
than rude style" (28).
    Sidney points out that much of the Bible is poetry – "David in his
Psalms, Solomon in his Song of Songs, in his Ecclesiastes and
Proverbs, Moses and Deborah in their Hymns, and the writer of
Job" (10) – to strengthen the case that poetry "being rightly applied,
deserveth not to be scourged out of the Church of God" (8). Poetry,
that is, is validated by its use in the Bible; Sidney does not argue
that the Bible is validated by its poetry. Affirming a more consistent Neoplatonism in his *A Defence of Poetry*, Percy Bysshe
Shelley (1792–1822) took a much more expansive view of poetry

and a much dimmer view of organized religion, especially Christianity. For Shelley it is "[t]he poetry in the doctrines of Jesus Christ" (126) that is the source of whatever is true and valuable in Christianity, whereas the beliefs of orthodox Christianity are nothing more than "the rigidly defined and ever-repeated idealisms of a distorted superstition" (120). It was the "poets among the authors of the Christian and Chivalric systems of manners and thought" who prevented the world from falling "into utter anarchy and darkness," but such poets are in no way responsible for the quite real "evil produced by these systems ... no portion of it can be imputed to the poetry they contain" (125–6).

Shelley shares the Neoplatonist belief (by no means confined to Neoplatonism) that ultimate reality cannot be conveyed in words or images. The spiritual insight attained by the poet is higher and more valuable than the poem in which he or she attempts to express that insight: "when composition begins, inspiration is already on the decline, and the most glorious poetry that has ever been communicated to the world is probably a feeble shadow of the original conception of the poet" (135). All poetry worthy of the name is finally about the same unchanging truths, so that Shelley can think of particular poems from diverse places and times "as episodes to that great poem, which all poets, like the co-operating thoughts of one great mind, have built up since the beginning of the world" (124). If Homer seems to affirm different beliefs and attitudes than Dante, and if Shakespeare seems to have a view of human life and the universe different from both, that is ultimately an illusion. A true poet "participates in the eternal, the infinite, and the one; as far as relates to his conceptions, time and place and number are not" (112). Shelley asserts that "a poet considers the vices of his contemporaries as the temporary dress in which his creations must be arrayed, and which cover without concealing the eternal proportions of their beauty." Ordinary human beings, according to Platonists and Neoplatonists alike, cannot understand or appreciate beauty and truth in their fullness, so poets must make concessions to the unenlightened: "Few poets of the highest class have chosen to exhibit the beauty of their conceptions in its naked truth and splendor; and it is doubtful whether the alloy of costume, habit, etc., be not necessary to temper this planetary music for mortal ears" (117).

Although the Neoplatonic notion that great poets have privileged access to a spiritual realm unattainable by reason continues to find adherents, it is difficult to imagine greater claims for poetry derived from that privileged access than those made by Shelley in *A Defence of Poetry*. Neoplatonism answers Plato's primary objection to poetry – that it tells lies about the gods – by asserting that, on the contrary, poetry brings one closer to the divine. In contrast to both, critics in the humanistic tradition, beginning with Aristotle, assume that poetry and literature in general are sources of insight into human life but have no special access to metaphysical or theological knowledge. Consistent Platonists and Neoplatonists, meanwhile, would argue that almost the only thing worth knowing about human life is the means by which human beings can transcend the everyday world and achieve intellectual or spiritual union with ultimate reality. The great novels of the nineteenth and twentieth centuries about human beings in society, from *Pride and Prejudice* through *War and Peace, Middlemarch, The Ambassadors, Ulysses,* and *The Magic Mountain,* may be defended much more easily from a humanistic perspective than a Neoplatonic. Some of the most influential and modernist critics, however, followed the Neoplatonists in defending literature on the basis of the moral and spiritual elevation it made possible, rather than on the ground of its ability to provide insights into human life.

2

Romanticism and Modernism

Romantics and neoclassicists had profound disagreements about why literature was important and about which works were most praiseworthy, but one reason their quarrels were so intense was that both groups did indeed believe that literature was important, important enough to be the cause of passionate debate. Meanwhile, increasing numbers of scientists, philosophers, economists, politicians, and ordinary citizens either ignored literature entirely or thought of it only as entertainment, not to be taken seriously in thinking about human life and its meaning. Some of the most influential Romantic poets and critics responded to the diminishing importance of literature in the general culture not by making limited but defensible contentions about the ways literature can illuminate life but by making far larger claims for literature and especially for poetry – and poets – than neoclassicists like Alexander Pope ever had. The modernists broke with the Romantics on many issues, but, more often than not, they followed the Romantics in responding to the larger culture's indifference or hostility by making outsize claims for literature in general and poetry in particular. Partisans of both Romanticism and modernism, including those who had no interest in Neoplatonism as a philosophy, adopted a view of literature paralleling Neoplatonism's notion that the ability to create and appreciate fine art puts one on a moral and spiritual plane far above the great majority of human beings, absorbed as they are by purely material concerns. Once such inflated claims were considered on their own terms rather than accepted as rhetorical flourishes seemingly justified by the initial failure of the larger culture to recognize the greatness of works like "Ode on a Grecian Urn" and *The Waste Land*, it was inevitable that there would be a critical reaction. The modernists themselves had carried out just such a reaction against the Romantics, even as they emulated their predecessors by linking the case for literature to their own claim to the moral and spiritual high ground. The acceptance of the postmodernist dismissal of literature's claim to special importance by not only those to whom reading itself seems old-fashioned but also by scholars and critics who might be expected to be among the defenders of literature surely derives in large part from a backlash to the inflated claims for literature and especially poetry made by both the Romantics and modernists.

In one of the key documents of English Romanticism, the Preface to *Lyrical Ballads*, William Wordsworth makes extravagant claims for poetry, although his characterization of the poet is comparatively restrained. The poet that Wordsworth describes in the main argument of the Preface is an impressive figure but without any supernatural attributes or inspiration: "He [the poet] is a man speaking to men: a man, it is true, endued with more lively sensibility, more enthusiasm and tenderness, who has a greater knowledge of human nature, and a more comprehensive soul, than are supposed to be common among mankind" (751). Wordsworth severely qualifies the Neoplatonic notion that the ability to create fine art is a sure indication of spiritual superiority when he asserts that "the Poet is chiefly distinguished from other men by a greater promptness to think and feel without immediate external excitement, and a greater power in expressing such thoughts and feelings as are produced in him" (753). It is true that Wordsworth himself believed the ability to feel deeply "without the application of gross and violent stimulants" was so important that, in his opinion, "one being is elevated above another, in proportion as he possesses this capability" (746). A reader persuaded by the Preface to the *Lyrical Ballads* might nevertheless feel that a poet, although fine in his way, was not the equal of a passionate nonpoet in the ability to express strong passions through language. The best poem the former could write "must, in liveliness and truth, fall far short of that which is uttered by men in real life, under the actual pressure of those passions, certain shadows of which the Poet thus produces, or feels to be produced, in himself" (751). If the nonpoet lived in the country, the superiority would be even greater because, Wordsworth asserts, in "low and rustic life ... the essential passions of the heart find a better soil ... and speak a plainer and more emphatic language," since "in that condition the passions of men are incorporated with the beautiful and permanent forms of nature" (743–4). Wordsworth nevertheless makes such exalted claims for poetry that it is difficult to imagine how his assertions could be supported or even what they might mean:

Poetry is the breath and finer spirit of all knowledge; it is the impassioned expression which is in the countenance of all Science. ... the Poet binds together by passion and knowledge the vast empire of human society, as it is spread over the whole earth, and over all time. ... Poetry is the first and last of all knowledge – it is as immortal as the heart of man. (752–3)

Samuel Taylor Coleridge, the other contributor to *Lyrical Ballads*, waited until the publication of *Biographia Literaria*, in 1817, "to declare once for all, in what points I coincide with his [Wordsworth's] opinions, and in what points I altogether differ" (10). Coleridge raises reasonable questions about Wordsworth's belief in the moral and literary superiority of rural life, commenting that his own experience in communities where "the *farmers* are the overseers and guardians of the poor" has "engender[ed] more than scepticism concerning the desirable influences of low and rustic life in and for itself." "It is not every man that is likely to be improved by a country life or by country labors," Coleridge observes drily (45). He is quite certain that "the phraseology of low and rustic life," although "so highly extolled by Mr. Wordsworth" is not to be found in his poems. In Coleridge's view "the language of Mr. Wordsworth's homeliest composition differs from that of a common peasant" (56) in obvious and striking ways, much to the advantage of the poems themselves. Similarly, Wordsworth was mistaken when he claimed in the Preface that there is "no essential difference between the language of prose and metrical composition" (Wordsworth 749), as his own poems demonstrate. Coleridge finds that if one were to exclude "all, that a literal adherence to the theory of his preface *would* exclude, two-thirds at least of the marked beauties of his poetry must be erased" (106). Strikingly, however, Coleridge raises no objections to the extravagant claims Wordsworth makes for poetry. Instead, in the course of explaining his own poetic creed, Coleridge offers a description of poetry at least as grandiose and with even less specific meaning than Wordsworth's formulations: "For poetry is the blossom and the fragrancy of all human knowledge, human thoughts, human passions, emotions, language" (26).

Those claims for poetry that Wordsworth and Coleridge asserted only in isolated statements Shelley argued for systematically and at length in his *Defence of Poetry*. He echoes and outdoes them both in the scope of his claims for poetry:

Poetry is indeed something divine. It is at once the center and circumference of knowledge; it is that which comprehends all science, and that to which all science must be referred. It is at the same time the root and blossom of all other systems of thought; it is that from which all spring, and that which adorns all; and that which, if blighted, denies the fruit and the seed and withholds from the barren world the nourishment and the succession of the scions of the tree of life. (135)

In explaining the grounds for such assertions, however, Shelley finds it necessary to expand the definition of poetry far beyond common usage. Thus, what is generally considered poetry, "arrangements of language, and especially metrical language" is only "poetry in a more restricted sense" (113). In the larger sense necessary to justify his claims, poets are not only those who write poetry but also

the institutors of laws, and the founders of civil society, and the inventors of the arts of life, and the teachers, who draw into a certain propinquity with the beautiful and the true, that partial apprehension of the agencies of the invisible world which is called religion. (112)

Thus, Shelley can assert that "The true poetry of Rome lived in its institutions" (125) rather than in the productions of Lucretius and Virgil, excellent poets in the more restricted sense though they were. If one accepts Shelley's extension of the meaning of poetry, then it is quite possible to understand how it could be that "Poetry ever communicates all the pleasure which men are capable of receiving: it is ever still the light of life; the source of whatever of beautiful or generous or true can have place in an evil time" (124). The trouble is that now "poetry" seems to have no specific meaning at all. And, even if one agrees with Shelley's claims for poetry in the broader sense, that still leaves unresolved the status of poetry in the usual sense. The famous last sentence of the *Defence* – "Poets are the unacknowledged legislators of the World" (140) – becomes little more than a tautology when one recalls that Shelley has already defined a legislative body's law-making – at least when it makes laws of which he approves – as "poetry in a universal sense."

Ralph Waldo Emerson's American version of Romanticism made even stronger claims for the poet and poetry than did Shelley, if that is possible. Like Shelley's *A Defense of Poetry*, Emerson's "The Poet" is an impressive literary work in its own right. As arguments on behalf of poetry and literature, however, both seem designed rather to inspire those already persuaded than to convince nonbelievers. Shelley exalts a general creative power he calls "poetry" to heights that it seems virtually impossible for actual poems, or at least any but the very greatest, to reach. Emerson's own conception of poetry is similarly broad, but so elevated that he can only "look in vain for the poet whom I describe" (465). Shelley is willing to grant the title of "epic poet" only to Homer and Milton, along with Dante, but Emerson's standard is even higher: "But when we adhere to the ideal of the poet, we have our difficulties even with Milton and Homer. Milton is too literary, and Homer too literal and historical" (465–6). On the other hand, Emerson is able to find what he identifies as poems everywhere in the natural world: "The pairing of the birds is an idyl, not tedious as our idyls are; a tempest is a rough ode, without falsehood or rant: a summer, with its harvest sown, reaped, and stored, is an epic song, subordinating how many admirably exe-cuted parts" (459).

For Emerson, as for the German idealist philosophers who then seemed to be on the cutting edge of intellectual progress, "The Universe is the externisation of the soul" (453), and the true poet is one who can bring home that metaphysical idea through the use of symbols. The poetic use of symbols is based on a thesis about the nature of reality: "Things admit of being used as symbols, because nature is a symbol in the whole, and in every part" (452). Twice, Emerson proclaims that "poets are thus liberating gods" (461, 462) because it is their mission to dramatize this all-important truth. If poets differ from the mystics who preach the same truth, it is only because the latter commonly err in taking "an accidental and individual symbol for an universal one" (463-4), thus making the key mistake, the source of "all religious error," that turns individual insight into dead doctrine: "The history of hierarchies seems to show, that all religious error consisted in making the symbol too stark and solid, and, at last, nothing but an excess of the organ of language" (464). Poets, like mystics, reveal that "the universe is the externisation of the soul," but in poetry "all symbols are fluxional" (463), thus preventing intuition from becoming dogma. Poetry, it seems, reaches the same spiritual heights as religion, only it does so without all the baggage of organized religion or even those "mystics" who treat their own insights as dogmas.

But it was not only Romantics who made extravagant claims for poetry. John Stuart Mill, asking himself in 1833 "What Is Poetry?," begins his inquiry by offering a definition very much in the spirit of Shelley's *Defence*: "poetry is either nothing, or it is the better part of all art whatever, and of real life too" (103). Mill explains that "poetry" can be found not only in poems but also in painting "if the feeling declares itself by such signs as escape from us when we are unconscious of being seen" (113). Architecture can also "partake of poetry" when church structures, for example, "express, or harmonize with, the feelings of devotion" (116). For Mill, poetry is the name for "the representation of *feeling*" (104), wherever it occurs. His 1838 essay "Writings of Alfred de Vigny" offered a somewhat less expansive definition, but one for which "Poetry" still means much more than poems; it is "the love of beauty and of imaginative emotion" (209). In the latter essay, Mill argued that poems themselves should be reserved for expressing feeling too deep for prose: "Hence, ever since man has been man, all deep and sustained feeling has tended to express itself in rhythmical language; and the deeper the feeling, the more characteristic and decided the rhythm" (236).

Like Mill, Matthew Arnold was no Romantic, yet, like Mill, he echoes the Romantics in making extreme claims for poetry. In "The Function of Criticism at the Present Time," he distances himself from the Romantics, asserting that "the English poetry of the first quarter of this century, with plenty of energy, plenty of creative force, did not know enough" (262). In "The Study of Poetry," however, Arnold reaffirms and attempts to justify Wordsworth's most extravagant claims for poetry:

Without poetry, our science will appear incomplete, and most of what now passes with us for religion and philosophy will be replaced by poetry. Science, I say, will appear incomplete without it. For finely and truly does Wordsworth call poetry "the impassioned expression which is in the countenance of all science"; and what is a countenance without its expression? Again, Wordsworth finely and truly calls poetry "the breath and finer spirit of all knowledge": our religion, parading evidences such as those on which the popular mind relies now; our philosophy, pluming itself on its reasonings about causation and finite and infinite being; what are they but the shadows and dreams and false shows of knowledge? The day will come when we shall wonder at ourselves for having trusted to them, for having taken them seriously; and the more we perceive their hollowness, the more we shall prize "the breath and finer spirit of knowledge" offered to us by poetry. (161–2)

Without mentioning Shelley, Arnold implies that he had a point in claiming that whatever was valuable in religion derived from its use of poetry: "The strongest part of our religion today is its unconscious poetry" (161), Arnold observes.

Like the Romantics, Arnold praises poetry in extravagant terms; but he distinguishes clearly between poetry – that is to say, poems – and fictional works in prose, which for Arnold cannot ever reach the spiritual heights attained by great poetry. Living during the years when the novels of George Eliot, Charles Dickens, Anthony Trollope, William Thackeray, Charlotte Bronte, and Emily Bronte were appearing and in the generation after the publication of the novels of Jane Austen and Walter Scott, Matthew Arnold takes almost no notice at all of novels of any kind in his numerous essays. Arnold was prompted by the success of a French acting company in London to remind his readers in "The French Play in London" that the "high poetry" of Shakespeare and the "Attic tragedians" was something different and far superior to French novels and plays (66). Arnold objects to those "who are disposed to class all imaginative producers together, and to call them all by name of poet" (67). The very fact that "the French [are] inclined to give this wide extension to the name poet" is evidence of "the inadequacy of their genius in the higher regions of poetry" (67–8). Matthew Arnold, who so often finds reasons to compare French culture favorably to English philistinism, draws the line at any attempt to muddle the difference between poetry and prose: "If they [the French] were more at home in those regions, they would feel the essential difference between imaginative production in verse and imaginative production in prose too strongly to be ever inclined to call both by the common name of poetry." Poetry, Arnold asserts, "is simply the most delightful and perfect form of utterance that human words can reach" (68). French culture may be superior to English in many respects, but the failure of the French to recognize the gulf separating poetry from prose ensures that French poetry cannot reach the heights of the greatest English poetry:

And if we find a nation doubting whether there is any great difference between imaginative and eloquent production in verse and imaginative and eloquent production in prose, and inclined to call all imaginative producers by the common name of poets, then we may be sure of one thing: namely that this nation has never yet succeeded in finding the highest and most adequate form for poetry. Because, if it had, it could never have doubted of the essential superiority of this form to all prose forms of utterance. (69)

Like almost all the Romantics and many of the modernist critics, Arnold thought of poetry as spiritually and aesthetically far superior to prose in general and the novel in particular. His underestimation of the novel and his overestimation of the unique spirituality of poetry vitiated his attempt to formulate a convincing alternative to

the philistine dismissal of literature without resorting to the extra-
vagances of the Romantics. Arnold attempts in "The Study of
Poetry" to identify the greatest poetry by reference to "touchstones"
exhibiting "high poetic truth and seriousness," claiming to derive
this standard from "Aristotle's profound observation that the superiority of poetry over history consists in its possessing a higher truth
and a higher seriousness" (171). Arnold's notion of "higher seriousness," according to which "Chaucer is not one of the great classics"
(176) whereas the author of "Elegy in a Country Churchyard" is a
classic ("He is the scantiest and frailest of classics in our poetry,
but he is a classic" [181]) relies on a misuse of the passage from
the *Poetics* in question. Arnold's paraphrase of Aristotle's text
suggests that poetry has a moral and spiritual depth that history
lacks, whereas the text itself suggests no such thing. Here is the
passage in question, as translated by W. Hamilton Fyfe for the Loeb
Library:

The real difference is this, that one tells what happened and the other
what might happen. For this reason poetry is something more scientific
and serious than history, because poetry tends to give general truths while
history gives particular facts.
    By a "general truth" I mean the sort of thing that a certain type of man
will do or say either probably or necessarily. (35)

Whether one feels that Fyfe's "more scientific" is exactly the right
choice as a translation for *philosophoteron* ("more philosophical"
is an obvious alternative), it is clear that Aristotle's text carries no
suggestion that there is anything particularly moral or spiritual
about poetry's ability to provide the kind of "general truths" that
history cannot. It is Arnold and not Aristotle who believed that
greatness in poetry is best identified by the tone of high moral
seriousness that marks "the perfect poetic accent" (185).
    In making this claim, Arnold was closer to the Romantics and
the more extreme modernists than to either Aristotle or the central
humanistic tradition. Neither the Romantic critics nor the more
zealous partisans of modernism were much interested in learning
about human life in all its variety – including even the life of the
middle class – from literature. Instead, they turned to literature

and especially to poetry to find a moral and spiritual stance that allowed them to confront a world that seemed hostile to their deepest intuitions. Perhaps that is why neither the Romantics nor many modernists were able to appreciate the achievements of prose fiction and especially the novel. Most novels, including many of the greatest nineteenth-century novels, provide little assistance in achieving the kind of spiritual elevation that religion had once made possible. Lyric poetry, on the other hand, might at least briefly lift one up to a spiritual realm far above a world apparently devoted to material concerns. Arnold himself famously supposed that poetry would eventually take the place of religion:

> The future of poetry is immense, because in poetry, where it is worthy of its high destinies, our race, as time goes on, will find an ever surer and surer stay. There is not a creed which is not shaken, not an accredited dogma which is not shown to be questionable, not a received tradition which does not threaten to dissolve. Our religion has materialized itself in the fact, in the supposed fact; it has attached its emotion to the fact, and now the fact is failing it. But for poetry the idea is everything; the rest is a world of illusion, of divine illusion. Poetry attaches its emotion to the idea; the idea *is* the fact. The strongest part of our religion today is its unconscious poetry. ("The Study of Poetry" 161)

The best-known statement in this passage is the one that seems most mistaken, the prediction that "as time goes on" poetry will become increasingly more important. The reasons that poetry has lost the public significance that it had in Arnold's day are many, and the most important have nothing to do with literary criticism. Conversely, it is all too easy to go from observing, unexceptionably, that, in the 130 years since "The Study of Poetry" appeared, poetry has not had the "immense" importance Arnold envisioned for it to assuming that poetry and literature have no role at all to play in contemporary culture.

The most influential modernist through the first half of the twentieth century, T. S. Eliot, rejected Arnold's invitation to accept literature as a substitute for religion. For Eliot, "The total effect of Arnold's philosophy is to set up Culture in the place of Religion, and to leave Religion to be laid waste by the anarchy of feeling"

("Arnold and Pater," 387). In Eliot's opinion "the humanistic point of view is auxiliary and dependent upon the religious point of view" ("The Humanism of Irving Babbitt," 427). English and American modernists made claims on behalf of poetry and literature scarcely less expansive than those of the Romantics or of Victorians like Matthew Arnold and Mill who declared poetry "the better part of all art whatever, and of real life too," but the modernists did not present literature as an alternative to religion. Many modernist critics did, however, think of art and literature as representing the only valid alternative to the values promoted by every other institution and seemingly shared by the great majority of the population. Some modernists, like Eliot, saw literature as a lesser ally of religion, some did not, but the great majority were certain that literary works provided access to a view of the world directly contradictory and vastly superior to the worldview of their non-literary brethren. This certainty was shared by English critics as different as F. R. Leavis and Herbert Read and by American critics such as the Southern conservative Allen Tate and the New York radical Philip Rahv.

F. R. Leavis's *New Bearing in English Poetry* (1932), was one of the first and most influential book-length arguments for the modernist poetry of T. S. Eliot and Ezra Pound. Leavis began his argument by declaring in the book's first sentence that "Poetry matters little to the modern world" (5). On the one hand, Leavis suggests that "poetry must be adequate to modern life" even though the sentiment is a cliché that "has often been said" (22). Leavis praises T. S. Eliot's work because "We have here, in short, poetry that expresses freely a modern sensibility, the ways of feeling, the modes of experience, of one fully alive in his own age" (76). Eliot's poetry is all the stronger because "its staple idiom and movement derive immediately from modern speech" (82). Yet a first-rate poet like T. S. Eliot cannot help being first and foremost "aware of a hostile and overwhelming environment" (104). Leavis praises unreservedly Ezra Pound's "Hugh Selwyn Mauberley," in large part because of its evocation of a view of "the modern world" shared by the critic: "the modern world of mass-production and leveling-down, a world that has destroyed the traditions and is hostile, not only to the artist, but to all distinction of spirit" (141). The view of the modern world Leavis here attributes to Pound is almost identical to the one he offers as his own in the concluding paragraphs of *New Bearings*, a view in which modernist art, especially poetry, stands in lonely, unqualified opposition to everything "below," especially the ideas and attitudes of those unmoved by modernist art and therefore necessarily incapable of appreciating "the finer values":

For not only poetry, but literature and art in general, are becoming more specialized: the process is implicit in the process of modern civilization. The important works of to-day, unlike those of the past, tend to appeal only at the highest level of response, which only a tiny minority can reach, instead of at a number of levels. On the other hand, the finer values are ceasing to be a matter of even conventional concern for any except the minority capable of the highest level. Everywhere below, a process of standardization, mass-production and leveling-down goes forward, and civilization is coming to mean a solidarity achieved by the exploitation of the most readily released responses. So that poetry in the future, if there is poetry, seems likely to matter even less to the world.
Those who care about it can only go on caring. (213–14)

Whereas F. R. Leavis was a polemicist who, despite his importance as a literary critic, always remained a dissident in the larger culture, Herbert Read (1893–1968) became so respectable that he was eventually awarded a knighthood (in 1963) for "services to literature." Certainly, Read was one of the most prolific and influential critics in England in the first half of the twentieth century. A respected modernist poet himself, as a critic Read was from the 1920s on a tireless and persuasive spokesman for modernist art and literature, publishing many books and appearing in prestigious journals such as the BBC's *Listener* and T. S. Eliot's *Criterion*. Reviewing an anthology of Read's essays in 1945, George Owell commented that "It would be difficult to over-praise Read as a popularizer and as a champion of unfashionable causes. I suppose no one in our time has done more to encourage young poets and keep the British public informed about artistic developments in Europe" (404). The "unfashionable causes" Read championed, specifically modernist art and poetry, were already becoming very much the fashion when Orwell wrote. Even in 1945, Read's criticism seemed to Orwell to suffer from its undiscriminating acceptance of all new literary and artistic movements. Orwell judged that Read's

purely critical work has a sort of diffuseness, a wateriness, which comes from being too open-minded, too charitable, too civilized, too anxious to keep abreast of modern thought and remain in touch with all movements simultaneously, instead of giving expression to the vehement likes and dislikes which must be present in his mind, just as much as in any other writer's. (405)

If Read was unable or unwilling to make harsh judgments about contemporary art and literature, he was more than willing to denounce almost everything else about his own society. For Read, as for other partisans of modernism, the championing of the values associated with modernist art and literature implied a condemnation of virtually every other aspect of modern life, especially all those people, the great majority, who did not share the same outlook. In *Anarchy and Order*, a collection of his writings defending anarchism, Read emphasized that "The same philosophy reappears in my literary criticism and in my poetry" (9). This "philosophy" conflated moral and aesthetic dissatisfaction with society with contempt for most of Read's fellow citizens, both rich and poor: "I despise this foul industrial epoch – not only the plutocracy which it has raised to power, but also the industrial proletariat which it has drained from the land and proliferated in hovels of indifferent brick" (58–9). Since "the existing social order is outrageously unjust," those who fail to follow Read's example and revolt must be "either morally insensitive or criminally selfish" (17). If Read's anarchism attracted few adherents, it was not because there were any flaws in his argument but rather because all too many people "ask for nothing better than to be sheep under a shepherd, soldiers under a captain, slaves under an overseer" (37). A true poet, however, was no sheep but instead an "agent of destruction": "To make life, to insure progress, to create interest and vividness, it is necessary to break form, to distort pattern, to change the nature of our civilization. In order to create it is necessary to destroy; and the agent of destruction in society is the poet" (58). Read himself proclaimed that "I shall endeavor to live as an individual, to develop my individuality; and if necessary I shall be isolated in a prison rather than submit to the indignities of war and collectivism" (59). Instead of being sent to prison, Read was given a knighthood, another indication that the blanket denunciations of the social order by modernist critics served more to establish modernist art and literature on a putative moral high ground than to provide any serious challenge to the political and economic arrangements they deplored so vehemently.

In the United States, the championing of modernist literature went hand in hand with condemnation of what was often called, derisively, "bourgeois culture." Philip Rahv's political stances changed over the years, but he never stopped claiming, both explicitly and by implication, that the price of a sympathetic understanding of modernist literature was a rejection of middle-class – "bourgeois" – values. Rahv was the dominant figure among the ex-Communist defenders of literary modernism at *Partisan Review*, which he co-edited with William Phillips. In "Twilight of the Thirties," a 1939 reassessment of the relations between literature and politics, Rahv praises modernism and the avant-garde while retaining a Marxist vocabulary and analysis. The opening sentences of the essay illustrate his perspective: "To speak of modern literature is to speak of that peculiar social grouping, the intelligentsia, to whom it belongs. The intelligentsia, too, is a modern product, created by the drastic division of labor that prevails under capitalism" (320). Rahv's disillusionment with the Soviet Union and the Communist Party does not lead him to discover formerly hidden merits in capitalism. He finds American society "intrinsically hostile, and at best indifferent, to the rights of the human personality and to everything imaginative, gratuitous, natural, and commercially devoid of advantages" (321). Given such a society, the seemingly nihilistic or antisocial aspects of modernist art appear as tokens of moral virtue: "it is precisely its integrity which is to a large extent synonymous with the 'antisocial' character of so much modern art" (322). If the old avant-garde, with its "proud self-imposed isolation of a cultivated minority" (321) is over, Rahv hopes that it may be reconstituted in "a new vanguard group whose members, not frightened by isolation, know how to swim against the current" (323–4). It would be best if a new "sufficiently organic, active, and broad revolutionary movement" would take the place of the discredited Communist Party, but if that is lacking the only choice of the artist with integrity is "to utilize the possibilities of individual and group secession from, and protest against, the dominant values of our time" (324). After World War II, Rahv no longer looked for a "broad revolutionary movement," but his contempt for the outlook of middle-class nonartists remained. Even in his contribution to "Our Country and Our Culture," the 1952 *Partisan Review* symposium marking a rapprochement between *Partisan* intellectuals and American society, Rahv continued to praise the avant-garde for "resisting the bourgeois incentives to accommodation" and to insist on its moral stature: "For what the avant-garde actually represents historically, from its very beginnings in the early nineteenth century, is the effort to preserve the integrity of art and the intellect amidst the conditions of alienation brought on by the major social forces of the modern era" (182).

In a 1980 *Partisan Review* essay discussing *Essays on Literature and Politics 1932–1972*, a posthumous collection of Rahv's essays, Christopher Lasch offered a handsome tribute to the achievements of Rahv and his journal:

> He and other editors of *Partisan Review* earned from American intellectuals a lasting debt of gratitude by exposing the totalitarian character of Soviet communism; attacking the sentimental nationalism associated with the culture of the Popular Front; analyzing the American literary tradition with a rare combination of sympathy and detachment, neither ignoring nor exaggerating its accomplishments; and, not least, helping to introduce American readers to the classics of European modernism. (184)

Rahv's assertion that literary criticism should be independent of any party line was an act of intellectual and moral courage at a time when the prestige of the Soviet Union and Communism was at its height. Lasch observes, however, that Rahv's defense of modernism was tied to his continuing belief in the Leninist notion of the vanguard party whose right to rule derives from its superior insight into history. If the official Communist Party had become a tool of a totalitarian dictatorship, then another vanguard had to be found:

> Rahv in his continuing search for "a new vanguard group" had to turn to the "modern artist," whose long-standing feud with the bourgeoisie he now tried to construe into the advance guard of a revolutionary culture. Rahv's commitment to modernism thus grew out of his unexamined commitment to Leninism. Both rested on the assumption that literary and political vanguards alone can lead the masses to the promised land. (188)

The criticism of the *Partisan Review* school headed by Rahv repeatedly intimated that the modernist masterpieces revealed the hollowness of middle-class morality. As Frederick Crews noted in a *New York Review of Books* essay on *Essays on Literature and Politics*, "What united Marx and Proust, Nietzsche and Joyce, Freud and Camus, was their equidistance from Iowa" (4). But if it was clear that middle-class standards were to be disdained, it was none too clear what standards, if any, would take their place. In a 1966 interview with the Brandeis undergraduate literary magazine *Folio*, Rahv deplored the prominence of "hipsters, militant homosexuals, and pornographers, who claim the title of avant-garde even while trying to 'make it' in a big way in the worldly world" (75). But if bourgeois morality was indeed beneath contempt, as modernist literature supposedly demonstrated, wasn't any and all defiance of its standards somehow justified? And if bourgeois moral standards could not be justified, then what principles of morality remained? The Marxism to which "all his life he was sternly faithful," in Mary McCarthy's words (146), had no answer, nor did a modernism whose only morality was a rejection of bourgeois standards. Feeling compelled to point out to the student interviewer that "The prohibition of murder is not a mere convention of society, a pious prejudice or some kind of bourgeois leftover," Rahv was unable to explain what moral principles made murder wrong; he merely remarked that the prohibition against murder "has existed in every society, however primitive" (78). Rahv's inability to offer a more convincing rationale suggests that Christopher Lasch had a point in observing that Rahv's commitment to a vanguard sensibility in both literature and politics made it impossible for him to notice "that the modernist movement contained at least the potential for a postmodernist attack on mind" (193).

If Philip Rahv felt that the modernist masterpieces provided the literary counterpart to Marxism's political and economic critique of capitalist society, Allen Tate argued even more passionately that literary modernism demonstrated the fundamental inhumanity of the system he pejoratively characterized as "finance capitalism" ("The Function of the Critical Quarterly" 54) and "monopoly capitalism" ("The Present Function of Criticism" 200). If Rahv was contemptuous of the bourgeoisie, Tate was scornful of those who hoped for "the realization of a *bourgeois* paradise of gadgets and of the consumption, not of the fruits of the earth, but of commodities" ("The Present Function of Criticism" 199). Rahv hoped for a revival of Marxism, Tate for a religious revival, but both were equally ready to condemn any literary work that seemed to be "the expression of a middle-class culture" ("The Present Function of Criticism" 201).

For Tate, the literary and the religious perspectives were in important ways one and the same. In his 1952 essay "The Man of Letters in the Modern World," the alienation of the man of letters from the modern world is caused by the modern world's rejection of religion and, therefore, of literature as well. For Tate, "the battle is now between the dehumanized society of secularism ... and the eternal society of the communion of the human spirit" (4–5). Poetry and literature make "communion" possible and are thus entirely opposed to the "secularism" of the modern world: "What we, as literary men, have been asked to support, and what we have rejected, is the action of society as *secularism* [emphasis in original], or the society that substitutes means for ends" (6). In Tate's view, the literature of the nineteenth century and the first half of the twentieth should be understood as a sustained protest against the evils of "secularism."

The roll call of the noble and sinister characters, our ancestors and our brothers, who exemplify the lesson, must end in a shudder: Julien Sorel, Emma Bovary, Captain Ahab, Hepzibah Pyncheon, Roderick Usher, Lambert Strether, Baron de Charlus, Stephen Dedalus, Joe Christmas – all these and more, to say nothing of the precise probing of their, and our, sensibility, which is modern poetry since Baudelaire. Have men of letters perversely invented these horrors? They are rather inevitable creations of a secularized society, the society of means without ends, in which nobody participates with the full substance of his humanity. (8)

In the same essay Tate provides another list making the same point:

Blake's "hapless soldier's sigh," Poe's "tell-tale heart," Rimbaud's nature careening in a "drunken boat," Eliot's woman "pulling her long black hair," are qualities of the life of Baudelaire's *fourmillante Cité*, the secularism of the swarm, of which we are the present citizens. (7)

In a 1968 essay, "Poetry Modern and Unmodern," Tate backs up the authority of Baudelaire with that of Herbert Read, whose knighthood surely certifies his superiority to the vulgarity with which he finds himself surrounded: "It is the civilization of the *fourmillante Cité* recently described by Sir Herbert Read as the 'most vulgar civilization in the history of mankind'" (235).

"The Man of Letters in the Modern World" suggests in passing and without documentation that "the black slaves of the Old South," unlike "the white slaves of Russia," possessed at least "the inalienable right to talk back" (15). The emphasis on the connection between religion and literature and the uncritical view of slavery both link the 1952 essay to Tate's contribution to *I'll Take My Stand*, the 1930 anthology defending "The South and the Agrarian Tradition," in the words of its subtitle. His essay was titled "Remarks on the Southern Religion" – but Tate's defense of religion on the grounds that it provides a fuller, more complete way of viewing reality than the abstractions used by science and technology could easily be taken for a defense of literature. The following quotation from "Remarks on the Southern Religion" substitutes "literature" for "religion," with the result that the passage is all the more convincing (words changed are in brackets):

For abstraction is the death of [literature] no less than the death of anything else. [Literature], when it directs its attention to the horse cropping the blue-grass on the lawn, is concerned with the whole horse, and not with (1) that part of him which he has in common with other horses, or that more general part which he shares with other quadrapeds or with the more general vertebrates; and not with (2) that power of the horse which he shares with horsepower in general, of pushing or pulling another object. [Literature] pretends to place before us the horse as he is.

Since this essay is not [literature], but a discussion of it, it does not pretend to put before you the complete horse. It does pretend to do the following: to show that the complete horse may be there in spite of the fact that this discussion cannot bring him forth. In other words, there is a complete and self-contained horse in spite of the now prevailing faith that there is none simply because the abstract and scientific mind cannot see him.

The modern mind sees only half of the horse – that half which may become a dynamo, or an automobile, or any other horsepowered machine. If this mind had much respect for the full-dimensioned, grass-eating horse, it would never have invented the engine which represents only half of him. The [literary] mind, on the other hand, has this respect; it wants the whole horse, and it will be satisfied with nothing less. (156–7)

Whether Tate is discussing religion or literature or the connection between the two, his argument on behalf of apprehending the fullness of lived reality rather than mere abstractions is an attractive and powerful one. And yet this preference for the concrete over the abstract, surely defensible and even admirable in literary criticism, becomes, when transposed into cultural criticism, a basis for not only condemning capitalism but also for defending slavery. The most serious charge made against the Agrarians' defense of the South has always been that it amounted to, or at least implied, a defense of segregation and slavery. In many cases, the defense was quite explicit. In "What Is a Traditional Society?" (1936), Tate argued for the moral superiority of the antebellum South to a market society based on free labor. According to Tate, a social order based on what he called "finance-capitalist economics" is intrinsically "hostile to the perpetuation of a moral code" (70), whereas a society based on slave labor is not. Indeed, Tate asserted that in a traditional society like the Old South, "it is possible to behave morally all the time," adding, "It is this principle that is the center of the philosophy of Jefferson" (69). Here, Tate would seem to have differed from the Jefferson who observed in his *Notes on the State of Virginia* "The whole commerce between master and slave is a perpetual exercise of the most boisterous passions, the most unremitting despotism on the one part, and degrading submissions on the other. . . . I tremble for my country when I reflect that God is just" (288–9).

It is hard to deny that there is a good deal that is attractive about the notion of a traditional society that includes, as Glenn Arbery puts it in his introduction to *The Southern Critics*,

such things as attachment to place from generation to generation, the traditions and communities that sprang up around such attachments, attunement to the rhythms of nature and its contingencies, strong bonds of kinship, a sense of the sacred, and indifference to an abstract idea of wealth understood in terms of monetary values. (2)

It is also undeniable that the technological change and personal mobility encouraged by the free market weaken the attachments and bonds Arbery and the Agrarians rightly prize. One of the greatest proponents of free markets, Friedrich Hayek, freely acknowledged in *The Fatal Conceit* that the rules that make possible the "extended human order created by a competitive market" (7) require the painful suppression of instincts formed during the long epoch when the typical unit in which human beings or their ancestors lived was "the face-to-face troop" (17). In modern society, the ethics appropriate to family life do not work for society as a whole. Life in a clan or tribe called for solidarity within the group and "instinctual aggressiveness toward outsiders" (13). The marketplace, however, does not divide people into friends or enemies but instead requires equality before the law for all. While noting and even emphasizing the deep-seated emotional appeal of using the ethics of the family, clan, or tribe to condemn contemporary capitalist society (an appeal that politicians of both extreme left and right have exploited), Hayek observed that the attempt to regulate a modern economy according to family or tribal ethics would inevitably "doom a large part of mankind to poverty and death" (27).

Philosophers or intellectuals, Hayek pointed out, are most in thrall to instinctive longings when they concoct ideal socialist or communist societies. For Hayek "atavistic longing after the life of the noble savage is the main source of the collectivist tradition" (19). The Agrarians saw themselves as opponents of rationalistic left-wing intellectuals; a number preferred the title "Tracts Against Communism" to "I'll Take My Stand." Yet just as left-wing intellectuals condemned capitalism for its moral flaws while ignoring or even justifying the atrocities of communist regimes, the Agrarians vehemently condemned industrial technology, and what Allen Tate called "finance-capitalist economics" while accepting or even justifying slavery and segregation. The leftists idealized Soviet Russia and the Agrarians the Old South, but both groups yearned for a society whose unity would eliminate the frustrations and alienation that accompany the unprecedented wealth and opportunities made possible by developed capitalist societies.

Art and literature have powerfully dramatized the conflicts, frustrations, and alienation of modern life, but it would be a mistake to take the guidance of literary intellectuals urging either a leap into an (imagined) utopia of the future or a return to a (largely mythical) past. The poetry of Wordsworth, Coleridge, Keats, and Shelley retains its power to teach and delight, just as the works of moderns like Joyce, Mann, and Eliot continue to reward our attention in the twenty-first century. The great works of the Romantic and modernist periods do not need to be defended by exaggerated claims for literature nor by denouncing every aspect of society that seems indifferent to or unaffected by literature. Defenders of Romanticism and modernism often wrote as though writers and sympathetic critics constituted a sect whose minority status only demonstrated the moral and intellectual nullity of the overwhelming majority. Romantics and modernists invoked the prestige of great literature to denounce technology and capitalism, sometimes democracy or the modern world in general, and almost always middle-class or bourgeois culture. Agreeing almost entirely with this critique, postmodernist theorists have gone one step further in refusing to grant literature an exemption from the overall condemnation. In English departments in the United States, this refusal has resulted in the rise of "cultural studies," a putatively all-inclusive superdiscipline founded on the denial of "literature" as an independent field of study with its own standards of judgment. Unwilling to make value judgments about literary or artistic quality, the theorists whose works provide the rationale for cultural studies are more than ready to condemn bourgeois culture, capitalism, and what they consider American "imperialism." Although Marxism is an influential ingredient in the theoretical framework of twenty-first-century cultural studies, it is not Rahv's old-fashioned Marxism, the Marxism of Lenin and Trotsky, or even the Marxism of Marx and Engels. The Marxism that informs contemporary postmodernism and cultural studies derives instead from the Frankfurt School of Theodor Adorno, Max Horkheimer, and Herbert Marcuse.

3

Theory and Cultural Studies

The Frankfurt School, whose major figures include Max Horkheimer (1895–1973), Theodor Adorno (1903–1969), and Herbert Marcuse (1898–1979), were avowedly Marxist theorists who developed their "critical theory" first in Frankfurt during the Weimar Republic and then in the United States, where they sought refuge after the Nazis came to power. Horkheimer and Adorno returned to Frankfurt in 1949, whereas Marcuse remained in the United States, gaining notoriety in the late 1960s and early '70s as a mentor and supporter of the New Left. The critical theory of the Frankfurt School accepted the orthodox Marxist belief that capitalism could and should give way to socialism. The critical theorists, however, rejected some of the basic tenets of Marxism, most notably the key thesis that the industrial working class was the revolutionary agent destined to overthrow capitalism. According to the Frankfurt School, socialist revolution in the West had become a practical impossibility but remained a moral necessity. The originality of the critical theorists derived from their willingness to ignore or discount all the economic, social, and political gains achieved in the twentieth century by the vast majority of the populations of Western democracies in favor of what Thomas Wheatland succinctly characterizes as "a nightmare vision of late capitalism, in which reason had become obliterated, freedom had been surrendered, and history could finally be perceived as a steady descent into barbarism" (*The Frankfurt School in Exile* 292).

In works such as Adorno and Horkheimer's *Dialectic of Enlightenment* (1944) and Marcuse's *One-Dimensional Man* (1964), the critical theorists asserted that Western societies in general and the United States in particular were totalitarian regimes comparable, despite democratic institutions and legal guarantees of freedom of speech and religion, to Nazi Germany and Stalinist Russia. Marcuse explained this strikingly counter-intuitive judgment in *One-Dimensional Man*:

> By virtue of the way it has organized its technological base, contemporary industrial society tends to be totalitarian. For "totalitarian" is not only a terroristic political coordination of society, but also a non-terroristic economic-technical coordination which operates through the manipulation of needs by vested interests. It thus precludes the emergence of an effective opposition against the whole. Not only a specific form of government or party rule makes for totalitarianism, but also a specific system of production and distribution which may well be compatible with a "pluralism" of parties, newspapers, "countervailing powers," etc. (3)

According to Marcuse, free speech as practiced in the United States and other Western democracies was not only no barrier to totalitarianism, it was also an impediment to the emergence of the ideal society in which reason would rule. In place of the liberal conception of legal freedom of speech that Marcuse denounced as "repressive tolerance," he proposed "liberating tolerance": "Liberating tolerance, then, would mean intolerance against movements from the Right, and toleration of movements from the Left." This kind of selective tolerance was justified because "true pacification requires the withdrawal of tolerance before the deed, at the stage of communication in word, print, and picture" ("Repressive Tolerance" 109). Just as Plato had insisted on the necessity of censorship in his ideal Republic, Marcuse argued that suppression of free speech was required in the twentieth century for the establishment of what he considered true freedom. Arguing that "the answer to Plato's educational dictatorship is the democratic educational dictatorship of free men," Marcuse commented that in a society (such as the

United States, in his view) that "has entered the phase of total administration and indoctrination," those who could be considered truly free and thus properly eligible to participate in political decision making "would be a small number indeed, and not necessarily that of the elected representatives of the people" ("Repressive Tolerance" 106).

Most proponents of cultural studies today would reject critical theory's characterization of almost all popular culture as "mass culture," but they do share the Frankfurt School's belief in the moral necessity for radical transformation of the Western capitalist democracies, a belief grounded not on the empirically testable claims about the economic "laws" on which the mature Marx rested his case but instead on concepts such as "alienation" and "reification," as well as on visions of an ideal socialism, notions for which empirical verification is impossible and irrelevant. Its supporters characterize the relation of cultural studies to Marxism in a variety of ways. According to Simon During, cultural studies is a form of "postmarxist theory" (33). *The Norton Anthology of Theory and Criticism* (NATC) refers to its "residual Marxism" (2479), while Hayden White asserts that "cultural studies is a neo-Marxist activity" (264). James Carey points to "obligatory Marxism or neomarxism" as the "background for ... cultural studies as they today are conventionally understood" (14). Critical theory's influence on the theories that provide the rationale for contemporary cultural studies is displayed not only in the field's obligatory leftism but perhaps even more importantly in the belief in the explanatory power of theory and the concomitant assurance that those who have mastered the theory are competent to make meaningful pronouncements on politics, economics, art, literature, and any other field of human activity. Their confidence in the supremacy of theory is another way in which both the Frankfurt School and proponents of cultural studies reveal how much they owe to the example of Plato.

In contemporary theory, Plato usually is presented as the source of the logocentrism and foundationalism that is at the root of all that is wrong with Western culture, but in practice, the politically engaged theorists whose ideas dominate cultural studies follow Plato (and the critical theorists) in preferring theory to literature on the grounds that only theory allows one to see through the prejudices, errors, and false certitudes that pervade the common culture and literature as well. Plato did not let the poets into his republic because even the best of them, or perhaps especially the best – Homer – spread ideas and attitudes in conflict with true philosophy. Today's theorists have their own idea of an ideal republic, not entirely different from Plato's. They seek a society in which theoretical reason will rule, unconstrained by the customs or "prejudices" of the past conveyed so seductively by novels, plays, and poem. Many see their theorizing as part of "a movement to eradicate gender, race, class, and sexual prejudice" (577), as feminist critic Devoney Looser puts it. In considering the significance of this "movement," it is important to distinguish between an effort to minimize the influence of views one considers prejudiced on the one hand and, on the other hand, a campaign "to eradicate" thoughts and feelings. The former is standard practice under liberal democracy, whereas the latter would require a cultural cleansing that only a totalitarian regime could carry out. If the great eradication were actually to occur – or, as it is called in Henry James's *The Princess Casamassima*, "the great rectification" (396) – there would be no place for such examples of humanistic criticism as Lionel Trilling's on *The Princess Casamassima*, George Santayana's on the *Divine Comedy*, Erich Auerbach's on the *Odyssey*, Helen Vendler's on Keats's Odes, or Marilyn Butler's on Jane Austen. Indeed, there would be no room for the epics of Dante and Homer, the plays of Shakespeare, the poems of Keats, or the novels of Jane Austen and Henry James, all of which preserve ideas and attitudes that would have to be eliminated even as remembered possibilities for the final eradication of "gender, race, class, and sexual prejudice" to succeed.

Such an eradication seems unlikely to occur in the United States, but the cultural studies movement is nothing if not ambitious. Its devotees claim the intellectual authority to study and judge every aspect of human life, since the theorizing they embrace is universally applicable. The scope of its ambition can be surmised from a consideration of the 2010 second edition of NATC. The NATC is a canon maker that establishes the framework of received opinion in departments of English and cultural studies. Despite its length – 2,758 pages – the NATC is most revealing in its omissions, the most significant of which occurs in the title. The NATC claims to deal with "theory," not with "literary theory" and with "criticism," not merely "literary criticism." Rarely has arrogance been expressed so economically. The strategic omission of the qualifying adjective "literary" intimates (without explicitly declaring) that professors who use the NATC are equipped to provide guidance to all those who employ any sort of theory, presumably including their colleagues in the social sciences and even those in physics and chemistry. Such pretension has not been seen since the heyday of the Hegelian system, which claimed the intellectual authority to give the law to every particular science and discipline, from physics to history and everything in between. Grand theory deserted philosophy with the demise of philosophical idealism early in the twentieth century, but it seems to have reappeared in the unlikely precincts of the English department.

In the preface, the editors blandly assert that the far-reaching claims of the new kind of "theory" are not only compatible with "questioning" and "skepticism" but are somehow derived from just those attitudes. They declare that "theory in its newer sense . . . entails a mode of questioning and analysis . . . skepticism toward systems, institutions, and norms." It requires "a readiness to take critical stands and to engage in resistance" (xxxiii). Resistance to what? We are not told. The editors concede that "This theory – or 'cultural critique' as it is more descriptively termed" may to those of "an earlier generation" seem more "like advocacy rather than disinterested inquiry" (xxxiv). The "Introduction to Theory and Criticism" explains that "critique calls for a critic at once suspicious and ethical, committed to a set of values different from, or directly opposed to, those expressed in the text" (2). So the contemporary critical theorist is skeptical about "norms," and yet, since he or she is (we are assured) also "ethical," some norms must be affirmed. Which ones? No answer. The reader does learn that the critic must have values "different from, or directly opposed to, those expressed in the text" under consideration (2). To be fair, this stance seems reasonable enough in studying some texts, such as *Mein Kampf*, but there are other texts, more likely to be encountered in literature courses, for which it seems less suitable. One wonders if it is absolutely necessary that the critic "engage in resistance" to the "set of values" of *Middlemarch* or *The Ambassadors* or *Beloved* in order to provide a theoretically sound interpretation. Perhaps it is "theory in its newer sense" that should be resisted.

The editors recognize that the sweeping claims they make on behalf of their favored approach will not be universally accepted. They acknowledge in the introduction that some might not agree with what might appear to be a "turn away from literature and its central concerns." To the editors, these dissenters can only be "'antitheorists,' as they are called." Called by whom besides the editors themselves? No answer. Once having defined anybody who dissents from postmodernist theorizing as opposed to theory of any sort, it is easy for the editors to dispose of the opposition by pointing out that "there is no position free of theory, not even the one called 'common sense'" (1). True enough, and yet there is certainly a distinction to be made between those theories (like nineteenth-century idealism or the postmodernist theory promoted by the editors) that reject common sense and those that attempt to clarify and refine it.

The first edition already skimped on criticism and ideas more than fifty years old, devoting almost half its 2,600-plus pages to movements after the New Criticism that flourished in the mid-twentieth century. The second edition, although more than a hundred pages longer, skews its selection even further, omitting many key texts found in the first edition, beginning with Plato's *Ion*, a dialogue that raises almost all the central questions about literary criticism. An excerpt from Plotinus's *Enneads* is also missing, thus depriving readers of an acquaintance with the classic text of Neoplatonism, essential not only because of its own great influence but because an awareness of Plotinus's interpretation of Plato allows one to better understand Plato's own thought. Other authors dropped from the new edition include Quintilian,

Macrobius, Hugh of St. Victor, Geoffrey of Vinsauf, Giambattista
Giraldi, Ronsard, Edward Young, Thomas Love Peacock (whose
satirical *Four Ages of Poetry* provoked Shelley to write his
Defence of Poetry), Theophile Gautier, C. G. Jung, Kenneth
Burke, Georges Poulet, and E. D. Hirsch. All these omissions
allow the editors to devote almost 1,500 pages to developments
after the New Criticism – including, especially, the rise of "theory
in its newer sense."

The additions to the new NATC include a category entitled
"Antitheory," thus conveying the impression of an admirable willingness to provide space for voices opposing the anthology's own
raison d'être. Yet only two of the nine critics (Stanley Fish, Gerald
Graff, co-authors Michael Hardt and Antonio Negri, bell hooks,
co-authors Steven Knapp and Walter Benn Michaels, Bruno
Latour, Plato, C. D. Narasimhaiah, Barbara Christian) classified
as "antitheorists" defend anything close to what the editors themselves identify as the core of the "antitheory" position: "a return to
studying literature for itself" (1). Stanley Fish, listed as an "antitheorist," is probably one of the best-known American proponents
(that is to say, theorists) of what he calls "anti-foundationalism,"
one of the key elements in the postmodernist worldview. Gerald
Graff is also listed as an "antitheorist." But in his own essay,
"Taking Cover in Coverage," he is an advocate for theory, objecting to "the established curriculum's poverty of theory" (1963) and
arguing for a new curriculum in which "theory courses should be
central, not peripheral" (1969). The title of Steven Knapp and
Walter Benn Michael's essay, "Against Theory," suggests that
its authors are taking on postmodernist theory in all its ramifica-
tions, but the essay itself is much narrower, concerning itself only
with "issues of belief and intention" (2492) and refraining from
any call for "a return to studying literature for itself." bell hooks's
essay "Postmodern Blackness" is devoted to "exploring the radical
potential of postmodernism as it relates to racial difference and
racial domination" (2512). The introduction to the selection from
Empire by Hardt and Negri claims that their "influential book
remains required reading for students of postmodernity and glob-
alization, particularly for their repositioning and reevaluation of

theories of the postmodern" (NATC 2618). The essay by Bruno Latour chosen for inclusion is summarized by NATC as follows: "In 'Why Has Critique Run Out of Steam: From Matters of Fact to Matters of Concern' (2004), he laments the appropriation of contemporary critique by conspiracy theorists, global capitalists, and right-wing extremists to such ends as debunking global warming" (2277).

C. D. Narasimhaiah and Barbara Christian are the only critics listed whose ideas bear any resemblance to the editors' description of "antitheory" as "a return to studying literature for itself." Narasimhaiah, it should be noted, does not criticize or even discuss postmodernist theory at all, focusing instead on the relevance for the critic of Indian literature of, for example, "a keen sense of the Indian past . . . a fair grounding in Indian Poetics" and "familiarity with literary masterpieces in Sanskrit and Prakrit" (1384). In her essay "The Race for Theory," Barbara Christian observes that "critics are no longer concerned with literature, but with other critics' texts" (2128) and objects strongly to contemporary theory's

linguistic jargon, its emphasis on quoting its prophets, its tendency towards "Biblical" exegesis, its refusal even to mention specific works of creative writers, far less contemporary ones, its preoccupations with mechanical analyses of language, graphs, algebraic equations, its gross generalizations about culture. (2129)

Christian, no advocate of any "return to studying literature for itself," argues that the true political impact of the new, supposedly revolutionary theorizing has been far from liberating: "The literature of blacks, women of South America and Africa, etc., as overtly 'political' literature was being preempted by a new Western concept which proclaimed that reality does not exist, that everything is relative, and that every text is silent about something" (2133).

Perhaps the most inexplicable choice for the "Antitheory" classification is the most famous and influential theorist in Western history: Plato. No explanation is given, and the introduction to the Plato selections offers no clue, instead deepening the mystery by stating the undeniable: "A monumental figure in the history of

Western philosophy, Plato looms nearly as large in the history of European literary theory" (41). One is driven to the suspicion that it is because the implications of Plato as consummate theorist are so unwelcome to the contemporary apologists for Theory that they feel compelled to classify Plato, against the evidence of the *Dialogues* (including those excerpted here), as a member of the other team. The parallels are straightforward. The most influential contemporary theorists are contemptuous of common sense, desire radical cultural and political change, and are confident that theory rather than literature provides the key to understanding human life. Plato likewise distrusted the commonsense ideas of his society and worked for revolutionary cultural and political change. Literature, he came to feel, was dangerous because it reinforced and intensified all the prejudices and attitudes he opposed. Plato was confident that it was theory, not literature, that should guide human life. There are, of course, some important differences between Plato's theories and contemporary Theory. Plato was the first and most influential "logocentrist" and "essentialist," making him a target for the reckless deconstructive extremism of Nietzsche, Heidegger, and Derrida (NATC contributors all). Plato's Socrates challenged traditional Greek culture by declaring that the state of one's soul was all-important, whereas the fate of one's body was a secondary matter. The NATC, judging by its "Alternative Table of Contents," thinks otherwise. The twenty-three "Issues and Topics" listed include "The Body," with eleven readings, but there are apparently no readings in which the soul or the inner self comes up as a central issue or topic. Plato himself was a literary genius whose key dialogues and myths remain compelling literary works, whereas an article written with ordinary clarity is a rare achievement for contemporary theorists.

A closer parallel to the contemporary theorists in the NATC may be the feminist protagonist of Henry James's *The Bostonians*, Olive Chancellor, for whom "almost everything that was usual was iniquitous" (11). For some of the new contributors, it is the political and economic order that is especially "iniquitous." Lisa Lowe finds herself in a world where "the contradictions of the national and the international converge in an overdetermination of neocolonial capitalism, anti-immigrant racism, and patriarchal gender stratification" (2524). Michael Hardt and Antonio Negri see postmodernism as "the logic by which global capital operates" (2632) and hope for a time when "taking control of the truth" will be in the hands of "constituent assemblies of the multitude, social factories for the production of truth" (2635). Other contributors find the usual attitudes about sex iniquitously stigmatizing: Lauren Berlant and Michael Warner are troubled by American "national heterosexuality" (2601), whose narrow judgmentalism sees to it that "promiscuity is so heavily stigmatized as nonintimate" (2610). Gayle Rubin, on the other hand, finding it unjust that "boy-lovers are so stigmatized" speaks up for "the community of men who love underaged youth" (2382–3). Judith Halberstam opposes "male dominance and heteronormativity" (2644).

At odds with the usual and normal, Henry James's Olive Chancellor "felt more at her ease in the presence of anything strange" (11), and this seems to be the case with the new contributors as well: their enthusiasms, if sometimes vague, are at least far from the conventional or usual. Lisa Lowe envisions "the formation of alternative social practices" (2534). Hardt and Negri look forward to a time when there will be "constituent assemblies of the multitude" (2635). Berlant and Warner are enthralled by a display of "erotic vomiting," commenting that on such occasions "sex appears more sublime than narration itself" (2614). Objecting to male masculinity, Halberstam reserves her praise for "powerful and affirmative forms of female masculinity" (2649). Gayle Rubin looks forward to a society in which "homosexuality, sadomasochism, prostitution, or boy-love" are no longer "taken to be mysterious and problematic in some way that more respectable sexualities are not" (2397). The narrator of *The Bostonians* does not directly challenge Olive Chancellor's views, and he gives her credit for being personally "distinguished and discriminating" (152). Granting that the contributors mentioned here possess similarly impressive personal qualities, and waiving any judgments about their ideas on politics or sexuality, one may still observe that literature plays little if any role in their arguments. That is understandable because those who yearn for transformative change that will bring about a new world free from the attitudes, ideas, and institutions of the present must regard the most acclaimed literary works in much the same way Plato regarded Homer: as misleading and dangerous influences to be ignored or, if possible, suppressed.

In 2005, about midway between the publication of the first edition of the NATC and the second, Columbia University Press published *Theory's Empire*, an anthology in which forty-nine critics, including such well-known figures as René Wellek, Anthony Appiah, Denis Donoghue, and Frank Kermode, offered powerful critiques of the most influential aspects of contemporary theorizing. The volume as a whole critiques the failure "to distinguish between 'a theory' as one approach among many, 'theory' as a system of concepts employed in the humanities, and Theory as an overarching 'practice' of our time," what "can today be referred to simply as Theory, emblazoned with a capital T" (1). The anthology is no compilation of "antitheory," if that is taken to mean an attempt to avoid thinking about theoretical issues. If, however, an "antitheorist" is one who does not do battle with common sense but instead takes it as a starting point, then the contributors to *Theory's Empire* should be considered "antitheorists." The introduction explains that its contributors "have to spell out and reinforce some rudimentary arguments concerning facts and beliefs, evidence and truth, knowledge and opinion that should by right be considered commonplaces but are more often unfamiliar to most of our students" (14).

A reader depending on the second edition of the NATC to learn about contemporary theory, however, would never learn that an anthology with contributions from many distinguished critics challenging the hegemony of "Theory" had been published by a major university press. Although many recent essays are added to the second edition, none of the additions is by any of the contributors to *Theory's Empire*. There are other weighty matters about which a reader who trusted this volume for a full presentation of contemporary theory and criticism would remain ignorant. Readers who turn to the section titled "Marxism" in the "Introduction to Theory and Criticism" would never learn that Marxism has been the ideology of some of the most murderous dictatorships in history or that Marx's predictions about the future of capitalism and socialism have been discredited by the history of the last century. Likewise, a reader of the "Psychoanalysis" section would never guess that the scientific standing of Freud's theory is today almost as low among psychiatrists as Marx's among economists.

Such wholesale omissions tell their own story clearly enough. If, however, one wants to consider the debate over contemporary criticism and theory from a larger historical and intellectual perspective, there is no better resource than the work of René Wellek. Immensely learned in many languages, Wellek discusses, in his magisterial eight-volume *History of Modern Criticism 1750–1950*, the most disparate critical approaches with fairness and acumen throughout, always supporting his characterizations and judgments with generous quotations from the critic under consideration. Wellek and Austin Warren's *Theory of Literature* compared the leading ideas of English and American critics with the most significant developments in European thought about literature, shaping several generations of critics.

René Wellek died in 1995, but there is little doubt as to where he would stand in the current debates about Theory. The coauthor of *Theory of Literature* was anything but an "antitheorist," and yet that is where he would have to be classified if, by some chance, he were ever considered for inclusion. If the editors of the NATC were to allow René Wellek to appear in the inevitable third edition, they would certainly be introducing a perspective on Theory almost entirely omitted from its earlier versions. Readings they might consider include his 1983 essay "Destroying Literary Studies" (included in *Theory's Empire*) or the title essay of his book *The Attack on Literature*.

The effect on the classroom study of literature of the outlook canonized in the NATC can be gauged by considering a representative example of an edition of a classic work designed for the classroom, the casebook of Jane Austen's *Emma*, edited by Alistair M. Duckworth in the "Case Studies in Contemporary Criticism" series published by Bedford/St. Martin's. In addition to the novel itself, this edition includes five essays exemplifying five critical approaches to *Emma*, as well as separate essays on the five critical schools represented: "Gender Criticism," "Marxist Criticism," "Cultural Criticism," "New Historicism," and "Feminist Criticism." An examination of each of these approaches in turn may provide some sense of the distance between humanistic criticism and the schools whose intellectual respectability in the postmodernist era is certified by their inclusion in such a casebook.

In the essay classified as "Gender Criticism," "'Not at all what a man should be!': Remaking English Manhood in *Emma*," Claudia L. Johnson argues that *Emma* rejects a conception of chivalric or sentimental masculinity Johnson associates with Edmund Burke in favor of an older masculine ideal. According to Johnson, Austen rejects "the chivalric pseudotraditionalism celebrated by Burke" (452) and, through her portrait of Mr. Knightley, redefines "English manhood instead as brisk, energetic, downright, 'natural,' unaffected, reserved, businesslike, plain-speaking; gentlemanly, to be sure, but not courtly" (453). Not that Johnson proposes that such an ideal of manhood be taken seriously today. She is willing to grant that *Emma* is a success, but what it succeeds in after laudably "diminishing the authority of male sentimentality" is not laudable at all: "reimmasculating [sic] men and women alike with a high sense of national purpose" (441). The novel deserves praise for what Johnson takes to be its critique of Burke's alleged "pseudotraditionalism," but its own message, Johnson concludes, has no relevance today but "harkens backwards still to the norms of manly independence which Burke's paean to Marie-Antoinette interrupted" (454).

The essay representing "feminist criticism," Devoney Looser's "'The Duty of Woman by Woman': Reforming Feminism in *Emma*," likewise praises *Emma* and Jane Austen in such a qualified way that the effect is, if not to damn, at least to patronize. Looser observes that Jane Austen "did not espouse the revolutionary idea of a feminist sisterhood" (581), adding that "[m]any feminists today rightly find the novel's acceptance of social ranking as troubling as its failure to envisage a female community across social barriers" (582). Austen is certainly not a feminist if feminism is understood as Looser understands it, "as a movement to eradicate gender, race, class, and sexual prejudice and to agitate for change" (577–8). Conversely, if feminism involves merely "attending to how women are limited and devalued within a culture" (577), then *Emma* can be placed "in the liberal feminist category" (582). Even though Austen, for reasons of her own, "chooses not to represent sisterhood within or across social levels," at least "she exposes the hypocrisy and potential damage of hierarchical female/female paternalism" (582). Looser ends her essay with condescension and faint praise: "Today we may see Austen's lessons about women's duty as too individually focused or too limited in scope to offer a model for feminist practice, but in her own time she implicitly argued for greater fairness among women within the existing social, political, and economic order" (592).

The essay by Beth Fowkes Tobin offering a Marxist perspective, "Aiding Impoverished Gentlewomen: Power and Class in *Emma*," echoes Plato's objections to poetry in its warning against dangerous lies seductively presented. All too many readers and critics, wrongly "assuming that human nature is transhistorical," have been fooled by Jane Austen, reading *Emma* as a story of the title character's "moral development from a selfish and narcissistic adolescent" to finally "a thoughtful and responsible adult aware of her own needs and those of others around her." Jane Austen herself has to shoulder much of the blame for the popularity of this interpretation. As Tobin puts it, "Austen encourages this humanist reading of moral development and in the process mystifies the economic and social relations she has so precisely depicted in her novel" (473). Tobin repeatedly warns against the novel's ability to mislead readers. The novel "has the effect of brushing away" legitimate concerns, it "subverts the seriousness" of women's problems by offering "solutions that deny the seriousness of the problem" and fails to admit that "impoverished middle-class women are victims of a capitalist system." Summing up, Tobin sees the author of *Emma* as "Ultimately an apologist for the landed classes" (485). Jane Austen remains, unfortunately from Tobin's point of view, a very successful apologist, since not only ordinary readers but even "many critics" continue to read the novel as "the story of moral and psychological development of an individual, ignoring [what to Tobin is all too obvious] the social, economic, and political content of the novel" (486). Like most people except for Marxists, these readers and critics live in illusion, governed by the "false consciousness" endemic to capitalist society and spread by, among other things, works of literature, and so it is unsurprising that as readers of *Emma* they are "not conscious of the ideological work the narrative performs" (486).

Paul Delaney, whose essay "'A Sort of Notch in the Donwell Estate': Intersections of Status and Class in *Emma*," is offered as an example of "cultural criticism," takes as his primary topic an issue discussed in the other essays as well, "Austen's specific position on the political spectrum." Delaney, the "cultural critic," differs from the gender, feminist, and Marxist critics by arguing that Jane Austen cares about "status" as well as class and gender. Emma's marriage to Mr. Knightley "subordinates both gender and class to a status ideal of benevolence" (521). Delaney's judgment of Jane Austen follows the model established in the feminist essay of faint praise and condescension: "It would be both anachronistic and futile to blame Austen for failure to envision other kinds of opportunities [other than marriage] for women in the public sphere." If Jane Austen fails to transcend the conventions of her time and place, she can at least be given credit for devising an ending in which those sometimes conflicting conventional values were reconciled, an ending in which, as Delaney puts it, "the contending claims of status, class, and gender can be most fully and reciprocally satisfied" (521).

Like the other essays, the representative of "new historicism" finds nothing in *Emma* to challenge contemporary preconceptions. The novel's "ideological imperatives" are disguised, but the authors of "'The Tittle-Tattle of Highbury': Gossip and the Free Indirect Style in *Emma*," Casey Finch and Peter Bowen, see through the "new narrative technology" (aka the use of free indirect discourse) employed by Jane Austen to hide "the novel's political impulsions" (556). Emma's Highbury appears in the novel as a place where "a democracy of independent and differing opinions" may be heard, but Finch and Bowen are not taken in. If "the norms of the community" seem to be "the natural realization of its citizens' desire," that impression only highlights Jane Austen's skill in employing "a new and formidable technology of truth" to conceal the reality of "overriding social imperatives" (556) in the service of "the high patriarchal truths the novel is concerned to put into place" (546).

The five critics representing five schools of thought seem united in their lack of interest in *Emma* as a work of art or in Jane Austen as one of the world's great novelists. They do care about Austen's politics and the sociopolitical impact of *Emma*, which most agree is to be deplored. The new historicist finds the novel affirming "high patriarchal truths" (546). Austen is simply "an apologist for the landed classes" (485) for the Marxist, but, according to the cultural critic, Emma's marriage to Mr. Knightley shows that Austen is more concerned with status than class. The gender critic finds Austen occupied with reaffirming an ideal of "manly independence" (454) that was passé in her own time. The feminist critic observes that Austen's putative "liberal feminism" is no model for today's feminists, given Austen's unwillingness to challenge "the existing social, political, and economic order" (592).

Indeed, four of the five essays agree in finding that Jane Austen used her skill as a writer to do things that were better left undone. The Marxist essay complains that Austen "mystifies" the very "economic and social relations" she depicts with precision (473). The new historicist finds Austen skillful in deploying a "technology of truth" to "disguise the ideological imperatives of the novel" (556). The cultural critic admires the novelist's ability to reconcile "the contending claims of status, class and gender" (521) but also suggests that the novel's concern with such claims betrays its failure to transcend or see through the dominant attitudes of her time and place. The gender critic says that Austen is successful in "reimmasculating men and women alike" (441), but it is hard to view this success as an achievement to admire. The feminist critic is alone in finding valuable if limited insight in the novel; she gives Austen credit for dramatizing "hierarchical female/female paternalism" but adds that Austen's imagination was not capable of "envisag[ing] a female community across social barriers" (582).

All five of the essays give the impression that *Emma* is a novel that offers no insights and raises no questions worth considering. Jane Austen, it appears, accepted rather unthinkingly the conventions of her place and time, and these conventions are affirmed in her novels, including *Emma*. A reading of the five casebook critics leaves one wondering why it is worth writing essays about *Emma* at all. One might wonder even more why it is a good idea to require students to read the novel and study it with the aid of a casebook. None of the five critics seems to have enjoyed reading the novel; certainly, their essays don't convey any sense of aesthetic delight or intellectual excitement. The five schools all share a refusal to consider the novel as a work of art that can both teach and delight.

Lionel Trilling, as it happens, wrote an essay on "*Emma* and the Legend of Jane Austen," included in his 1965 collection, *Beyond Culture*. Trilling's approach to *Emma* differs in a number of ways that together characterize some key differences between criticism in the humanistic tradition and the "schools" represented in the casebook. Trilling assumes that *Emma* has something to teach him, something that it requires all the effort of the critic to grasp. *Emma*, he emphasizes, "is a very difficult novel." If, at first glance, Jane Austen is easier to understand than Proust or Joyce or Kafka, a closer examination reveals that *Emma* ultimately offers more resistance to interpretation, since "sympathetic" re-readings of *Ulysses* leave one "less puzzled," while even reading *Emma* again and again will not allow "us to flatter ourselves that we have fully understood what the novel is doing" (32).

Trilling, like the casebook critics, observes that the novel does not present "the real England" (49) but instead a sort of ideal England that exists nowhere except in Austen's fiction. He does not, however, view this disjunction as a fault to condemn. For Trilling, the presentation of Highbury as a kind of "idyllic world" (47) is a literary device "which has the effect of emphasizing by contrast the brilliant modernity" (42) of Emma herself, who throughout the novel engages in "conscious self-definition and self

criticism" and feels "the need to make private judgments of reality" (41). Emma Woodhouse, Trilling felt, was his contemporary,
since "there is no reality about which the modern person is more
uncertain and more anxious than the reality of himself" (41). The
ability of Emma to ultimately judge her own errors and to join
with Mr. Knightley in a marriage of equals celebrated by their
friends seems to Trilling to convey not an ideological fantasy but a
vision of "the hope of victory in the battle that the mind must
wage, and it speaks of the expectation of allies in the fight, of the
possibility of community" (49).

Trilling's essay is a characteristic expression of the humanistic
tradition not only in its affirmation that literature both teaches and
delights but also in its demonstration of the way the two are
intertwined, as in the best works they always are. The casebook
critics feel no need to learn anything important from Jane Austen
because their theories have already made everything clear. Devoney
Looser, the feminist critic, expresses an ideal seemingly shared by
all the five critical schools represented when she describes feminism
as "specifically a movement to eradicate gender, race, class, and
sexual prejudice" (577–8). All these "prejudices" have not been
eradicated from Austen's Highbury, so any pleasure a reader might
take from its depiction is to be deplored. In contrast, Trilling has no
qualms about observing that Jane Austen's presentation of a world
where nothing goes terribly wrong, where innocence is safe, is a
source of pleasure: "The quiet of Highbury, the unperturbed spirits
of Mr. Woodhouse and Miss Bates, the instructive perfection of
Mr. Knightley and Mrs. Weston, constitute much of the charm of
Emma" (47).

On their side, it is precisely the "charm of *Emma*" that worries
the casebook critics. They fear it might somehow encourage readers to wonder if a society where all the desired "eradications" have
taken place would be so ideal after all. Trilling, however, finds in
the Highbury of Jane Austen an ideal world that challenges the
abstractions of theory with the living world of the novel. Emma's
journey from the opening scene in which she confronts with mixed
feelings the marriage of her beloved governess to Mr. Weston to
self-knowledge and her own marriage to Mr. Knightley offers

"the possibility of controlling the personal life, of becoming acquainted with ourselves, of creating a community of 'intelligent love'" (49). By the standards of the casebook critics, *Emma* is a dangerous book, as any work must be whose art is powerful enough to reopen questions that contemporary ideology considers closed. Trilling examines *Emma* at least as closely as the later critics, observing that the England represented in Jane Austen's novels "was not the real England" and cautioning that "The error of identifying it with the actual England ought always to be remarked" (49). Trilling nevertheless finds something to be learned, a vision of human life whose authority and significance is not derived by adherence to an ideology or a theory but instead conveyed through art.

The prospects for humanistic criticism are not bright if one must turn to Lionel Trilling, who died in 1975, to find an alternative approach to the schools exemplified by the casebook critics. Fortunately, that is not necessary. Although Trilling is probably the best-known critic in the humanistic tradition of the past fifty years, the tradition survives, although not necessarily under that name. The last essay in the *Emma* volume of "Case Studies in Contemporary Criticism" is introduced by the series editor, Ross C. Murfin, in an essay titled "Combining Perspectives on *Emma*." Murfin declares that the reason for the inclusion of Butler's essay "is to demonstrate the permeability" of "contemporary critical approaches" and thereby demonstrate "how supposedly disparate assumptions can be held simultaneously" (594). The essay in question, a revised version of an introduction to the 1991 Everyman's Library edition of *Emma* by Marilyn Butler, is better understood as an example of a kind of criticism the editor apparently does not recognize – humanistic criticism.

Marilyn Butler has no doubt that *Emma* both teaches and delights. "Any Austen novel," she declares, "is likeable, accessible, among the friendliest of classics" (598). When she asks "why do readers continue to experience so much pleasure when the heroine accepts the right man?," it is not because she is afraid that the seductiveness of the novel will mislead unwary readers into ideological errors. Instead, she suggests that readers experience aesthetic "pleasure" because of the formal unity achieved: "Perhaps the happiest interpretation of *Emma* makes it a Mozartian formal dance, like *Cosi fan tutti* or *The Marriage of Figaro*" (598). In contrast to the notion that Austen's *Emma* affirms the provincial value of her own place and time and thus has nothing to say to those of other times and places, Butler notes that "Jane Austen's novels, generally taken in the British Isles as the most parochial of great novels, have readers in Japan, India, and Nigeria who can easily identify with their essential subject-matter" (598). If *Emma* is popular, it is also, as Trilling emphasized, difficult. It is all too easy to assume that the novel as a whole supports Emma Woodhouse's "insistence of a village hierarchy based on 'old family'" (602) values. A careful reader becomes aware early that Emma is "a self-interested and hence thoroughly unreliable narrator" (602). To appreciate Emma more accurately, one must attend to the novel as a whole, ready to find things unanticipated by one's school or theory:

Austen's art is always much less concerned with the direct expression of attitudes, emotions, experiences, than with elaborate displacements through which a great range of thought, feeling, and minute observation is being quietly registered. By displaying the humanity of her fools and gossips, Austen escapes the doctrinaire tendencies of so many of her contemporaries, and works her best surprises. (612)

It is a very good thing that critics like Marilyn Butler continue to write, and it is much to the credit of the editor of the *Emma* casebook, Alistair Duckworth, that her essay is included with the rest. It is unfortunate, however, that the humanistic tradition in criticism, although practiced by fine critics like Butler, is no longer recognized as one of the critical options available to professors or students. Another "Casebook of Contemporary Criticism," this one on *The House of Mirth*, includes, like the *Emma* volume, Marxist, Feminist, and "cultural criticism," and adds examples of "deconstruction" and "psychoanalytic criticism" (dropping new historicist and gender). The editor, Shari Benstock, comments that "all five of them [essays on *The House of Mirth*] could be categorized as feminist" (319). As in the *Emma* volume, the humanistic approach is not recognized as a possible alternative, nor is there any essay comparable to that of Marilyn Butler's, which exemplifies the humanistic approach even though it is not so characterized.

Why has the humanistic tradition become invisible to the academic powers that be? Perhaps for the same reason that literature itself has become unfashionable in the prestigious departments where cultural studies hold sway. Humanistic criticism holds that we can gain insights about human life from novels and poems that theories, even the best, cannot provide. Plato understandably excluded the Homeric poems from his republic. The theorists who dominate English departments, it appears, have their own idea of an ideal republic, not entirely different from Plato's. They, or many of them, want, or think they want, a society in which theoretical reason will rule, unconstrained by the customs or "prejudices" of the past conveyed so seductively by novels, plays, and poems. How this revolution will be carried out the critics do not explain, although we do have some examples from recent history of attempts to eradicate the past and create a new society along such lines. (Mao's cultural revolution, Cambodia under Pol Pot, and North Korea under Kim Il-Sung and his son come to mind.) It is certainly clear, however, that books like *Emma* will either have to be banned or at least thoroughly discredited if the eradication is to be successful.

The primary distinction in literary criticism today is not between those committed to the study of the Great Books and those interested in popular art and literature. That division lies instead between those whose commitment to politics is so all-embracing that the very notion of independent literary judgment becomes inconceivable and those who instead believe the ability to appreciate and judge works of art and literature by standards independent of politics is a key achievement of a truly liberal education. The former are more likely to consider themselves practitioners of cultural studies than of literary criticism. Richard Posner may be not too far wrong in suggesting that the aim of cultural studies "is to knock literature off its pedestal and find vehicles easier than literary works for making political points" (8).

The latter believe that, without independent standards of literary greatness, it is all too easy to grant authority only to works that reinforce the contemporary consensus, whatever that may be. These standards, worked out over centuries in a still unfinished conversation, are a common heritage that cannot be claimed by one political movement or another, or so the humanistic tradition would contend. According to the dominant voices in postmodernist cultural studies, however, "greatness" is a meaningless construct, and, in any case, literature and art, great or otherwise, provide nothing that cannot be explained better, or explained away, by Theory.

4

Aristotle and the Humanistic Tradition

Aristotle's response to Plato provides a model for humanistic criticism that remains valid today. Aristotle's case for literature is all the stronger because he tacitly accepts Plato's rejection of the notion that poets have special access to divine truth, a claim defended by the Neoplatonists and revived by the Romantics. Literature, Aristotle believes, can tell us important things about human life but little about the universe. Plays and epic poems can provide valuable insight into the sorts of things that certain sorts of people are likely to do in certain sorts of situations. Whereas Plato believed that the culture of his time was wrong about the most important things, Aristotle was willing to give due deference (although not unquestioning acceptance) to the common sense of his society, both about the value of literature and about moral questions. The humanistic tradition in literary criticism remains Aristotelian both in its view of literature as a source of insight about human life and in its willingness to judge grand theory by the norms of common sense. When literary criticism has relied overmuch on one or another overarching theory – including Aristotle's own – for its intellectual authority, it has not only broken with common sense, but it has forfeited its role as the tradition within which the insights of novels, poems, and plays are worked out, made explicit, and their implications for personal lives and society debated.

For more than a thousand years, it was not Aristotle's *Poetics* but Horace's *The Art of Poetry* that was the most influential work of Western literary criticism. Horace's observation that the best writer is one "who has managed to blend usefulness with pleasure," whose work "delights his reader at the same time as he instructs him" (108) is the classic formulation of the dual emphases of the humanistic tradition. Unlike Aristotle, however, Horace made no attempt to work out what the relationship might be between pleasure and instruction. The best neoclassical critics admired both *The Art of Poetry* and the *Poetics*, but their admiration did not prevent them from thinking for themselves. Alexander Pope and Samuel Johnson remain important to the humanistic tradition for many reasons, among the least of which is their acceptance of Aristotle as a supreme authority. Alexander Pope's "An Essay on Criticism" is rightly considered an exposition of neoclassical ideas, but its permanent importance derives from its unsurpassed demonstration of the connections between the ethics of criticism in particular and morality in general. For Pope, the ethics of criticism have nothing to do with evaluating writers according to the degree of moral uplift in their works and everything to do with judging a work on its literary merit alone, without regard to irrelevant criteria, such as whether the author is a wealthy aristocrat or a poor commoner, whether the book is by a foreigner or a native, or whether it has sold many or few copies. Similarly, Samuel Johnson in his "Preface to Shakespeare" argued for what today is misleadingly called "the canon" on grounds identifiably neoclassical but still valid today. Although believers have no doubts about the divine authorship of the canonical works of their religion, literary excellence, Johnson observes, "is not absolute and definite, but gradual and comparative. Literary judgment is not deductive; it is based entirely on "observation and experience" (59). A work that has maintained a reputation for greatness over many centuries has done so for no other reason than "because frequent comparisons have confirmed opinion in its favor" (60).

In the nineteenth century, critics like Matthew Arnold and Henry James – the latter's literary criticism is often neglected because of the preeminent stature of his fiction – absorbed what was valid in the Romantic critique of neoclassicism but returned to the humanistic notion that literature is important not for what it tells us about God or ultimate reality but for what it reveals about human life. In "Literature and Science," Arnold happily admitted that science was a better guide to the nature of the universe than was literature but argued that literature provides a "criticism of life" (68) that science could not. James declared in "The Art of Fiction" that "The only reason for the existence of a novel is that it does attempt to represent life" (46). The prominent New Critic Cleanth Brooks defended literature on similar grounds when he argued in *The Well Wrought Urn* that a good poem "must return to us the unity of the experience itself as man knows it in his own experience" (212–13).

Aristotle's seminal importance to the humanistic tradition becomes clear when one reads the *Poetics* as a response to Plato's critique of literature in the *Republic*. The *Poetics* has unfortunately too often been read in isolation from its intellectual context, which seems reasonable enough if one thinks of the *Poetics* as a set of rules whose validity derives simply from Aristotle's unparalleled ability to grasp universal truths about poetry and literature in general. This approach was the one adopted by the French neoclassicists in the seventeenth century and briefly revived in a different form by the Chicago critics in the mid-twentieth century. The significance of the *Poetics* for the humanistic tradition, however, does not derive from the universal applicability of the "rules" it supposedly establishes but rather in the approach to literature it exemplifies. The humanistic tradition in literary criticism retains Aristotle as an exemplar while rejecting the neoclassic notion of Aristotle as a rule maker whose authority could not be challenged.

One of Plato's chief accusations against literature is that the poets tell lies about the gods. Aristotle does not respond to this claim directly, but he answers it by a device more effective than any argument; he simply assumes throughout the *Poetics* that poets, having no special knowledge about the gods or ultimate reality, are only worth attending to because their poems provide insight into human life. Aristotle's comparison of poetry to history takes it for granted that both deal with human life, but history only "tells what happened" whereas poetry tells "what might happen." Poetry, that is, reveals "the sort of thing that a certain type of man will do or say either probably or necessarily" (35). This is quite a modest claim by comparison to the contentions of poetry's earlier admirers, who assert that poets "know all arts and all things human that have to do with virtue and vice, and the divine things too," according to Socrates in the tenth book of the *Republic* (281). Even while praising poetry above history, Aristotle implicitly rejects not only the claim that poets have special access to the divine but also the notion that poets have any special knowledge about "virtue and vice." Poets, in Aristotle's view, do not possess encyclopedic knowledge of "all arts," nor any special knowledge at all beyond an awareness of "the sort of thing that a certain type of man will do or say either probably or necessarily."

What good is such knowledge, if it can even be called knowledge at all? For those concerned only with keeping their souls in good order, an awareness of the way other people behave is not very important. Knowledge of how other people are likely to act seems like the knowledge of "what is going to come" in the procession along the wall of the cave for which the cave dwellers in Socrates's allegory award "honors, praises and prizes" (*Republic* 195) but which from the viewpoint of anyone who has escaped the cave and seen the world outside seems entirely worthless. Knowledge about what a certain sort of person is likely to do "probably or necessarily" is, in any case, inexact knowledge. There is no clear boundary between one "sort of person" and another "sort." Even if the "sorts" could be clearly distinguished, it would still be the case that learning what one sort of person is likely but not guaranteed to do would not count as real knowledge by the standards affirmed in Plato's *Republic*. Socrates asserts that the pupils receiving an ideal education "should never attempt to learn anything imperfect, anything that doesn't always come out at the point where everything ought to arrive" (210). The only kind of knowledge worth having, according to Socrates in the *Republic*, is "knowing what is always," not "what is at any time coming into being and passing away" (206). The kind of knowledge that Aristotle claims literature can provide, knowledge of the way people behave, is utterly unimportant and does not really deserve to be called knowledge, according to the Socrates of the *Republic*.

Rejecting, tacitly but firmly, the claim that poets have special insight into what Socrates in the *Republic* calls "the divine things," Aristotle unnecessarily limits his understanding of literature by refusing to consider the dramatic presentation of the relation of gods to human beings in, for example, the works of Homer, Sophocles, and Euripides. Yet the Homeric epics and the tragedies of Sophocles and Euripides all dramatize relationships between human beings and the gods, and the relationships between the human and the divine are as much part of the poems as are relationships between human beings. The failure to discuss the role of the gods in Homer's epics and in the tragedies of Sophocles and Euripides is a major omission in the *Poetics*. A reader who depended on Aristotle's discussion to gain a general understanding of the *Iliad*, the *Odyssey*, the Oedipus plays, or *Iphigenia in Tauris* would be seriously misled, since such a reader would never learn that relationships between gods and human beings are important elements in all these works.

In Euripides's *Iphigenia in Tauris*, Orestes is commanded by Apollo to go to the island of Tauris and steal the statue of Athena he will find there; Apollo promises that if Orestes follows orders, the god will see to it that the Furies will stop punishing Orestes for killing his mother Clytemnestra. Aristotle comments that "the fact that the god told him [Orestes] to go there, and why, and the object of his journey lie outside the outline-plot" (67). For Aristotle, those aspects of the play that "lie outside the outline-plot" are apparently not worth considering. And yet it can be argued that the main interest of *Iphigenia in Tauris* is its dramatization of a world in which the gods come to seem, in Orestes's words, "no more trustworthy than fleeting dreams." When Orestes sums up this conclusion, he arrives at a point of view that seems central to the play but would be unnoticed by a critic whose perspective was bounded by the *Poetics*:

> The gods themselves, even those we call prophetic,
> Are no more trustworthy than fleeting dreams. The world
> Of gods is as chaotic as our mortal world.
> What galls one is that, while still of sound mind, he should,
> By heeding the words of prophets, plunge himself into
> A depth of ruin only experience can fathom. (148)

Aristotle praises Sophocles's play *Oedipus the King* for placing whatever is "inexplicable in the incidents" in the play "outside the tragedy" (57). It certainly is "inexplicable" to ordinary understanding why Oedipus should be fated to kill his father and marry his mother, and it is true that the action of the play takes place long after Laius and Jocasta attempt to thwart Apollo's prophecy about the newborn Oedipus. Yet one of the important ways in which Sophocles's drama differs from that of Euripides is the difference between the Apollo of Sophocles's Oedipus and the much less mysterious, much less awe-inspiring Apollo of *Iphigenia in Tauris*. Apollo himself does not appear in either play, but neither work can be fully understood without taking into account each play's presentation of the relation of the gods to human beings.

Aristotle remains persuasive on the larger point that the value of poetry and literature generally lies in its ability to provide insight into human life rather than in any alleged access to the divine. The humanistic tradition has followed Aristotle in turning to literature to learn about human life while rejecting the notion that poets have special access to the gods or God, but it has not followed him in ignoring poetic representations of religion and "divine things." Religion is itself part of human life, and most humanistic criticism since Aristotle has taken it for granted that the depiction of the role of religion and religious feeling in human life is as valid a subject for literature as love or war. Furthermore, although critics in the humanistic tradition do not turn to literature for revelation (although the sacred writings of religions may very well include works with literary qualities), many go beyond Aristotle in turning to literary works for insight into the imaginative consequences of a particular view of the world. Belief in Homer's gods is no longer what William James would call "a live hypothesis" ("The Will to Believe" 476), but it is still possible to gain from the *Iliad* some sense of what might count in human life in a universe seemingly ruled by amoral forces in which a shadowy existence after death provides no compensation for suffering and loss in earthly life. Humanistic criticism does not judge literary works by the religious beliefs they affirm, but it does judge their literary merit in part by considering the degree to which the work succeeds in carrying out the imaginative logic of its premises. Its success in doing so allows readers to grasp imaginatively the consequences of a viewpoint that otherwise might be understood only as an abstract proposition.

George Santayana's eloquent praise of Homer and Dante in "The Absence of Religion in Shakespeare" for the completeness of their imaginative worlds is a representative example of humanistic criticism, because Santayana is paying tribute to their literary accomplishments, not to their metaphysical acumen:

> Homer is the chief repository of the Greek religion, and Dante the faithful interpreter of the Catholic. Nature would have been inconceivable to them without the supernatural, or man without the influence and companionship of the gods. These poets live in a cosmos. In their minds, as in the mind of their age, the fragments of experience have fallen together into a perfect picture, like the bits of glass in a kaleidoscope. Their universe is a total. Reason and imagination have mastered it completely and peopled it. (95)

Santayana himself emphasizes that his judgment that one cannot "find in Shakespeare all that the highest poet could give" because Shakespeare is "without a philosophy and without a religion" (100) is an aesthetic judgment, not the expression of a preference for a religious worldview as opposed to a nonreligious one:

> For what is required for theoretic wholeness is not this or that system but some system. Its value is not the value of truth, but that of victorious imagination. Unity of conception is an aesthetic merit no less than a logical demand. ... Without such a conception our emotions cannot be steadfast and enlightened. Without it the imagination cannot fulfill its essential function or achieve its supreme success. (100–01)

One does not have to agree with Santayana's conclusion that Shakespeare failed to provide "all that the highest poet could

give" to agree with his implicit assumption that literary criticism is
justified in taking account of the imaginative universe of a creative
writer, even though the critic is concerned with literary and aesthetic issues rather than metaphysical judgments.

Should literary criticism, and especially humanistic criticism,
concern itself with the truth of a writer's metaphysical judgments?
Aristotle votes no by means of his eloquent silence in the face of
Plato's denunciations of the poets for telling lies about the gods.
Santayana says no ("what is required . . . is not this or that system
but some system"), but his one-time student T. S. Eliot seems at
first to take a different tack in his essay "Religion and Literature."
Eliot argues that "Literary criticism should be completed by
criticism from a definite ethical and theological standpoint"
(343). Writing as a Christian as well as a poet and critic, Eliot
declared "What I believe to be incumbent upon all Christians is
the duty of maintaining consciously certain standards and criteria
of criticism over and above those applied by the rest of the world"
(353). In both statements, Eliot distinguishes criticism that is
specifically literary from another kind that is "incumbent upon
all Christians" – and presumably members of other religions – and
that derives "from a definite ethical and theological standpoint."
So perhaps Eliot is not really at odds with the humanistic tradition
of literary criticism that turns to literature for insight into human
life rather than for knowledge of ultimate reality. He merely
believes that literary criticism "should be completed" by another
kind of criticism, one whose criteria are not literary but instead
"ethical and theological."

Yet Eliot's point would be easier to accept if he had not linked
ethical and theological concerns as equally distinguishable from
literary standards. Eliot may be right in "Religion and Literature"
when he argues that "our religion imposes our ethics" (347),
but, in any case, it remains possible to discuss moral and ethical
issues in their own terms without appealing to religious revelation.
Most humanistic critics have taken it for granted that literary merit
does not depend on the truth of a writer's religion or metaphysics.
Humanistic criticism since Aristotle has, however, contended
that the literary standing of novels, plays, and poems is based in

part on the moral insight they convey. Critics such as Samuel Johnson, Matthew Arnold, Henry James, Edmund Wilson, and Lionel Trilling go to literary works for representations of human life that provide bases for qualifying, refining, and clarifying, but not overturning, traditional moral standards.

Aristotle himself assumes throughout the *Poetics* that moral standards are uncontroversial, so that he is able to write without elaboration or explanation that a skilled tragedian will avoid plots showing "wicked people passing from bad fortune to good," since such plots do not "satisfy our feelings or arouse pity and fear" (45). This assumption is another tacit departure from Plato, one of whose major objections to literature is precisely its powerful affirmation of conventional moral standards. Aristotle takes it for granted that good literature will not outrage the moral sensibility of its audience.

Another issue on which Aristotle differs from Plato without explicit disagreement is the intellectual value of representation or "imitation." The *Poetics* considers representation an aid to learning, since a good representation selects those aspects of its subject that are essential to its identity and omits unnecessary details. The representation, by focusing on what is most important and leaving out what might distract, makes it possible for students of the representation to classify what is being represented with other members of its class that differ from it in unimportant details but that share the aspects the representation has identified as essential. (Fyfe's translation obscures this point by leaving out the article in the key sentence: "The reason why we enjoy seeing likenesses is that, as we look, we learn and infer what each is, for instance, 'that is so and so'" [15]. Gerald Else's translation of the same sentence clarifies: "For that is why people enjoy seeing the reproductions: because in their viewing they find they are learning, inferring what class each object belongs to: for example that 'this individual is a so-and-so'" [125]. Else points out that "what Aristotle means by 'learning and inferring' is not the recognition that 'this person is that person,' but that he is 'that *kind* of creature'" [131–2]).

"Representation" is the word W. Hamilton Fyfe uses for Aristotle's "mimesis" in his translation of the *Poetics*, whereas

Allan Bloom uses "imitation" for the same Greek word in his translation of Plato's *Republic*. Each choice is appropriate for the text being translated, since Plato certainly intends mimesis to convey the negative implications that "imitation" has in English, whereas, for Aristotle, a representation is an accomplishment that is a source of knowledge. For Plato, an imitation is self-evidently inferior to the original. Knowledge is to be gained by comprehending the truly real, the Forms, of which visible entities are only imitations. In the tenth book of the *Republic*, Plato compares poetry to painting – the painted couch is inferior both to the couch made by a craftsman, on which one can at least sit or lie, and both are inferior to the ideal couch, which can be known only by the mind, not by the senses. Just as paintings are inferior to the objects they portray, so poems are inferior to what they describe. The former are inferior to the latter both in regard to the degree of reality they possess and in the knowledge to be gained by studying them.

Poetry is superior to history, according to Aristotle, just because the historian must stick to particular facts that reveal what happened once and will never happen again in exactly the same way. Poetry, on the other hand, is free to omit irrelevant details and identify a sequence of events that may well recur. The difference between history and poetry is that "one tells what happened and the other what might happen" (35). There is no guarantee, of course, that the poet will necessarily succeed in isolating a sequence that reveals a significant recurrent pattern in human life. Aristotle's approach, here and elsewhere, assumes that one must make judgments about the quality of literary works. Writers will be more or less successful in selecting the essential from the nonessential, and the knowledge their work might provide about human life will vary accordingly. There is no definite formula for distinguishing between plots that do convey knowledge and those that mislead. All Aristotle can do is provide some general guidelines based on his knowledge of Greek drama and epic poetry.

Whereas Aristotle was once acclaimed and later condemned for establishing a set of unchallengeable rules, his approach is better understood as calling for individual judgment about the literary merit and relevance to human life of particular works from audiences and certainly from would-be critics. Plato requires no such judgments, since in his philosophy no poetry, from the greatest, like Homer's epics, to the most insignificant, is or could be a source of knowledge. Literary merit plays no part in Plato's system, since by definition knowledge as opposed to mere opinion can only be found by seeking out the changeless reality of the Forms. Platonic philosophy leaves no more room for considering the qualities that make for literary excellence than do such influential contemporary approaches as Marxism, New Historicism, and cultural studies in general.

Aristotle, in contrast, is the founder of the humanistic tradition's insistence that the judgment of literary works is an inescapable part of the critic's task. Yes, such judgments are opinions, but some opinions are better supported by the evidence and by the reasons offered on their behalf than other opinions. Certainty may not be possible, but discussions about literary merit are not therefore a waste of time.

Horace's "Art of Poetry" affirmed that literature should both delight and teach, a formula that is still not a cliché, if only because so many influential theories have insisted that literary works do only one or the other. Horace's influence, however, has not been entirely beneficial. Often, single lines were quoted and requoted out of context, eventually assuming a meaning quite different from what they originally possessed. For example, in isolation, the observation that "A poem is like a picture" was taken to mean that poems should above all provide descriptions that would approximate the effect of a picture or painting. In context, however, Horace's point is entirely different; poems are like pictures in that some are more impressive the more closely they are examined, whereas others that are striking at first seem mediocre when considered more carefully:

A poem is like a picture; one strikes your fancy more, the nearer you stand; another, the farther away. This courts the shade, that will wish to be seen in the light, and dreads not the critic insight of the judge. This pleased but once; that, through ten times called for, will always please. (481)

Some of his phrasing suggests that delighting is one thing and teaching another and, furthermore, that the teaching is a simple matter of explicit advice giving: "Poets aim either to benefit, or to amuse, or to utter words at once both pleasing and helpful to life. Whatever you instruct, be brief" (479). It was the recovery of the *Poetics* that provided a model of humanistic criticism in which the knowledge literature provides could be seen as the implications of the work as a whole rather than as separable "instructions." Conversely, Horace's warning that affluent would-be poets should be careful to avoid so-called critics who are really self-interested flatterers remains pertinent:

> Like the crier, who gathers a crowd to the auction of his wares, so the poet bids flatterers flock to the call of gain, if he is rich in lands, and rich in moneys put out at interest. But if he be one who can fitly serve a dainty dinner, and be surety for a poor man of little credit, or can rescue one entangled in gloomy suits-at-law, I shall wonder if the happy fellow will be able to distinguish between a false and a true friend. (485)

Alexander Pope followed Horace in emphasizing the moral issues involved in literary judgments. Pope's "An Essay on Criticism," an eighteenth-century version of Horace's "Art of Poetry," makes clear the extent to which literary criticism and especially literary judgment require moral discipline as well as intellectual acumen. The "Essay on Criticism" can be itself criticized both for regarding Aristotle's *Poetics* as a set of unchallengeable rules and for identifying these supposed rules with the natural order – "Learn hence for Ancient *Rules* a just Esteem;/ To copy *Nature* is to copy *Them*" (255) – but Pope's conception of the moral issues involved in literary criticism, based in large part on Horace, retains its validity today. Pope observes that the mere willingness to take pleasure in another's work has a moral component. A certain generosity of spirit is necessary to appreciate and delight in what is indeed well done; the critic must give up a lesser kind of delight, the "malignant dull Delight" that comes from finding fault with what deserves praise:

> A perfect Judge will *read* each Work of Wit
> With the same Spirit that its Author *writ*,
> Survey the *Whole*, nor seek slight Faults to find,

> Where *Nature moves,* and *Rapture warms* the Mind;
> Nor lose, for that malignant dull Delight,
> The *gen'rous Pleasure* to be charm'd with Wit. (266–7)

Pope encourages the critic to forgo the sense of superiority gained by discovering flaws in a work that is generally admired. Instead, the critic is encouraged to see the work as sympathetically as possible and thus, by entering into the "Spirit" of another in attending to a literary work, to foster the ability to enter imaginatively into another's point of view in situations outside literature. Pope makes it clear, however, that imaginative sympathy does not preclude clear judgment. His point is that the critic should give each work the benefit of the doubt, should begin with an attempt to adopt the author's point of view and judge the work on its own terms. Pope is advocating what today might be called "immanent criticism."

Literature can be a solvent for prejudices, but only if the critics who communicate the findings of literature to the larger culture do not allow those prejudices to deform their literary judgments. Critics go wrong if they allow themselves to be influenced by a prejudice against foreigners or against one's fellow citizens: "Some *foreign* Writers, some our *own* despise" (285). It is a mistake to assume that what is popular must be excellent and equally mistaken to take it for granted that a bestseller must be mediocre:

> The *Vulgar* thus through *Imitation* err;
> As oft the *Learn'd* by being *Singular*;
> So much they scorn the Crowd, that if the Throng
> By *Chance* go right, they *purposely* go wrong; (288)

If one task of a literary critic is to make available to the larger culture the testimony of literature on human life, then critics have an obligation to report accurately on the authority of that testimony by accurately assessing the literary merit of the witness. If a play or novel or poem is deemed authoritative mainly because it supports political or philosophical doctrines favored by the critic, then, insofar as the verdict of the critic is accepted, the culture as a whole is prevented from weighing properly the testimony the play or novel or poem has to offer. If literature has something distinctive to contribute to the understanding of human life, it is because plays, fiction, and poems make possible ways of looking at life unique to literature. To judge the authority of literary works by appealing to the very doctrines whose views are to be tested by reference to literature is to engage in an egregious begging of the question. Judging a literary work according to whether it seems to further a political party or cause is perhaps the most obvious example of such abdication of the obligations of a critic. If critical stances simply mimic political arguments, then literary critics are failing to make the distinctive contribution literary criticism can provide when critics turn to literature to examine, qualify, and refine the ideas about human life underlying political programs. No such contribution is possible when "Parties in *Wit* attend on those of *State*,/and publick Faction doubles private Hate" (290). It is doubtless impossible for the critic to avoid all prejudices, but he or she is obliged to make the attempt.

Pope's "An Essay on Criticism" assumes a small society in which poets and critics know each other. Good manners are important; not so important that etiquette should trump truth, but enough that unpleasant truths should be presented so as to give the least offense possible:

> 'Tis not enough your counsel still be *true*,
> *Blunt Truths* more Mischief than *nice Falshoods* do;
> Men must be *taught* as if you taught them *not*;
> And Things *unknown* propos'd as Things *forgot*:
> Without *Good Breeding*, *Truth* is disapprov'd;
> That only makes *Superior* Sense *belov'd*. (305–6)

Failures of etiquette might prevent good criticism from having its proper influence, but bad criticism not the result of simple ignorance or stupidity is due to "*Pride*, the *never-failing Vice of Fools*" (264). It is pride that prevents critics from experiencing "The *gen'rous Pleasure* to be charm'd with Wit" (267), and it is pride that leads them to ignore the work as a whole and instead focus on a personal hobby-horse: "Most Criticks, fond of some subservient Art,/Still make the *Whole* depend upon a *Part*"(269).

In his "Preface to Shakespeare," Samuel Johnson observed that there are no "principles demonstrative and scientifick" that provide a formula allowing one to determine with certainty which literary works are excellent and which mediocre. Literary excellence, Johnson asserts, "is not absolute and definite, but gradual and comparative" (59). The absence of "principles demonstrative and scientifick" does not mean, however, that it is impossible to distinguish between better and worse literary productions. It does mean that there is no unmistakable essence, no specific marker that distinguishes great works from all others. The only basis for the judgment of one literary work is comparison with others:

> As among the works of nature no man can properly call a river deep or a mountain high, without the knowledge of many mountains and many rivers; so in the productions of genius, nothing can be stiled excellent till it has been compared with other works of the same kind. (60)

Johnson makes these observations to justify a feeling of "reverence due to writings that have long subsisted," writings that have passed the only "test" appropriate for works of literature, "length of duration and continuance of esteem" (60). Johnson, like Aristotle and unlike Plato, believes that the judgments of the general public, when confirmed by generations, are usually well-founded. There is no scientific authority available to override the decisions of the public, but the judgment of one period or era may be compared to the judgments of other periods and other times. If almost all judgments concur, then the probability increases that they are right: "What mankind have long possessed they have often examined and compared, and if they persist to value the possession, it is because frequent comparisons have confirmed opinion in its favour" (60). Johnson gives weight to "continuance of esteem" because he is willing to believe that most other readers, like himself, more often than not make their literary judgments in good faith and after reflection. The ordinary reader is not infallible, but errors derived from particular fads or fashions are likely to cancel each other out over time. (Conversely, if, like Plato, one believes that most people are ruled by irrational emotions, or like most Marxists one finds the masses ruled by false consciousness, or like many feminists one believes that patriarchy has made it impossible for work by women to be judged fairly, then the "continuance of esteem" would mean nothing more than that a particularly esteemed work caters to long-lasting prejudices that only the right kind of revolution will eventually erase.) Literary criticism in the humanistic tradition is written for the general reader, as well as for critics and scholars, in the faith that human beings are capable of being persuaded, eventually, by appeals to reason and evidence.

Johnson makes a skeptical argument to support respect for traditional opinion. There are no certainties or absolutes, he argues, when it comes to literary evaluation. Works whose greatness has been acknowledged for at least a "century, the term commonly fixed as the test of literary merit" should indeed be provisionally granted due respect, but it is not impossible, although unlikely, that the verdict of the ages might be wrong. Johnson is unwilling to accept the greatness of Shakespeare as a given even though his fame has lasted more than one hundred years, since "human judgment, though it be gradually gaining upon certainty, never becomes infallible; and approbation, though long continued, may yet be only approbation of prejudice or fashion" (61). Johnson is justifying what today is often called "the canon," but he is doing so in a way that reveals why that term is so misleading. The notion of a "canon" of great books is based on an analogy with the canon of sacred books that make up the Hebrew and Christian Bibles. Believers who accept the "canon" of their religion do not believe that it is merely probable that the books making up the canon of sacred texts are indeed sacred; they accept the canon as an article of faith. Once accepted, the choice of the sacred texts making up a religious canon is not routinely up for debate in succeeding generations. The decision to include a particular work among the sacred texts is not justified on the basis of comparison to other candidates for inclusion; instead, it is believed that the putatively sacred texts are marked by some indication of divine inspiration or authorship. The sacred texts of a religion do not require validation by nonbelievers to be accepted as sacred by members of the faith. In contrast, the literary "canon" is always up for debate; testimony from readers of widely divergent backgrounds and beliefs is always relevant, and absolute certainty is neither possible nor expected.

Against those who assume that reasoned public discussion is impossible, either because most human beings are irredeemably bigoted or stupid or both or because achieving even limited knowledge about anything is impossible even for experts, the humanistic tradition assumes that meaningful discussion open to general readers as well as scholars is not only possible but is the best means of arriving at valid judgments of literary merit. The most influential restatement since Pope and Johnson of the notion that literary critics should not judge literary works by the degree to which they affirm the critic's own opinions but only according to literary standards remains Matthew Arnold's championship of critical "disinterestedness" in his 1864 essay, "The Function of Criticism at the Present Time." Arnold, however, expands the scope of literary criticism far beyond imaginative literature. Much of what Arnold calls literary criticism would today be called cultural criticism. Unlike contemporary proponents of cultural studies, however, Arnold does not justify his expansive notion of criticism by an appeal to theory. In *Culture and Anarchy*, he describes himself as "a plain, unsystematic writer, without a philosophy" (137). He cannot rely on the authority of philosophical or scientific theories but must instead "keep close to the level ground of common fact" (192):

> But an unpretending writer, without a philosophy based on interdependent, subordinate, and coherent principles, must not presume to indulge himself too much in generalities. He must keep close to the level ground of common fact, the only safe ground for understandings without a scientific equipment. (192)

Even if one feels that Arnold protests too much in such passages, it remains true that his case for an expanded conception of literary criticism does not depend on the validity of a specific theory of society or the universe.

In "The Bishop and the Philosopher," one of the essays for which "The Function of Criticism" served as the introduction, Arnold describes his critique of Bishop Colenso's book questioning the historical veracity of the Pentateuch, the first five books of the Hebrew Bible, as an example of "literary criticism," a kind of criticism that is neither theological, historical, nor philosophical:

Literary criticism's most important function is to try books as to the influence which they are calculated to have upon the general culture of single nations or of the world at large. Of this culture literary criticism is the appointed guardian, and on this culture all literary works may be conceived as in some way or other operating. All these works have a special professional criticism to undergo: theological works that of theologians, historical works that of historians, philosophical works that of philosophers, and in this case each kind of work is tried by a separate standard. But they have also a general literary criticism to undergo, and this tries them all, as I have said, by one standard – their effect upon a general culture. (41)

In "The Function of Criticism" Arnold offers his critique of Bishop Colenso as an example of disinterested criticism. Arnold, like Bishop Colenso, is in theological terms a liberal; neither makes it a matter of faith to believe in the complete factual and historical accuracy of the Bible. He imagines a fellow liberal scandalized by Arnold's willingness to question Bishop Colenso's "speculative confusion":

I criticized Bishop Colenso's speculative confusion. Immediately there was a cry raised: "What is this? Here is a liberal attacking a liberal. Do you not belong to the movement? are you not a friend of truth? Is not Bishop Colenso in pursuit of truth? Then speak with proper respect of his book. . . . Do you want to encourage to the attack of a brother liberal his, and your, and our implacable enemies . . .?" (277)

Against this imagined remonstrance, Arnold insists that "the practical consequences of a book are to genuine criticism no recommendation of it, if the book is, in the highest sense, blundering" (278). He is "bound by my own definition of criticism: *a disinterested endeavor to learn and propagate the best that is known and thought in the world*" (283; emphasis in original), and from this perspective Bishop Colenso's book simply does not count: "To criticism, therefore, which seeks to have the best that is known and thought on this problem, it is, however well meant, of no importance whatever" (278).

Presumably, if the critic should be "disinterested" in evaluating a book of theology, one should also be disinterested in evaluating a work of literature according to the highest standards, those set by "the best that is known and thought in the world." It is not immediately clear, however, that Arnold's notion of "criticism" refers to literary criticism in particular. Arnold opens "The Function of Criticism at the Present Time" by quoting a passage from an earlier essay in which "criticism" refers to intellectual activity in any field:

"Of the literature of France and Germany, as of the intellect of Europe in general, the main effort, for now many years, has been a critical effort; the endeavour, in all branches of knowledge, theology, philosophy, history, art, science, to see the object as in itself it really is." (258)

Literary criticism in the form of the New Criticism would later take up Arnold's call to see the literary work "as in itself it really is," but Arnold himself, it is clear, is not especially concerned with the criticism of poems and plays in this passage. Philosophers, theologians, historians, and scientists, as well as artists, are all engaged in the same "endeavour"; why then should literary criticism have the position of "the appointed guardian" of culture that Arnold claims for it in "The Bishop and the Philosopher"?

The preeminence that postmodernist cultural studies claims for itself on the basis of the reach of its grounding theories Arnold claims for literary criticism on the basis of the superiority of imaginative literature and especially poetry over both religion and science as a "criticism of life." In his 1882 essay "Literature and Science," Arnold vindicates the importance of a humanistic education, including the study of ancient art and literature, not despite but because of the increasing importance of science. Arnold stresses the ability of the "criticism of life" implicit in great works of literature to assist us in the necessary task of relating "the results of modern science to our need for conduct, our need for beauty":

[W]e shall find that this art, and poetry, and eloquence, have in fact not only the power of refreshing and delighting us, they have also the power, – such is the strength and worth, in essentials, of their authors' criticism of life, – they have a fortifying, and elevating, and quickening, and sugges-tive power, capable of wonderfully helping us to relate the results of modern science to our need for conduct, our need for beauty. (68)

Arnold grounds the importance of literary criticism, even criticism of nonliterary works, in the prior importance of literature itself as the source of the most meaningful "criticism of life," thus rejecting in advance the postmodernist affirmation of Theory over literature and reaffirming his place in the humanistic tradition of literary criticism.

The notion of literature as, above all, a "criticism of life" is itself vulnerable to criticism, however, not least because Arnold provided so few convincing examples of what he meant by the phrase. His emphasis in "The Study of Poetry" on "high seriousness" as one of the touchstones of the best poetry comes close to insisting on a specifically Victorian moral earnestness as an essential attribute of greatness in literature. Arnold's lifelong insistence on the gulf between poetry and even the best novels – in "George Sand" (1884), he insisted that "The novel is a more superficial form of literature than poetry" (189) – and his concomitant failure to take account of the novels of Jane Austen, Charles Dickens, George Eliot, and their peers, made it all the more difficult for him to explain how literature's "criticism of life" would work in any detail. Arnold's late essay "Count Leo Tolstoi," one of the very few that discusses a novel, provides a tantalizing illustration of what Arnold might have accomplished if he had treated the English novels of his time with the attention he accords in this essay to *Anna Karenina*. Arnold observes that Tolstoy "deals abundantly with criminal passion and with adultery" but does so without special pleading of any kind. On the one hand, "We are not led to believe ... that Anna is wonderfully exalted and ennobled by her passion for Wronsky" [sic], but, on the other, there is no titillation. Anna dies a suicide; she is not a misunderstood saint, but neither is she at all contemptible: "But then Anna, let us remember, is to the last, through all the fret and misery, still Anna; always with something which charms; nay, with something, even, something in her nature, which consoles and does good" (292). Arnold powerfully contrasts the view of life presented in *Anna Karenina* with Flaubert's novel of adultery, *Madame Bovary*. Both authors offer a way of looking at human life, both offer a "criticism of life." Arnold finds the way of *Anna*

Karenina vastly superior because Tolstoy provides us with a fuller, more generous, and ultimately more truthful view of the world than does Flaubert, despite all his powers of precise and accurate observation, in *Madame Bovary*:

> Emma Bovary follows a course in some respects like that of Anna, but where, in Emma Bovary, is Anna's charm? The treasures of compassion, tenderness, insight, which alone, amid such guilt and misery, can enable charm to subsist and to emerge, are wanting to Flaubert. He is cruel, with the cruelty of petrified feeling, to his poor heroine; he pursues her without pity or pause, as with malignity; he is harder upon her himself than any reader ever, I think, will be inclined to be. (293)

Matthew Arnold, who so rarely was willing to give his critical attention to the novel, joins hands with Henry James, the great champion of the novel, both in his appreciation of *Anna Karenina* and even more in his critique of *Madame Bovary*. Arnold found it difficult to think of a novel as a work of art on the same plane as poetry, whereas James insisted on the novel as a genre capable of the highest art. In this insistence, James was a modernist in the line that goes from Flaubert to Joyce, Proust, and Mann. But James was a modernist with a difference, a modernist in something of the same way that Matthew Arnold was a "Liberal" but "a Liberal tempered by experience, reflection, and renouncement" (*Culture and Anarchy* 88). Arnold was a liberal, but he was unwilling to accept liberalism as an ideology. Henry James's writings on *Madame Bovary* illustrate his ability to understand and appreciate the achievement of modernism without accepting the extreme claims of what might be called the ideology of modernism, with its absolutist condemnation of virtually all aspects of the modern world and its equally extreme elevation of art, especially modernist art, to absolute moral and cultural authority.

Madame Bovary is generally recognized as an exemplary "modernist" novel, one of the first demonstrating that a novel, despite its length, could be a work of art as tightly organized as a great poem or painting. Novelists like Thackeray, Dickens, and Trollope saw nothing wrong with interrupting their narratives to make authorial comments about their characters or to point out in an explicit, straightforward fashion the intended message of the work as a whole. Balzac and Tolstoy similarly felt free to speak directly to the reader, whatever the cost to artistic unity of such authorial digressions. In *War and Peace*, of course, the authorial commentary is so extensive that it cannot be called a "digression" but instead a major element of the work. Since its publication, *War and Peace* has been considered a masterpiece that makes its own rules, but James considered it a deeply flawed work, masterpiece or not. Tolstoy may have been an "epic genius," but *War and Peace*, James warned would-be novelists, served "execrably, pestilentially, as a model" ("The New Novel" 134). In contrast, in *Madame Bovary*, there are no authorial comments at all, no digressions, no interruptions or digressions from the narrative.

For Henry James, such restraint was exemplary; in refusing to speak directly to the reader, Flaubert affirmed the self-sufficiency of the novel itself. *Madame Bovary* demonstrates the ability of a work of art to convey its meaning through artistic means alone, without explanations, without guideposts. For James, the willingness of an Anthony Trollope, for example, to break from his narrative and address the reader directly was "a betrayal of a sacred office," "a terrible crime." Trollope's offense is worse than other digressions because Trollope explicitly "admits that the events he narrates have not really happened, and that he can give his narrative any turn the reader may like best" ("The Art of Fiction" 46). But no matter how interesting or even profound the thoughts of the author, inserting them profanes the "sacred office" of the novelist. James famously linked *War and Peace* with Thackeray's *The Newcomes* and Dumas's *The Three Musketeers* because all three included what to James were violations of the novel's artistic integrity. No doubt Tolstoy was an incomparably more significant figure than Thackeray or Dumas, and *War and Peace* was a much greater achievement than all of Thackeray and Dumas's works taken together; *The Newcomes*, *The Three Musketeers*, and *War and Peace* could, nevertheless, be classed together as "large, loose baggy monsters," since the authors of all three had been willing to profane their "sacred office" with "queer elements of the accidental and the arbitrary" (*"The Tragic Muse"* 1107).

James repeatedly compares the painter to the novelist; in "The Art of Fiction" he declares that "the analogy between the art of the painter and the art of the novelist is, so far as I am able to see, complete" (46). At a time when poetry was the only kind of literature recognized as a high art on a level with painting, James's comparison of the novelist to the painter was one way to emphasize "the fact that fiction is one of the *fine* arts, deserving in its turn of all the honours and emoluments that have hitherto been reserved for the successful professions of music, poetry, painting, architecture" (47). It was, James believed, "impossible to insist too much on so important a truth" (34). One of the most important parallels James draws between a painting and a novel as works of art is that the artistic excellence of each depends much more on the ability of the creative artist to create a complex unified structure in which each part contributes to the whole than in the intrinsic importance of the subject itself. Although the importance of a unified visual composition was generally recognized in regard to painting, the importance of the same sort of unity was much less appreciated in regard to the novel, so much so that some of the most highly regarded fictions were, in James's view, works without any high degree of artistic unity. James acknowledges that, in a painting poorly composed, "There may in its absence be life," just as there is "life" in *War and Peace* and *The Three Musketeers*, but he emphasizes that "a picture without composition slights its most precious chance for beauty" ("*The Tragic Muse*" 1107). In "Gustave Flaubert," James describes Flaubert as a great "painter of life"; as in a great painting, there is nothing extraneous, no episode or passage that does not play its role in the overall composition:

The form is *in itself* as interesting, as active, as much of the essence of the subject as the idea, and yet so close is its fit and so inseparable its life that we catch it at no moment on any errand of its own. That verily is to *be* interesting – all round; that is to be genuine and whole. The work is a classic because the thing, such as it is, is ideally done, and because it shows that in such doing eternal beauty may dwell. (325)

In *Madame Bovary*, Flaubert has realized James's ideal of a novel that is the equal in artistic achievement to a great painting, and

James's praise is unstinting: "*Madame Bovary* has a perfection that not only stamps it, but that makes it stand almost alone; it holds itself with such a supreme unapproachable assurance as both excites and defies judgment" (325).

Flaubert himself seemed to be not so much a human being who wrote novels but rather a novelist who was incidentally a human being: "He was born a novelist, grew up, lived, died a novelist, breathing, feeling, thinking, speaking, performing every operation of life, only as that votary." James, however, immediately qualifies his characterization without granting anything more to Flaubert's mere humanity: "It was not indeed perhaps primarily so much that he was born and lived a novelist as that he was born and lived literary, and that to be literary represented for him an almost overwhelming situation" (315). The difference between being a "novelist" and being "literary" is more significant than it may appear. For James, the novelist is comparable not only to the painter but also to the historian. Like the historian, the novelist is committed to telling the truth about human life, so that when Trollope remarks to the reader that he can "give his narrative any turn the reader may like best," it "shocks" James "every whit as much in Trollope as it would have shocked me in Gibbon or Macaulay" because Trollope's remark "implies that the novelist is less occupied in looking for the truth (the truth, of course I mean, that he assumes, the premises that we must grant him, whatever they may be) than the historian. ... To represent and illustrate the past, the actions of men, is the task of either writer" ("The Art of Fiction" 47). As a literary man, Flaubert "cared immensely for the medium, the task and the triumph involved" ("Gustave Flaubert" 316), but he had only disdain for the way of life of his own place and time, the France described in *Madame Bovary* and *Sentimental Education*. James considers Flaubert a literary man rather than a novelist because his masterpiece, *Madame Bovary*, which was written with overwhelming dedication and achieved an unsurpassable artistic unity, presented a false, one-sided view of human life. James was unwilling to accept Flaubert's verdict on the way of life described in *Madame Bovary* even though that judgment has the authority that great art can provide. James notes the unsparing completeness of Flaubert's indictment:

Besides being the history of the most miserable of women, *Madame Bovary* is also an elaborate picture of small *bourgeois* rural life. Anything, in this direction, more remorseless and complete it would be hard to conceive. Into all that makes life ignoble, and vulgar, and sterile M. Flaubert has entered with an extraordinary penetration. The dullness and flatness of it all suffocate us; the pettiness and ugliness sicken us. Every one in the book is either stupid or mean. . . . ("Charles de Bernard and Gustave Flaubert" 173–4)

Unlike the twentieth century partisans of modernism who were only too ready to accept artistic indictments of the bourgeois world as authoritative, James acknowledges Flaubert's artistic achievement but still questions his view of life. Flaubert's outlook suffered from "the primary defect of his mind, his want of a general sense of proportion." ("Correspondence de Gustave Flaubert" 304). This defect led him to exaggerate the limitations of the middle-class world into a vision of a kind of hell on earth that had only tenuous connections with the actualities of bourgeois life, in the provinces or elsewhere. Because most of his fellow citizens failed to care for literary excellence as he did, he felt justified, James observes, in making "in regard to his contemporaries, the accusation of malignantly hating it [literature]. This universal conspiracy he perceived, in his own country, in every feature of manners" ("Gustave Flaubert" 304). Flaubert's vision was distorted by

the strange weakness of his mind, his puerile dread of the grocer, the *bourgeois*, the sentiment that in his generation and the preceding misplaced, as it were, the spirit of adventure and the sense of honor, and sterilized a whole province of French literature. That worthy citizen ought never to have kept a poet from dreaming. ("Correspondence de Gustave Flaubert" 311).

James himself yielded to none in his commitment to literature and in his love for the works he considered truly excellent, and yet he saw that Flaubert's contempt and even hatred of those who felt differently could not be justified. Flaubert, James observed,

passed his life in strange oblivion of the circumstance that, however
incumbent it may be on most of us to do our duty, there is, in spite of a
thousand narrow dogmatisms, nothing in the world that any one is under
the least obligation to like – not even (one braces one's self to risk the
declaration) a particular kind of writing. ("Correspondence de Gustave
Flaubert" 313)

James contends that Flaubert's hatred of the bourgeoisie not only
distorted his view of the world around him but also limited him as
an artist. *Madame Bovary* is so relentless in presenting Emma
Bovary's adulteries in a sordid light that, James suggests, "it
would make the most useful of Sunday-school tracts" if it were
not "the reverse of what is called family reading" ("Charles de
Bernard and Gustave Flaubert" 169). That is, the novel's simplistic morality allies it with "tracts" that make no claim to literary
standing rather than with what James calls the "moral imagination" ("Charles de Bernard and Gustave Flaubert" 166) – with no
allusion, as far as one can tell, to Edmund Burke's use of the
phrase in his *Reflections on the French Revolution* – that is one
of the marks that distinguishes high art from mere entertainment
or (possibly high-minded) propaganda.

   Furthermore, Flaubert's disdain for the people whose stories he
is telling makes it impossible for him to grant a meaningful inner
life to any of them. He can evoke contemporary middle-class life
with stunning surface accuracy, but he is unable to sympathetically imagine or depict what lies beneath that surface. Flaubert's
domain is what James calls "the visible," but he fails signally to
capture the inner life, what James calls "the invisible": Flaubert's
style is inimitable, but "even a style rich in similes is limited when
it renders only the visible. The invisible Flaubert scarcely touches;
his vocabulary and all his methods were unadjusted and alien to
it" ("Gustave Flaubert" 312). James's most telling criticism of
Flaubert is not that he revealed what was better kept hidden but
rather that he stopped at the surface:

Let Flaubert always be cited as one of the devotees and even, when people
are fond of the word, as one of the martyrs of the plastic idea; but let him
be still more considerately preserved and more fully presented as one of
the most conspicuous of the faithless. For it was not that he went too far, it

was on the contrary that he stopped too short. He stopped forever at the public door. ... He should at least have listened at the chamber of the soul. ("Correspondence de Gustave Flaubert" 313)

One of the great humanistic critics, James saw no contradiction between a concern equal to Flaubert's with artistic form and a belief that the most important quality of a novel was its ability to reveal truths about human life. James was happy to acknowledge that Flaubert's exemplary craftsmanship allowed him to succeed magnificently in rendering accurately the surface of life, "the visible," while the artistic limitations of many of the American novels James encountered prevented them from conveying any truths at all. Literary technique was extremely important to James, but it was never an end in itself. Reviewing *Azarian*, a novel whose overwrought writing provoked James to a statement of first principles, he emphasized that a novel's "foremost claim to merit, and indeed the measure of its merit, is its *truth*" ("Harriet Elizabeth (Prescott) Spofford: *Azarian: An Episode*" 607). James rebukes novelists who make it "easy" for themselves because they recognize no obligation to make their narratives correspond to anything real: "The manner in question is easy, because the writer recognizes no standard of truth or accuracy by which his performances may be measured. He does not transcribe facts, – facts must be counted, measured, weighed, which takes far too much trouble" ("*Azarian*" 609). Another novelist's attempt to make an impact through extravagant stylistic effects alone drives James to feel a certain kinship with Gradgrind, Dickens's notorious disparager of all things artistic: "Like Mr. Gradgrind in Dickens's *Hard Times*, what the novel-reader craves above all things is *facts*. No matter how fictitious they may be, so long as they are facts" ("Elizabeth Stoddard: *Two Men: A Novel*" 616).

If Flaubert fell short of the truth through an unwillingness or inability to sympathize with the characters of *Madame Bovary*, American novelists like Rebecca Harding Davis, determined above all to arouse pity, conveyed much less truth. James distinguishes "the objective novel," which appeals to the reader's sympathy and also to "the reader's sense of beauty, his idea of form

and proportion, his humanity, in the broadest sense" from the
novels of Davis and her school, which aim at "instructing us,
purifying us, stirring up our pity" ("Rebecca Harding Davis:
Dallas Galbraith" 225). It may very well be the case that a truthful
view of human life may arouse a mood of what James finely calls
"intelligent sadness": "Nothing is more respectable on the part
of a writer – a novelist – than the intelligent sadness which forces
itself upon him on the completion of a dramatic scheme which is
in strict accordance with human life and its manifold miseries"
("Rebecca Harding Davis: *Waiting for the Verdict*" 222). Novels
"in strict accordance with human life," however, provide no outlet for the "luxurious need for tears" to which the novels of
Rebecca Harding Davis cater in the belief, no doubt sincere,

that there exists in the various departments of human life some logical
correlative to that luxurious need for tears and sighs and sad-colored
imagery of all kinds which dwells in the mind of all those persons,
whether men or women, who pursue literature under the sole guidance
of sentimentality, and consider it a sufficient outlet for the pursuit.
("Rebecca Harding Davis: *Waiting for the Verdict*" 221–2)

For humanistic criticism, the importance of literature is linked
to the significance of human life itself. If one is a nihilist or a
mystic, ordinary human life would not seem to have any particular interest or importance, and it follows that one would not be
interested in learning what literature might reveal about life.
Conversely, one may believe that ending poverty or promoting
equality is so important that, in comparison, literary concerns are
trivial. But the pressing importance of moral and political action
need not lead to the denigration of literature. Writers like Rebecca
Harding Davis may believe that literary questions are merely a
distraction from the serious business of life, since all that matters is
arousing emotions that will lead to social change. James points
out in reply that it is quite possible to appreciate the importance of
both art and life without denigrating the claims of either:

Quite as much as she, we believe that life is a very serious business. But it
is because it is essentially and inalienably serious that we believe it
can afford not to be tricked out in the fantastic trappings of a spurious

and repulsive solemnity. Art, too, is a very serious business. ("Dallas Galbraith" 228)

James also believed that it was possible both to be true to art and also to enter sympathetically into the life of Flaubert's despised *bourgeois*, who was even a larger part of life in America than in France. If American novelists, including himself, had not written about the "business man" that was only because the world of business was "as special and occult to the outsider as the world, say, of Arctic exploration – as impenetrable save as a result of special training." For James

the typical American figure is above all that "business man" whom the novelist and the dramatist have scarce yet seriously touched, whose song has still to be sung and his picture still to be painted. He is often an obscure, but not less often an epic, hero . . . the American "business man" remains, thanks to the length and strength of the wires that move him, *the* magnificent theme *en disponibilité*. ("The Question of the Opportunities" 655–6).

Reviewing Rebecca Harding Davis's *Dallas Galbraith* in 1868, James observed that "the day of dogmatic criticism is over." A critic is, after all, "simply a reader like all the others," differing from the rest simply because he or she is "a reader who prints his [or her] impressions." Critics had come, however reluctantly, to concede that they had no special authority others were bound to recognize: "No critic lays down the law, because no reader receives law ready made" ("Rebecca Harding Davis: *Dallas Galbraith*" 223). One might think that such comments might lead to a plea that critics, recognizing their limitations, be less judgmental, more willing to describe than evaluate. James, however, goes in another direction. He argues that critical humility, the awareness that no one "tells the whole truth," should instead lead critics to be "clear and emphatic" in their individual judgments:

No writer pretends that he tells the whole truth; he knows that the whole truth is a synthesis of the great body of small partial truths. But if the whole truth is to be pure and incontrovertible, it is needful that these various contributions to it be thoroughly firm and uncompromising. The critic reminds himself, then, that he must be before all things clear and emphatic. ("Rebecca Harding Davis: *Dallas Galbraith*" 223).

James was not just being polite when, in his best-known critical essay "The Art of Fiction," he praised Walter Besant's willingness to discuss critical principles while disagreeing almost entirely with his ideas about the novel:

Mr. Besant has set an excellent example in saying what he thinks, for his part, about the way in which fiction should be written. . . . Other labourers in the same field will doubtless take up the argument, they will give it the light of their experience, and the effect will surely be to make our interest in the novel a little more what it had for some time threatened to fail to be – a serious, active, inquiring interest. (45)

Criticism for James was an ongoing conversation: "Discussion, suggestion, formulation, these things are fertilizing when they are frank and sincere" (45). At its best, criticism was itself an art, "the most postponed and complicated of the arts, the last qualified for and arrived at, the one requiring behind it most maturity, most power to understand and compare" ("James Russell Lowell" 548).

It was the New Criticism of Cleanth Brooks and Robert Penn Warren, of John Crowe Ransom and Allen Tate, that finally convinced professors of literature that poems, plays, and fiction could be discussed, analyzed, and evaluated as works of literature rigorously enough to justify literary criticism as an academic discipline. The older emphasis on bibliographical and historical studies provided little or no guidance in distinguishing good poems or novels from bad other than personal taste or sensibility. Judgments about poetry and literature were ultimately nonrational and inexplicable; you either got it or you didn't. There was a general feeling in many English departments in the first half of the twentieth century in the United States that members of many groups, including people from non-English-speaking countries, Americans of African descent (despite having been born and raised in the United States), and Jews from anywhere, couldn't get it. It therefore followed that aspirants for teaching positions from such groups, no matter how intelligent they might seem, were not really qualified to teach in prestigious departments of English. (It took the personal intervention of President Nicholas Murray Butler to get Lionel Trilling promoted from instructor to assistant professor at Columbia.) The New Criticism changed all that by demonstrating that the literary quality of poems and stories could be analyzed, discussed, and demonstrated by close reading and analysis of the text. Almost anybody willing to make the effort could come to understand how a poem or a short story worked. Poetic greatness was no longer something mysterious, capable of being grasped only by those with the right blood or proper cultural heritage. It was open to inspection, analysis, and debate. Criticism was not merely arbitrary impressionism but a conversation that anyone who could give reasons for their opinions could join and a discipline that could be taught and practiced by professors from any race or ethnicity. Critics like Barbara Christian, for example, had no difficulty making use of the techniques of the New Criticism in her 1985 book *Black Feminist Criticism: Perspectives on Black Women Writers* to convey the literary achievements of authors such as Toni Morrison, Gwendolyn Brooks, and Paule Marshall.

The New Criticism first gained national attention in the 1940s, although the criticism of precursors like I. A. Richards and T. S. Eliot had been appearing since the '20s. Brooks's *Modern Poetry and the Tradition* came out in 1939, and Ransom published *The New Criticism* in 1941. Probably most influential in spreading the New Criticism to classrooms throughout the United States were the "Understanding" anthologies: Brooks and Warren's *Understanding Poetry* (1938), *Understanding Fiction* (1943), and *Understanding Drama*, edited by Brooks and Robert Heilman (1948). Although its effect in the academy was to democratize the classroom, opening up the study of literature to all those willing and able to make the requisite effort, the New Criticism was censured for its putatively reactionary political implications by liberals like Alfred Kazin. In *On Native Grounds* (1942), Kazin characterized the New Criticism as "a forbidding neoclassicism that combined strangely with estheticism and fulfilled itself in reaction" (426). The New Criticism was a "Formalist cult" (436) that "made a fetish of form," which for the New Critics was not merely a key aspect of any literary work but something much more portentous, "a symbol of order in a world that had no

order ... the last orthodoxy in the absence of all other orthodox-
ies" (431). Kazin referred to the New Critics as "the Formalists"
(425), suggesting that their focus on form alone included a refusal
to see any connection between literature and the rest of human
life: "These critics made readers conscious of 'the integrity of a
work of art,' but they did this at the expense of withdrawing
literature itself into chill and airless corners of human life" (437).

The New Critical emphasis on irony, ambiguity, and paradox
did, indeed, cast suspicion on poems and stories whose literary
rank seemed to be based less on literary merit than on the affirmation of an unironic, easy-to-understand political message confirming the politics of those doing the ranking. Not that the New
Critics were alone in this suspicion. Lionel Trilling argued in
The Liberal Imagination that the novels of writers like Sinclair
Lewis and John Steinbeck were ranked far above their literary
deserts only because their messages affirmed the progressive
worldview. But at least Trilling was himself a liberal, if a contra-
rian one, and a Northerner. Some of the original New Critics, on
the other hand, were Southerners, and at least three of the major
figures (Ransom, Warren, and Tate) were on record supporting
the culture of the South against the North in *I'll Take My Stand:
The South and the Agrarian Tradition* (1930), an anthology that
both criticized the industrialized, capitalist North (along lines that
would later be taken up by environmental critics usually associated with the left) and defended segregation as part of the
Southern way of life. It was all too easy to move from justified
opposition to the racism expressed in *I'll Take My Stand* to an
unjustified attack on the New Criticism's focus on "the text itself"
as somehow both politically reactionary and implicitly racist.

A consideration of the career of Robert Penn Warren goes a
long way to demonstrate that there was no necessary connection
between racism and either loyalty to the South or the New
Criticism. Of course, only three of the "Twelve Southerners"
who contributed to *I'll Take My Stand* could be called New
Critics (John Crowe Ransom, Allen Tate, and Robert Penn
Warren) and partisans of literary modernism, and some of the
most prominent New Critics were not Southerners at all (for

example, Robert Heilman, Austin Warren, and R. P. Blackmur).
Robert Penn Warren, however, was not only a renowned poet
and novelist but also one of the original Agrarians and one of the
most prominent New Critics. Already, in his contribution to
I'll Take My Stand, "The Briar Patch," Warren had gone too
far for Donald Davidson, who tried to have "The Briar Patch"
removed from the book. In that essay, Warren anticipated the
position of the protagonist in Harper Lee's 1960 novel *To Kill a
Mockingbird*; Atticus Finch did not condemn segregation but
did declare to the jury that at least "in our courts all men are
created equal" (205). In "The Briar Patch," Warren accepted
segregation and used lower-case ("Let the negro sit beneath his
own vine and fig tree" [264]) but insisted that "justice from the
law is the least that he [the African American] can demand for
himself or others can demand for him" (252). Warren warned
that "the white workman must learn ... that he may respect
himself as a white man, but, if he fails to concede the negro
[sic] equal protection, he does not properly respect himself as a
man" (260).

To Glenn Arbery, editor of *The Southern Critics: An Anthology*
(2010), Donald Davidson, never a New Critic and a segregation-
ist to the end, was isolated from the other Agrarians, including
Warren, "in part because he retained a loyalty to the South that
the others had long before modified or abandoned" (241). One
may well ask, however, if it was truly disloyalty to the South to
ask, as Warren did in 1961, "Does the man who, in the relative
safety of mob anonymity, stands howling vituperation at a little
Negro girl being conducted into a school building, feel himself at
one with those gaunt, barefoot, whiskery scarecrows who fought
it out, breast to breast, to the death, at the Bloody Angle in
Spotsylvania, in May, 1864? Can the man howling in the mob
imagine General R. E. Lee, CSA, shaking hands with Orval Faubus,
Governor of Arkansas?" (*The Legacy of the Civil War* 57).

By the 1950s, Warren had come to see desegregation as "just
one small episode in the long effort for justice," as he wrote in
Segregation: The Inner Conflict in the South (1956). In that book
and in *Who Speaks for the Negro?* (1965), Warren confronted

the full implications of his beliefs. *Segregation* ends with a self-interview, in which Warren identifies himself as "a Southerner" who is "afraid of the power state" and thinks that "the Northern press sometimes distorts Southern news" (63) but who is nevertheless "for desegregation" (64), in large part because "I don't think you can live with yourself when you are humiliating the man next to you" (63). The continuity between the lesson Warren in 1930 thought the "white workman" needed to learn and what by 1956 he had learned for himself illustrates the larger truth that Warren's stand for racial equality in the 1950s and '60s did not require him to abandon the New Criticism or the South. The New Criticism rejected doctrinaire thinking and emphasized the difficulty of drawing unambiguous morals from human relationships when understood, as the best literature made possible, in their full complexity. In both *Segregation* and *Who Speaks for the Negro?*, Warren makes his own belief in racial equality clear while presenting a gallery of portraits of specific individuals, black and white, from all sides of the political and ideological spectrum, with a wealth of concrete details and without self-righteousness.

Perhaps the most characteristic and certainly one of the best examples of the New Criticism in practice is Cleanth Brooks's *The Well Wrought Urn: Studies in the Structure of Poetry* (1947). Brooks analyzes ten well-known works from the seventeenth through the twentieth centuries, convincingly disproving the notion that the New Criticism was useful, if at all, only in considering poetry in the schools of either John Donne or T. S. Eliot and demonstrating that close reading could be carried on without ideological animus. More than sixty years after they first appeared, Brooks's readings of poets as various as Robert Herrick, Thomas Gray, John Keats, and Alfred, Lord Tennyson remain persuasive. Alfred Kazin had complained that the New Critics refused to see the poet as, in Wordsworth's phrase, simply "a man speaking to men" (*On Native Grounds* 433). Brooks answered him in his chapter "What Does Poetry Communicate?" in the course of an analysis of Robert Herrick's "Corinna's Going a-Maying." Brooks points out that a careful study of Herrick's poem does not result in "locating an idea or set of ideas which the poet has communicated with certain appropriate decorations" but rather in a view of "the poem itself as a process of exploration" (74). Brooks demonstrates that it is impossible, if one takes the poem seriously and attentively, to dismiss it as simply another "statement of the *carpe diem* theme" (67), as one would be likely to do, given the premise that Herrick should be thought of as speaking or communicating to the reader in a conversational way. Instead, the poem is better thought of as a "process of exploration" in which Herrick works out the conflict-ing claims of pagan and Christian attitudes in relation to the spring rites that the poet both calls Corinna to join and also deprecates as only "the harmless follie of the time" (68). Brooks feels no need to share with the reader his judgment as to whether it is pagan or Christian values that are superior, but he does make a strong case that the poem affirms both in different ways, making it difficult if not impossible to summarize the "meaning" of the poem. Attempts to do so are likely to result in something similar to what Brooks calls "my clumsy paraphrase":

All right, let's be serious. Dismiss my pagan argument as folly. Still, in a sense we are a part of nature, and are subject to its claims, and participate in its beauty. Whatever may be true in reality of the life of the soul, the body does decay, and unless we make haste to catch some part of that joy and beauty, that beauty – whatever else may be true – be lost. (72)

Surely, Brooks's summary is "clumsy" enough to discourage read-ers from taking it as a rough equivalent of Herrick's poem, thereby reinforcing the point – perhaps the central thesis of the New Criticism – that a poem of the quality of "Corinna's Going a-Maying"

communicates so much and communicates it so richly and with such delicate qualifications that the thing communicated is mauled and dis-torted if we attempt to convey it by any vehicle less subtle than that of the poem itself. (73)

This is not a "formalist" approach, looking only or even primarily at meter, rhyme scheme, and other technical devices, but rather an approach willing to be respectful to works of another place and time by devoting one's full attention to them. Contrary to the caricatures of the New Criticism claiming that it ruled out any reference to the author and thus any notion of the poet as "a man speaking to men," Brooks identifies the tensions of the poem while searching for

possible resolutions which would have appealed to Herrick the Anglican parson who lived so much of his life in Devonshire and apparently took so much interest, not only in the pagan literature of Rome and Greece, but in the native English survivals of the old fertility cults. (71)

Throughout *The Well Wrought Urn*, Brooks's criticism of each poem is based on the same act of faith that grounds his analysis of "Ode on a Grecian Urn": "namely, to assume that Keats meant what he said and that he chose his words with care" (155). The New Criticism is humanistic criticism, both because it involves listening carefully and respectfully to voices from other places and times, thereby enlarging and complicating one's sense of human experience, and also because in finding the "characteristic unity of a poem" in the way "the poet has 'come to terms' with his experience" (207) it demonstrates the way literature teaches about human life, by example and indirection rather than by explicit statement.

If the resolution of conflicting attitudes without giving short shrift to what is valid in each side in a poem or a novel may provide a model encouraging one to do justice to opposing views or emotions and yet arrive at a conclusion, it is also true that the crude application of aesthetic standards such as unity to political and social life is often disastrous. If the old South seemed to speak with a united voice, that was in large part because discordant voices were silenced by legal and extralegal coercion, including lynchings. The narrator of Milan Kundera's *The Book of Laughter and Forgetting* observes that the 1948 communist coup in Czechoslovakia was welcomed at the time by "the more dynamic, the more intelligent, the better" half of the population because of the appeal of the "great dream," "an idyll of justice for all," "a realm of harmony ... where every man is a note in a magnificent Bach fugue and anyone who refuses his note is a mere black dot, useless and meaningless, easily caught and squashed between the fingers like an insect" (8). Likewise, ideas that are attractive in politics do not necessarily work in literary criticism. In "Criticism as Pure Speculation" (1941), Ransom, arguing against organic unity as a standard, claimed that his emphasis on "local texture" not directly related to a poem's "logical structure" (138) meant that a poem could be considered "so to speak, a democratic state ... whereas a prose discourse ... is a totalitarian state" (137). It is quite possible, however, to prefer democracy to totalitarianism in politics while taking organic unity as an ideal in art and literature, the kind of unity that, as Cleanth Brooks put it, "triumphs over the apparently contradictory and conflicting elements of experience by unifying them into a new pattern" (*The Well Wrought Urn* 214).

Edmund Wilson, a critic superficially at odds with the New Criticism, affirms eloquently the human significance that the form of a lyric poem, for example, can have:

A lyric gives us nothing but a pattern imposed on the expression of a feeling; but this pattern of metrical quantities and of consonants and vowels that balance has the effect of reducing the feeling, however unruly or painful it may seem when we experience it in the course of our lives, to something orderly, symmetrical and pleasing; and it also relates this feeling to the more impressive scheme, works it into the larger texture, of the body of poetic art. The discord has been resolved, the anomaly subjected to discipline. ("The Historical Interpretation of Literature" 268)

Edmund Wilson and Lionel Trilling emphasized the connections between a writer's life and his or her work or between the work and the political and cultural world of which it was a part, whereas it was "the work itself" that was the focus of the New Critics. The differences between critics like Wilson and Trilling and critics like Cleanth Brooks and Robert Penn Warren once seemed momentous, but today it is the similarities that are striking – as is the contrast between the humanistic criticism founded by Aristotle and the cultural studies underwritten by contemporary Theory.

5

Edmund Wilson and Lionel Trilling

Edmund Wilson and Lionel Trilling were both humanistic critics. Both were influenced at different times and in different degrees by Marxist and Freudian theorizing, but it would be a mistake to categorize the writings of either as Marxist or Freudian criticism. Trilling never ceased to believe in the fundamental rightness of Freudian theory, and Wilson wrote major works under the influence of not only Freud but also Marx. Yet even when each was most influenced by doctrine, their criticism was still based on the humanistic supposition that literature provides insights into human life that cannot be supplied by any theory, no matter how brilliant. Neither, it should be noted, thought of himself as a "humanist" whose mission was the propagation of "humanism." Although one or the other might occasionally use "humanism" as a convenient way to refer to an outlook stressing the moral and intellectual value of the humanities, it was the special distinction of both Wilson and Trilling to elude in their critical practice all "isms" whatever.

Edmund Wilson remained loyal throughout his career to the view "that every valid work of art owes its power to giving expression to some specific human experience and connecting it with some human ideal." Attributing this view to the neglected critic Paul Rosenfeld in the closing essay of *Classics and Commercials*, Wilson commented that he and Rosenfeld "had in common a fundamental attitude and invoked a common cultural tradition, which it is easiest to call humanistic" ("Paul Rosenfeld: Three Phases" 875). In his moving essay "'Mr. Rolfe'" in *The Triple Thinkers*, Wilson recalls that his Greek instructor at the Hill School, Mr. Rolfe, had represented the "humanistic tradition: the belief in the nobility and beauty of what man as man has accomplished, and the reverence for literature as the record of this" (254) and reflects that he himself has been "trying to follow and feed it at a time when it has been running low" (255). At Columbia University, Lionel Trilling devoted a large part of his professional career to Columbia's Great Books program, a program "consciously humanistic in its emphasis and which insisted in the traditional humanistic way that the best citizen is the person who has learned from the great minds and souls of the past how beautiful reason and virtue are and how difficult to attain" ("The Uncertain Future of the Humanistic Educational Ideal" 165). If in his later works, beginning with *Beyond Culture* (1965), Trilling emphasized the ways in which contemporary culture was subverting "the traditional humanistic way," it was not because he himself had come to reject the humanistic ideal but because he wanted to clarify and defend it.

Their insistence on continuing to exercise independent literary judgment even when most under the spell of either Marx or Freud is perhaps the most obvious reason Edmund Wilson and Lionel Trilling are virtually nonpersons in the academy today. The second edition of *The Norton Anthology of Theory and Criticism* (NATC) is 2,758 pages long, but it has no room for Lionel Trilling. Edmund Wilson has one essay in the 2010 NATC; it is classified under "Marxism" (xxi) and "Ideology and Hegemony" (xxvii). Other critics appearing in both categories are Louis Althusser, Antonio Gramsci, Stuart Hall, Fredric Jameson, and Lisa Lowe – strange company for Wilson, who even during his comparatively brief Marxist period insisted that "Marxism by itself can tell us nothing whatever about the goodness or badness of a work of art. ... the man who tries to apply Marxist principles without real understanding of literature is liable to go horribly wrong" ("Marxism and Literature" 204). But it is probably a mistake to read too much into the NATC's categorizing when it classifies the greatest theorist of Western culture, Plato, under "Antitheory" and Marx and Engels under "Ideology and Hegemony" but not "Marxism."

The criticism of Wilson and Trilling is indeed hard to classify unless one recognizes them as members of a humanistic tradition capacious enough to study the connections between literature and society while also insisting that poems, plays, and novels should be judged on their own merits as works of art. Each insisted on making connections between literature and the larger society, and yet neither was willing to reduce literary criticism to a subdivision of psychology, sociology, or anything else. Wilson did not possess "a mind so fine that no idea could violate it," as T. S. Eliot wrote in praise of Henry James ("Henry James" 151), and yet his writing, if not his politics, remained almost unscathed from his encounters with Marx and Freud. The Freudianism of *The Wound and the Bow*, for example, is worn so lightly that the validity of the perceptive analyses of the connections between the life and the work of Dickens, Kipling, and the other writers Wilson considers does not depend at all on acceptance of the Freudian formulas. Like Matthew Arnold, both Wilson and Trilling believed that good literature was not only a source of refined pleasure for an elite but also a rich source of insight about human life that could and should be made available to as many readers as possible. Trilling and Wilson succeeded in carrying out this humanistic program at least as well as any American critics of the twentieth century. The contemporary academy's lack of interest in both critics is explained in large part by the postmodernist skepticism about the importance of literature itself. The NATC considerably understates the degree of opposition to the tradition of Arnold, Trilling, and Wilson when it acknowledges that Arnold's "ideal of literary and cultural humanism ... is one that radical critics and contemporary literary theorists have sought to complicate or undermine" (691).

Trilling was never more clear about the superiority of literature to even the best doctrines than in the book that made his reputation, a book whose title taken by itself might lead one to think that the author was interested in dividing the products of the imagination into political categories – the liberal imagination, the conservative imagination, perhaps the radical imagination, the fascist imagination, and the like. But, of course, that impression would be mistaken. Trilling was concerned above all with what he called, following Edmund Burke, "the moral imagination." Burke had insisted in *Reflections on the Revolution in France* that the revolution would end in tyranny unless supplemented and corrected by "a moral imagination, which the heart owns, and the understanding ratifies" (171). Burke's prescient warning was ignored by fellow Whigs like Charles James Fox and Americans like Thomas Jefferson, who expected a new world of "liberty, equality, fraternity" but instead got the Reign of Terror and Napoleon.

In *The Liberal Imagination*, Trilling was at pains to point out the gap between the kind of imagination expressed in the greatest modern literature and the attitudes and ideas about human beings associated with modern liberalism. It was the former that seemed to him profound and true, although disturbing, the latter shallow and false, although reassuring. In his preface, Trilling memorably asserted the importance of literature as "the human activity that takes the fullest and most precise account of variousness, possibility, complexity, and difficulty" (xxi). Literature thus opposes the inevitable one-sidedness of all political doctrines, even the most benign – one of the reasons why Plato banned the poets from his ideal republic. Trilling, however, focused on the relationship between literature and liberalism, both because he was himself a political liberal and because in the late 1940s it was easy to believe that "liberalism is not only the dominant but even the sole intellectual tradition" in the United States (xv).

Trilling did not take issue with what he identified as the characteristic liberal attitudes: "a ready if mild suspiciousness of the profit motive, a belief in progress, science, social legislation, planning, and international cooperation, perhaps especially where Russia is in question," even asserting that "these beliefs do great credit to those who hold them" ("The Function of the Little Magazine" 98). Yet these beliefs are mysteriously connected to other attitudes that do no great credit to anybody. In the essays that make up *The*

Liberal Imagination, Trilling explored what he called the "characteristic paradox" of liberalism; its goal "of a general enlargement and freedom and rational direction of human life" seems unambiguously admirable, and yet, as a movement liberalism "drifts toward a denial of the emotions and the imagination" (xx). Finding "no connection ... between our liberal educated class and the best of the literary mind of our time" ("The Function of the Little Magazine" 98–9), Trilling argued that it was liberalism, not "the literary mind," that needed to change. Liberals proudly favor legislation supposed to help the poor, yet Trilling observes that liberalism seems incapable of acknowledging the full humanity of poor people: "We who are liberal and progressive know that the poor are our equals in every sense except that of being equal to us" ("*The Princess Casamassima*" 88). The possibility that feeling pity for others often involves and even feeds a feeling of unearned superiority in oneself is unlikely to be considered by political activists. Writers anxious to speak for the poor but without access to what Trilling calls "the deep places of the imagination" ("The Function of the Little Magazine" 99) are no help either; Trilling observes in his essay "*The Princess Casamassima*" that "the literature of our liberal democracy pets and dandles its underprivileged characters" but nevertheless – or therefore – fails "to make them more than the pitied objects of our facile sociological minds" (87).

In contrast, a great writer like Henry James, speaking for no one but himself, succeeds in *The Princess Casamassima* in representing "the poor as if they had dignity and intelligence in the same degree as people of the reading class" (87). Trilling finds the special distinction of James's fiction in its "moral realism," a quality that has little to do with political attitudes and much with imaginative depth. Trilling refers to it as James's "particular gift of human understanding" (88), a gift that allows him in *The Princess Casamassima* to imagine individuals like the radical leader Paul Muniment, in whom "a genuine idealism coexists with a secret desire for personal power" (90). Surveying the literary scene at mid-twentieth century, Trilling makes an observation that seems equally true today:

We have the books that point out the bad conditions, that praise us for taking progressive attitudes. We have no books that raise questions in our minds not only about conditions but about ourselves, that lead us to refine our motives and ask what might lie behind our good impulses. ("Manners, Morals, and the Novel" 219–20)

To those who answer that what lies behind is unimportant as long as the impulses are good, Trilling answers in "Manners, Morals, and the Novel" that it is imperative that we become "aware of the dangers which lie in our most generous wishes," since "the moral passions are even more willful and imperious and impatient than the self-seeking passions" (221). But if even "generous wishes" are no guarantee of moral soundness, how can we learn to distinguish between what only makes us feel good about ourselves and what is truly good? Trilling's answer is the cultivation of "the moral imagination" through the study of literature and, particularly, the novel: "For our time the most effective agent of the moral imagination has been the novel of the last two hundred years" (222). The twenty-first century already provides enough examples of the enlistment of the "moral passions" on behalf of indiscriminate killing to make Trilling's reflections as relevant as ever.

The publication in 2008 of a new edition of *The Liberal Imagination* with an introduction by Louis Menand is predicated, one would assume, on the belief that Trilling's work speaks to the twenty-first century. Yet this new edition has a complicating factor: a reader must choose whether to read the essays in the spirit encouraged by Trilling's own preface or as instructed by Prof. Menand's introduction. Trilling hoped that his criticism would succeed "not in confirming liberalism in its sense of general rightness but rather in putting under some degree of pressure the liberal ideas and assumptions of the present time" (xvi). Louis Menand assures his readers that no such reexamination is necessary. According to Menand, Trilling believed in the obsolete notion that "there are more and less politically hygienic works of literature, and the function of criticism is to identify them and to explain why they tend to have good or bad political consequences" (x). This idea is outdated because (again according to Menand) "since the 1960s ... cultural taste has largely been liberated from politics" so that nowadays "educated people tend to be culturally promiscuous and permissive" (xi). Trilling's ideas about the "moral imagination" and "moral realism," unmentioned in Menand's introduction, have become retrograde and may be safely ignored. What one should take away, according to Menand – the "more difficult lesson of the way Trilling treats literature in *The Liberal Imagination*" – is the awareness "that there is no stable point outside a culture from which to critique it." Although Menand calls this the "more difficult lesson," it turns out that it is not so difficult after all. It is "something that is easy to see once you look at culture in the way anthropologists do." So it is this "anthropological perspective" (xii) that is the real insight to be gleaned from Trilling's work. It is "the most valuable piece of his intellectual legacy" despite, or rather because, it makes one skeptical of "the critical program for which he became celebrated" (xiv).

Menand claims to be praising Trilling, but if the truly valuable lesson to be learned from *The Liberal Imagination* is the "anthropological perspective," one wonders why one would go to a literary critic rather than to the anthropologists themselves. But why bother even with them? Menand's "more difficult lesson" is a mere corollary of the general proposition that all truth is relative, a notion that almost all students absorb even before they get to college, as Allan Bloom observed with some disapproval in 1987. Lionel Trilling believed that the "moral imagination" as expressed in literature could, indeed, provide a basis for criticizing and questioning political and social movements, including those that seem so unambiguously righteous as to be beyond criticism. Louis Menand is confident that today "educated people tend to be culturally promiscuous and permissive" (xi), so that concepts like the "moral imagination," "moral realism," and even "literature" seem outdated. If Louis Menand is right, *The Liberal Imagination* goes against the grain in the twenty-first century even more than when it was first published in 1950 – and is even more necessary.

Edmund Wilson did not worry about the gap that for Trilling was so troubling between the great literature of the twentieth century and the attitudes associated with American political liberalism. In part, this was because Trilling was more committed to liberalism than Wilson, who first turned to Marxism and then to an apparent disgust with all politics, expressed most vehemently in the introduction to *Patriotic Gore* (1962) and in *The Cold War and the Income Tax* (1963). But the differences between Trilling and Wilson were not only political; they also differed in their view of the political availability and relevance of great literature. Trilling believed that some great literature, specifically the modern masterpieces, could be made relevant to a decent politics only with great difficulty and cautious circumspection, since the most obvious political implications of such literature seemed to him dangerously antisocial. Edmund Wilson had no such fears.

Responding in "Archibald MacLeish and the Word" (1940) to the lament of Archibald MacLeish, then Librarian of Congress, that antiwar novels like *A Farewell to Arms* had "done more to disarm democracy in the face of fascism than any other single influence" (qtd. 479), Wilson did not make Trilling's point that great fiction can have spiritual authority and significance even if its apparent political implications are unclear or even disastrous. Instead, Wilson makes a case that the straightforward political message of the literature cited by MacLeish is after all quite defensible. He asks MacLeish "were there not, in short, very good reasons why anyone who served in the last war should have considered the Allied slogans an imposture?" (480). Far from justifying literature as an end in itself whose value is ultimately personal and spiritual rather than social and political, Wilson affirms the humanistic view of literature as "a technique for understanding, a medium for putting on record, the vicissitudes of human experience, a medium and a technique which must constantly be renewed to meet the requirements of changing experience" (482–3).

In *Axel's Castle*, an introduction to the modern masters whose work Trilling thought so great and yet so troubling, T. S. Eliot's "The Waste Land" is presented as an indictment of "the sterility of the Puritan temperament" (715). Wilson rejects the possibility that the poem may represent little more than "the mere gloomy moods of a New Englander regretting an emotionally undernourished youth," arguing that it captures "the desolation, the aesthetic and spiritual drouth, of Anglo-Saxon middle-class society," but even so the poem does not seem to challenge Wilson's own view of the world. Even when Wilson takes "The Waste Land" to refer more generally to "our post-War world of shattered institutions, strained nerves and bankrupt ideals" (716), the implication seems to be that Eliot is not so much raising radical and perhaps unanswerable doubts about the meaning of life as he is dramatizing attitudes and emotions that, for a number of straightforward reasons, are particularly characteristic of a specific place and time. Wilson finds the *anomie* of Eliot as expressed in "Ash-Wednesday" irritatingly personal rather than disturbingly prophetic: "And I am a little tired at hearing Eliot, only in his early forties, present himself as an 'agèd eagle' who asks why he should make the effort to stretch his wings" (733).

Perhaps the highpoint of *Axel's Castle* is its fifth chapter, "Marcel Proust." Without obfuscation or oversimplification, Wilson succeeds in bringing out the significance of Proust's masterpiece and its main character for the general reader, who is also Edmund Wilson:

> We acquire a curious affection for even the most objectionable characters in Proust: Morel, for example, is certainly one of the most odious characters in fiction, yet we are never really made to hate him or to wish that we did not have to hear about him, and we feel a genuine regret when Mme. Verdurin, with her false teeth and her monocle, finally vanishes from our sight. This generous sympathy and understanding for even the monstrosities which humanity produces, and Proust's capacity for galvanizing these monstrosities into energetic life, are at the bottom of the extraordinary success of the tragic-comic hero of Proust's Sodom, M. de Charlus. (737–8)

In *Axel's Castle* and in later essays, Wilson made the literature of high modernism available to the general reader not by slighting its complexity but by refusing to accept its technical innovations as ends in themselves and, instead, pointing to their human meaning as responses to modern life. Wilson returns to Proust in his essay on "Marxism and Literature" to illustrate his point that literary works need not deal with the class struggle to achieve moral significance:

When Proust, in his wonderful chapter on the death of the novelist Bergotte, speaks of those moral obligations which impose themselves in spite of everything and which seem to come through to humanity from some source outside its wretched self (obligations 'invisible only to fools – and are they really to them?'), he is describing a kind of duty which he felt only in connection with the literary work which he performed in his dark and fetid room; yet he speaks of every moral, esthetic, or intellectual passion which holds the expediencies of the world in contempt. (205)

Although the chapters in *Axel's Castle* on such major figures as Eliot, Proust, Yeats, and Joyce have not only retained their value but have acquired a new significance as reminders of the human meaning of works buried under mountains of academic commentary, Wilson is at his best on lesser-known writers. Although he gives the impression of having read everybody, he had little to say in his prolific career about Shakespeare, Homer, Dante, Tolstoy, or Mann, and his "Dissenting Opinion on Kafka," challenging Franz Kafka's stature as one of the great writers of the twentieth century, made almost no impact. Unlike Trilling, Wilson was neither especially enthralled nor unduly troubled by the modernist masterpieces. The difference in the two critics' responses to the modern literature of alienation is exemplified by their reactions to Kafka. The "terrible imagination" of a modernist like Franz Kafka speaks intimately and with irresistible "power" of an inner experience Trilling seemed to know only too well:

if ever we have experienced the sense that life is empty and meaningless, if ever we have suffered from the feeling that our behavior is compelled, that our will is not our own, or that it has ceased to function, we can scarcely withstand the power of Kafka's terrible imagination of man's existence. ("The Hunter Gracchus" 122)

Edmund Wilson, on the other hand, confessed that he was constitutionally unable to take Kafka seriously:

Now, it may make a good deal of difference whether one was born, like the present writer, before the end of the nineteenth century, when stability and progress were taken for granted, instead of in a period when upheaval and backsliding seemed the normal conditions of life; but, with much admiration for Kafka, I find it impossible to take him seriously as a major writer and have never ceased to be amazed at the number of people who can. ("A Dissenting Opinion on Kafka" 777)

If Wilson's criticism sometimes fails to do justice to a major writer, his treatment of minor figures is unexcelled. His criticism offers a gallery of portraits in which writers, if only they write well, are presented with respect and sympathetic understanding, no matter how slight or anomalous their work might be. One example is the portrait of the author of *Alice in Wonderland* in "C. L. Dodgson: Poet and Logician." Wilson makes a strong case for the larger importance of the Alice books "as studies in dream psychology," arguing that they "do not suffer by comparison with the best serious performances in this field – with Strindberg or Joyce or Flaubert's *Tentation de Saint Antoine*" (441). He goes on to evoke the world of Alice as

the world of teachers, family and pets, as it appears to a little girl, and also the little girl who is looking at this world. The creatures are always snapping at her and chiding her, saying brusque and rude and blighting things (as if their creator himself were snapping back at the authorities and pieties he served); and she in turn has a child's primitive cruelty. (441–2)

And yet Alice is "always a sensible and self-possessed little upper-class English girl, who never fails in the last resort to face down the outlandish creatures that plague her" (442). Lamenting that there "is no Charles Lutwidge Dodgson for grown-ups," Wilson calls for an edition of his writings that would include, besides the Alice books, Dodgson's *Curiosa Mathematica*, his *Dynamics of a Particle*, his letters, and "his articles on local events at Oxford and his journal of his trip to Russia" (443).

Wilson is unparalleled in evoking the atmosphere and spirit of unusual figures like Thomas Love Peacock, the friend of Shelley whose novels feature "the conversation in a country house, with much passing of port and claret, among highly intellectual guests, each of whom appears as the exponent of some current tendency or doctrine reduced to its simplest terms and carried to its most absurd lengths" ("The Musical Glasses of Peacock" 793–4). The various doctrines "more or less cancel one another out," leaving the reader with Peacock's own "classical common sense" – a quality whose value "should by no means be less today, at a time when extreme ideas are being violently put into practice" (794), an observation that remains as valid in the twenty-first century as when Wilson made it in 1947. Edna St. Vincent Millay is not considered a major poet today, and it may be that Wilson's estimate of her poetry was overly influenced by his affection for her, but his moving tribute to his one-time lover stands as an eloquent articulation and reaffirmation of the humanistic view of literature:

> [I]n giving supreme expression to profoundly felt human experience, she was able to identify herself with more general human experience and stand forth as a spokesman for the human spirit, announcing its predicaments, its vicissitudes, but, as a master of human expression, by the splendor of expression itself, putting herself beyond common embarrassments, common oppressions and panics. This is man who surveys himself and the world in which he moves, not the beast that scurries and suffers; and the name of the poet comes no longer to indicate a mere individual with a birthplace and a legal residence, but to figure as one of the pseudonyms assumed by that spirit itself. ("Epilogue 1952: Edna St. Vincent Millay" 607)

The eighteenth-century rationalism that was part of Wilson's intellectual equipment from the beginning and which he never abandoned perhaps kept him from appreciating fully those writers like Kafka whose vision either transcended or at least differed radically from that outlook, but it is also true that Wilson's essays demonstrate his own insistence on judging for himself, whether he is considering "classics" or "commercials" like the latest bestseller. Ready to condemn Somerset Maugham despite "his swelling reputation" ("The Apotheosis of Somerset Maugham" 725) as "a half-trashy novelist, who writes badly, but is patronized by half-serious readers, who do not care much about writing" (731), Wilson finds that the religious bestseller *The Robe*, despite being written with "an almost unrivaled fabric of old clichés" (637) – the title of the essay is "'You Can't Do This to Me!' Shrilled Celia" – nevertheless has an imaginative integrity that gives the novel "a certain purity" and makes the author worthy of "a certain respect" (639). Lloyd Douglas, the author, "has imagined the whole thing for himself," and thus "his book, on a lower level, has the same kind of dramatic effectiveness as Bernard Shaw's *Saint Joan*" (638).

Perhaps because Wilson cannot be definitively linked with any
one critical method or political ideology, it has been difficult for
his admirers to explain exactly why his criticism remains fresh and
rewarding today, especially since research and criticism on almost
all the figures he discusses has increased exponentially since his
own essays and books were written. One way to grasp Wilson's
achievement is to compare his own work with that of the critics he
himself respected. In *Classics and Commercials*, he offers a tribute
to his late Princeton classmate T. K. Whipple, the author of two
books on American literature, *Spokesmen* (1928) and the posthumously published *Study Out the Land* (1943). Wilson calls his
classmate "the first of our critics to study the new novelists and
dramatists and poets at the same time appreciatively and calmly,
to try to see the work of each as a whole and to make some sort of
summary of it" ("T. K. Whipple" 537). Whipple, like Wilson and
many other literary intellectuals, turned left in the 1930s, but,
unlike many others, the two managed, in the end, to keep their
balance. Wilson praises Whipple for managing to write criticism
that remained "unhysterical and unstampeded" despite having
digested "even a considerable dose of Marxism" (538). Wilson's
generous praise describes his own criticism even more accurately
than it does Whipple's fine work.

Two essays in *Classics and Commercials* praise George
Saintsbury, an English critic whose opinions were very different
from Wilson's – "in religion he was Church of England and in
politics an extreme Tory" – but who wins Wilson's praise because
"his prejudices were rarely allowed to interfere with his appetite
for good literature, wherever and by whomever written" ("George
Saintsbury's Centenary" 715). Wilson even argues that Saintsbury's
extreme political opinions give his criticism a dramatic interest it
would not have otherwise, "provided by the recurring conflict
between Saintsbury's Tory principles and the productions of those
of his subjects who hold contrary opinions. The thrill for the reader
results from Saintsbury's displays of gallantry in recognizing and
applauding the literary merit of writers whose views he abhors"
("George Saintsbury: Gourmet and Glutton" 763–4). Similarly,
Wilson's late masterpiece *Patriotic Gore* gains in dramatic quality

as the reader waits to see if Wilson will treat Lincoln, Grant, Alexander Stephens, and Oliver Wendell Holmes, Jr. with the reductivism that the "sea-slug" theory of history announced in the preface would seem to demand. (He does not.) And Wilson's treatment of Saintsbury himself exemplifies the "gallantry" he admires. Wilson seems to be characterizing his own work when he notes both Saintsbury's limitation and his strength: "it is true, as has sometimes been said of him, that he does not plumb the deepest literature deeply. But at least he has arrived by himself at his reasons for the greatness of the greatest. He never takes merits for granted" ("George Saintsbury's Centenary" 717).

Both Lionel Trilling and Edmund Wilson found themselves at odds with the cultural trends of the 1950s and '60s. It was Trilling, however, who formulated concepts that clarified not only his own dissatisfaction but also help us in understanding the direction of Wilson's work in those decades. Trilling lamented that the American writers of the '50s lacked interest and curiosity about their own society and thus failed to fulfill the minimal task of a novelist, "the job, that is, of giving us reasonably accurate news of the world, of telling us the way things are." For Trilling "the novelist, in his ideal character, is the artist who is consumed by the desire to know how things really are, who has entered into an elaborate romance with actuality" ("Two Notes on David Riesman" 99–100). American writers and intellectuals were all too ready to turn away from the messy compromises inevitable in liberal democratic politics to a dream of "a perfect and absolute form of government which shall make impossible the conflict of wills of actual politics" ("Two Notes on David Riesman" 97). For Trilling, however, the fundamental issue was not political but cultural and even spiritual; American intellectuals, including writers, wanted to "deny the idea of the *conditioned*" because "somewhere in our mental constitution is the demand for life as pure spirit" ("William Dean Howells" 79). Even though the attraction to the "idea of unconditioned spirit" in itself had no direct political implications, Trilling found the best evidence for this attraction in the difference between the intellectuals' response to the "failures and injustices" of capitalism and communism. As a good liberal, Trilling had no doubt that "the wide disrepute into which capitalistic society has fallen all over the world" was indeed "justified by the failures and injustices of capitalism," but he added that

> if we want to understand the assumptions about politics of the world today, we have to consider the readiness of people to condemn the failures and injustices of that [capitalist] society as compared with their reluctance to condemn the failures and injustices of Communist society. The comparison will give us the measure of the modern preference for the unconditioned – to the modern more-or-less thinking man, Communist society is likely to seem a close approximation to the unconditioned, to spirit making its own terms. ("William Dean Howells" 80)

The source of the attraction to "unconditioned spirit" was the "idea of the self" that was central to both modern literature and the culture influenced by it. This "idea of the self" Trilling identified in *The Opposing Self* could be set apart from other conceptions by "one distinguishing characteristic" that to Trilling seemed "pre-eminently important: its intense and adverse imagination of the culture in which it has its being" ("Preface" unpaged). It is a testament to the acuteness of Trilling's sensibility and the power of his ideas that these formulations can assist in understanding not only the trends of those times but also the career of even such a distinguished and strikingly distinctive figure as Edmund Wilson.

Wilson's essays and criticism of the 1950s and '60s suggest that he, like the novelists and writers whose failure to at least bring "news of the world" was lamented by Trilling, could no longer sustain interest in the society of his own time and place. In "The Author at Sixty," Wilson declared that when "I look through *Life* magazine, I feel that I do not belong in the country depicted there, that I do not even live in that country." Asking "am I, then, in a pocket of the past?" he could only offer the bare possibility that "my feelings and thoughts may be shared by many" (239). On the basis of this passage alone, one might suppose that Wilson's point has to do with *Life* magazine rather than with American society in general, but a survey of his writings in the 1950s and '60s suggests that he was no longer interested in "giving us reasonably accurate news of the world, of telling us the way things are," as he had been in the '20s, '30s, and '40s. *The Bit Between My Teeth*, subtitled "A Literary Chronicle of 1950–1965," does not include among its forty-three essays any that deal with an American novel, short-story collection, or drama from those fifteen years.

Wilson's introduction to *Patriotic Gore* (1962), his study of the literature of the Civil War, expresses a disillusionment not only with Marxism but with politics of any kind. Struggles between social groups or nations should be understood, Wilson now argues, not in terms of the political principles advanced by each group and not in terms of class struggle, as he had once believed, but by analogy to the "life at the bottom of the sea" as presented in a Walt Disney film, in which "a primitive organism called a sea slug is seen gobbling up smaller organisms through a large orifice at one end of its body; confronted with another sea slug of an only slightly lesser size, it ingurgitates that, too" (xi). Wilson has come to feel that the culture and society of the United States differs only minimally from totalitarian societies like the Soviet Union in its lack of concern for the particular human being, for the selfhood of the individual. The reductivism of the introduction is not continued, fortunately, in the portraits of individual lives that follow, but there is a sense in which what Trilling called the "idea of the self" that is characterized above all by "its intense and adverse imagination of the culture in which it has its being" skews Wilson's view of the Civil War and its significance not only in the preface but in the text that follows.

The first half of *Patriotic Gore* ends with a long portrait of Alexander Stephens, the vice-president of the Confederacy, who is presented as a figure who deserves respect as the intellectual and moral equal of Lincoln himself: "Abraham Lincoln and Alexander Stephens, who commanded one another's respect and who in intellect and career were peers, have come by this time to stand, in the crisis of the Civil War, at two opposite moral-political poles" (432). Although it is Lincoln who opposes slavery and Stephens who defends it, Wilson makes it clear that he prefers Stephens's "moral-political pole" because, for Wilson, there is an even more important issue: it is Stephens, not Lincoln, who speaks for self-hood. Lincoln is the kind who "hunts as one of a pack," whereas

Stephens "differs essentially from Lincoln in being usually at odds with the pack" (433). Stephens's "resolve to be himself and nothing but himself" (433) leads him to take risks that Lincoln would reject as imprudent. For Wilson, the fundamental issue is "the question of the exercise of power, of the backing up of power by force, the issue of the government, the organization, as against the individual, the family group – for the South that fought the war was a family group" (434). Wilson cannot but wonder "whether it may not be true, as Stephens said, that the cause of the South is the cause of us all" (434). Wilson argues that the cause of the South and the cause of the North are analogous to two opposing drives to be found in individuals of his own time, and it is clear that his own sympathy is with the former rather than the latter: "There is in most of us an unreconstructed Southerner who will not accept domination as well as a benevolent despot who wants to mold others for their own good" (435).

In considering the significance of the chapter on Alexander Stephens, it is important to remember that *Patriotic Gore* does not end with a ringing declaration that "the cause of the South is the cause of us all." Instead, the book goes on for almost another 400 pages. Over the second half of this long book, the notion that "the cause of the South is the cause of us all" and that the cause of the North and the Union is to be identified with despotism and domination is altered and qualified and finally transformed into a very different notion. Wilson's insightful analysis of the prose style of Lincoln and Grant leads him to identify the Union with an idea different from both despotism and revolt, the notion of responsibility. Observing that "Grant and Lincoln, in writing and speaking, were distinguished by similar qualities: lucidity, precision, terseness" (649), Wilson characterizes their prose as "the language of responsibility" (650). The last chapter of *Patriotic Gore* constitutes an eloquent tribute to Oliver Wendell Holmes, Jr., in which he again links the concept of responsibility with allegiance to the Union, to the United States. He praises Holmes not so much, if at all, because of his legal philosophy, but rather as an example of personal integrity, "one who was never corrupted, never discouraged or broken" (782). Despite Holmes's philosophical skepticism amounting almost to nihilism, he nevertheless lived out his "conviction that the United States had a special meaning and mission to devote one's whole life to which was a sufficient dedication for the highest gifts" (796). Wilson explains Holmes's decision to leave most of his personal wealth to the government of the United States in the last sentence of the book:

> The American Constitution was, as he came to declare, an "experiment" – what was to come of our democratic society it was impossible for a philosopher to tell – but he had taken responsibility for its working, he had subsisted and achieved his fame through his tenure of the place it had given him; and he returned to the treasury of the Union the little that he had to leave. (796)

If *Patriotic Gore* is a great book, Lionel Trilling's ideas help us understand its greatness. Edmund Wilson felt intensely the attraction of the "opposed self," the self at odds with organized society and government, and his introduction to the book demonstrates a proportionate disgust with the actuality of the United States and its government in the era of the Cold War. Yet, in its tracing out of individual lives and its careful analysis of specific texts, the body of *Patriotic Gore* dramatizes the authority of "the conditioned." The greatness of Oliver Wendell Holmes, Jr., the reader cannot help feeling, derives from his willingness, despite his philosophical skepticism, to accept his own country, with all its political corruption and cultural mediocrity, as nevertheless an entity for which one might take responsibility insofar as an individual can do so. For devotees of "unconditioned spirit," it might seem mere folly for one to dedicate "the highest gifts" to such an inevitably flawed, entirely contingent enterprise. Yet Wilson convinces the reader that it is not folly at all, not only through the eloquence of his closing passage but especially because this conclusion has been reached only after acknowledging fully and even extravagantly the attractions of the opposed self that cannot be satisfied with anything less than unconditioned spirit.

Both Trilling and Wilson made free use of "we" and "us" in describing their responses to literary works. Their ability to do so convincingly is not only testimony to a lost cultural unity, now seemingly fragmented beyond repair, but to their common rejection of any Neoplatonic or Romantic pretensions to spiritual superiority. (In a representative essay in *The Shores of Light*, "The Nietschean Line," Wilson rejected the "diluted and inconsistent Nietzscheanism" [396)] of figures like H. L. Mencken, Clive Bell, and Norman Douglas, whose criticisms of bourgeois civilization were based on "a genial understanding that he and we belong to a rare superior order of beings" [397].) A significant difference between the critical stances of Wilson and Trilling is expressed, however, in the different use each makes of the plural subject. Wilson's "we" is the editorial "we," implying that the views expressed are ones that would be held by all reasonable people if they were to examine the relevant evidence. Wilson assumes that his reader, like himself, approaches each work with an open mind, ready to be persuaded, and perhaps even seduced, by literary manipulation but ultimately able to tell the difference between "a novel worth reading" and "a piece of pure rubbish" – his characterization of Kay Boyle's World War II novel *Avalanche* ("Kay Boyle and the Saturday Evening Post" 575). Reviewing the Soviet novelist Leonid Leonov's *Road to the Ocean* in *Classics and Commercials*, Wilson takes it for granted that his own responses are likely to be similar to those of most readers: "We are conscious from the beginning that the characters are types, but we do not at first sight take them for the conventional types of Soviet fiction. . . . We give him [the author] the benefit of the doubt" ("Leonid Leonov: The Sophistication of a Formula" 673). Wilson assumes that the reader, like the critic, is capable of reflection, of recognizing that one's initial response may be mistaken: "The ending, however, is twisted to conform to Soviet propaganda: It is not till we come to the end that we are definitely let down by Leonov, but then we are badly let down. . . . Looking back, we become aware that these people have never been real in the first place, and that we have simply been distracted from minding it by the technical agility of the author" ("Leonid Leonov" 673–4). From the first, Wilson maintained that even the great modernist masterpieces were within the reach of the general reader. In "The Poetry of Drouth," his 1922 review of "The Waste Land," one of the first and still one of the most perceptive considerations of the poem, Wilson insisted that "for all its complicated correspondences and its recondite references and quotations, 'The Waste Land' is intelligible at first reading." Wilson points to the human meaning of Eliot's images, making the case that one need not recognize "any but the most obvious of Mr. Eliot's allusions to feel the force of the intense emotion which the poem is intended to convey" (870).

Lionel Trilling, in contrast to Wilson, typically uses "we" to implicate himself and his readers in some questionable moral or intellectual assumption. Much of the dramatic interest of Trilling's essays derives from his invocation of opinions that contrast with the views he wishes to ultimately propose. What makes for drama is Trilling's acceptance, through his use of the plural personal pronoun, of a certain responsibility for the opinions whose wrongness he demonstrates in the course of the essay. Here are some examples, chosen almost at random: "In Defense of Zola" begins with the assertion that "We all believe that we know all about Zola, whether we have read him or not" (15) before going on to argue that, contrary to the received opinion, Zola's works possess "moral and imaginative force" (18). The significance of D. H. Lawrence's claim that "The most exquisite literature in the world is written in the English language" is explicated by comparison to "our tendency to a solid Unesco attitude about cultures, which makes it morally wrong (undemocratic) to think of one culture as better than another" ("A Ramble on Graves" 29). Trilling characterizes the particular quality of Fanny Price, the protagonist of Jane Austen's *Mansfield Park*, a work whose greatness he intends to demonstrate, by first of all noting his own and his readers' antipathy to her: "Fanny Price is overtly virtuous and consciously virtuous. Our modern literary feeling is very strong against people who, when they mean to be virtuous, believe they know how to reach their goal and do reach it" ("*Mansfield Park*" 186). The authority of Trilling's conclusions is connected to the dramatic suspense such passages create; the reader waits to see how Trilling will manage to do justice to the position that he rejects even as he acknowledges it as in some degree his own, while still bringing out the superior wisdom of the opposed view, the view that he has only now come to appreciate, apparently, through the experience of re-reading the text in question. Just as Edmund Wilson works through the claims of the opposed self to finally acknowledge and affirm the claims of responsibility in *Patriotic Gore*, so Lionel Trilling, in essay after essay, works through ideas that are not merely "straw men" but to some extent his own to arrive finally at a different, enlarged conception that yet does not dismiss entirely "our" original opinion, the one held by "us," the one "we" believe.

In "That Smile of Parmenides Made Me Think," Trilling conveys the significance of George Santayana's way of "looking at life in detachment, from a 'height,'" by contrasting it to contemporary attitudes: "To look within is permitted; to look around is encouraged; but best not to look down – not realistic, not engaged, not democratic" (165–6). Yet Trilling, even though he seems by implication to praise the capacity for looking at things from a height, does not himself adopt this attitude in the essay. Instead, he suggests that he, like the reader, "experiences the unsanctioned altitude" of Santayana's letters "with as much guilt as pleasure" (166). Observing that readers may find it "easy" to dislike Santayana's apparent assumption of superiority, he points out that he has his "own antagonism to Santayana" (166). And Trilling goes on throughout the essay to include himself among those who find Santayana troubling or difficult; he himself is among the "Americans" Santayana makes uncomfortable: "What does alienate Americans from Santayana is the principles upon which his rejection of America is founded. That is, what troubles us is not his negations of America, but the affirmations upon which he based his sense of himself" (170). Trilling makes clear his admiration for Santayana and concludes that "for Santayana himself, his effort of self-definition had, in some ways, an amazing success" (177). But, even at the end of the essay, it seems clear that Trilling, probably like most of his readers, is not interested in achieving that kind of success for himself.

Edmund Wilson renounced his early enthusiasm for Marxism after *To the Finland Station* and after *The Wound and the Bow* did not again make use of Freudian theory in any significant way, but he was not interested in the kind of "cultural self-criticism" that marked not only Trilling's individual essays but his whole career. The possibility that malign, socially destructive ideas and attitudes might gain increased influence through their apparent endorsement by writers and critics associated with high culture did not trouble Wilson as it came to trouble Trilling. Wilson found "The Vogue of the Marquis de Sade," for example, interesting material for an essay, but the only "danger" he found with the fascination Sade held for French intellectuals was that "so much has been recently written about him that the subject is in danger of becoming a bore" ("The Vogue of the Marquis de Sade" 158). Although Wilson notes the existence of "the Sade cult" (159) and rejects the occasional attempts of the "cult" to "disguise the compulsive and inveterate sadism of the life and works of the Marquis de Sade" (167), he himself is glad that Sade's works are now considered legitimate objects of intellectual and academic study. From Wilson's own point of view, the study of de Sade, with his unapologetic "lust for cruelty" (170), can be justified for two reasons, both straightforwardly humanistic. The Marquis de Sade has "his definite importance in the history of Western thought, and there is a gap if we leave him out" (169). Rousseau's thought was tremendously influential but one-sided: "the Rousseauist doctrine was in need of a correction, a contradiction, that it got with a vengeance in Sade." And Wilson finds another, less academic reason for the Marquis's importance. The Jacobins of the French Revolution and the Bolsheviks of the Russian Revolution, and not them alone, justified violence, cruelty, and arbitrary power by claiming that everything they did was for the sake of bringing about a world of peace and plenty. Sade is worth studying because "the Marquis de Sade still stands as a reminder that the lust for cruelty, the appetite for destruction, are powerful motivations that must be recognized for what they are" (170).

Lionel Trilling's exemplar, Matthew Arnold, praised Edmund Burke in "The Function of Criticism at the Present Time" for his "return upon himself" when he considered the possibility that his animadversions on the French Revolution might be mistaken. Lionel Trilling's most striking "return upon himself" was not a single passage but rather his repeated warnings about the ways in which the great works of fiction and poetry he had championed in *The Liberal Imagination* as urgently needed correctives had become themselves in need of correction and qualification. Trilling asserted in *The Liberal Imagination* that there was "no work more necessary" than organizing "a new union between our political ideas and our imagination" ("The Function of the Little Magazine" 100), specifying that it was the modernist masters whose fiction and poetry provided the most intimate access to "the deep places of the imagination." These masters – Trilling cites "Proust, Joyce, Lawrence, Eliot, Yeats, Mann (in his creative work), Kafka, Rilke, Gide" – had written novels and poems whose implications seemed hostile to both liberalism and democracy, but Trilling had no doubt that they are "the best of the literary minds of our time." It is their work to which "our liberal educated class" should attend, not the "large literature of social and political protest" that may be "earnest, sincere, solemn" but "has neither imagination nor mind" ("The Function of the Little Magazine" 98–9). Trilling was himself a liberal, but he was confident that an increase in the influence of modernist literature could only enrich liberalism, make it less doctrinaire, less simplistic in its view of human beings. Trilling's sense of what a fuller appreciation of modernist literature might contribute to the culture seems very similar to his view of what a deeper understanding of Freud's ideas might supply. The optimistic psychologies of Karen Horney and Erich Fromm seem to be more in accord with liberal notions, but Freud's view is ultimately more useful to liberalism in the long run because it is more truthful. In Trilling's telling in "Freud and Literature," the Freudian view of human beings seems very close to the view of human life in great literature and especially in the modern masters. The insights of psychoanalysis and literature are comparable "in point of subtlety and complexity, of interest and tragic power." According to Trilling "the human nature of the Freudian psychology is exactly the stuff upon which the poet has always exercised his art" (34). There is no antagonism but instead a deep affinity between psychoanalysis and literature. Freud's psychology is not a reductive scientism but rather "a view which does not narrow and simplify the human world for the artist but on the contrary opens and complicates it" (57). Trilling's eloquent description of Freud's outlook could just as easily be a summary of the view of human life presented in the works of Joyce, Mann, and the other modern masters:

> Despite popular belief to the contrary, man, as Freud conceives him, is not to be understood by any single formula (such as sex) but is rather an inextricable tangle of culture and biology. And not being simple, he is not simply good; he has as Freud says somewhere, a kind of hell within him from which rise everlastingly the impulses which threaten his civilization. He has the faculty of imagining for himself more in the way of pleasure and satisfaction than he can possibly achieve. Everything that he gains he pays for in more than equal coin; compromise and the compounding with defeat constitute his best way of getting through the world. His best qualities are the result of a struggle whose outcome is tragic. Yet he is a creature of love. (57)

Fifteen years later, in *Beyond Culture*, Trilling was still convinced as to the profound truth of Freud's view of human beings and the world, but he was no longer so certain that the influence of art and culture was entirely benign. In "Freud and Literature," Trilling had described Freud's view of the self as "an inextricable tangle of culture and biology." Given the example of Trilling's model, Matthew Arnold, one might expect Trilling to hope that culture could be untangled from biology so that culture rather than biology would become the supreme factor in human life. For Arnold, "culture" was always an honorific term, to be identified with "the best that has been thought and said." Since Arnold, Trilling notes, the prestige of "culture" has only increased, even though Arnold's conception has been replaced by a conception drawn from the social sciences. Trilling observes in "Freud: Within and Beyond Culture" that the notion of culture as an entire way of life has made culture into "a kind of absolute" for anthropologists and even some psychoanalysts who have adopted the "principle of cultural autonomy," so that cultures are "to be thought of as self-contained systems not open to criticism from without" (92).

Trilling rejects this anticipation of multiculturalism, calling on Freud's emphasis on the power of biology not so much because it is scientifically true but because he wants it to be true. Trilling recognizes that an emphasis on the power of biology is usually considered "a reactionary part of Freud's thought" (97), but in his view it is "so far from being a reactionary idea that it is actually a liberating idea" (98). In *The Liberal Imagination*, Trilling had made clear his dissatisfaction with certain aspects of American culture, especially those associated with implicit or explicit support for Stalin's dictatorship, but he had not described "culture" itself as in need of correction. The struggle against Stalinism could be carried on within culture. Against V. L. Parrington, Trilling argued that "A culture is not a flow, nor even a confluence; the form of its existence is struggle, or at least debate – it is nothing if not a dialectic" ("Reality in America" 9). In countering the simplistic view of human life that liberalism seemed to endorse, Trilling could feel that he was not speaking only for himself but also for a significant if not large segment of the culture – the anti-Stalinist left in general and in particular the intellectual circles associated with *Partisan Review*. In *Beyond Culture*, he seems unable to point to any group that shares his viewpoint. It is now the "adversary culture" that is taken by both supporters and opponents to speak for art and literature, and one might have thought that Trilling could take his place as one of the most thoughtful and eloquent spokesmen of the adversarial viewpoint. In *The Liberal Imagination*, Trilling was able to criticize certain cultural attitudes associated with political liberalism without renouncing his own commitment to liberalism. Trilling's critique of the "adversary culture," however, is much more damning that his critique of liberalism ever was. Now, almost in desperation, he turns to biology as the only source of resistance to "cultural omnipotence":

We reflect that somewhere in the child, somewhere in the adult, there is a hard, irreducible, stubborn core of biological urgency, and biological necessity, and biological *reason*, that culture cannot reach and that reserves the right, which sooner or later it will exercise, to judge the culture and resist and revise it. (99)

In "Freud: Within and Beyond Culture," Trilling still claims that in affirming the power of the biological self against culture he is not really renouncing his own commitment to literature and high culture since literature, although itself an important part of culture, takes the side of the self against culture: "In its essence literature is concerned with the self; and the particular concern of the literature of the last two centuries has been with the self in its standing quarrel with culture" (102). This claim rings hollow, however, in the light of Trilling's awareness that, in his own place and time, art and literature is represented by the "adversary culture," which does not represent a real alternative to the dominant culture but only the appearance of one. In the preface to *Beyond Culture*, Trilling revises the claims made for literature in *The Liberal Imagination* much more radically than he does in his Freud essay. He has come to "the view that art does not always tell the truth or the best kind of truth." Art – which surely includes literature – Trilling now feels, "might well be subject, in the interests of autonomy, to the scrutiny of the rational intellect" (unpaged).

To what extent "the rational intellect" can be identified with "biological *reason*" remains unclear, despite Trilling's italicization of the latter. What is clear, however, is his recognition that the adversary culture, through its very success in affirming the liberation of the self, has in practice made it much more difficult for particular selves, specific human beings, to achieve "autonomy of perception and judgment" (unpaged). In *The Liberal Imagination*, Trilling could counter Stalinist ideology with the experience of art and literature, but, by 1965, that is no longer possible. In the preface to *Beyond Culture*, Trilling observes that "In our adversary culture such experience as is represented in and proposed by art moves toward becoming an idea, even an ideology, as witness the present ideational and ideological status of sex, violence, madness, and art itself" (unpaged). In his 1972 Jefferson Lecture, Trilling concerned himself not with the place of literature in our culture but with the standing of "Mind in the Modern World." And, although for Trilling one indication of the decline of mind is that among professors of literature "there is now a significant body of opinion which holds that literature, so far from having an educative power, can only obscure truth and impede virtue" (110), he himself does not argue that an important means of restoring the power of mind might be a renewed appreciation for the ability of literature to tell the truth and encourage virtue. Instead, it seems only too clear that "the contemporary ideology of irrationalism" that celebrates "the attainment of an immediacy of experience and perception which is beyond the power of rational mind" (123) derives a large part of its appeal and authority from the modernist literature Trilling had hailed in *The Liberal Imagination*. After all, according to "On the Teaching of Modern Literature," the lead essay of *Beyond Culture*, "Nothing is more characteristic of modern literature than its discovery and canonization of the primal, non-ethical energies" (17). Taking this literature as the voice of a wisdom superior to traditional bourgeois morality, "we consider the primitive forbidden ways of conduct which traditionally in tragedy lead to punishment by death ... as being the path to reality and truth, to an ultimate self-realization" (19). Modernist literature, or at least criticism explicating and affirming modernist literature, proclaimed the superiority of authenticity to sincerity with the result that "much that culture traditionally condemned and sought to exclude is accorded a considerable moral authority by reason of the authenticity claimed for it, for example, disorder, violence, unreason" (*Sincerity and Authenticity* 11). In such a climate of opinion, it is not so surprising – though still "appalling" – that "the doctrine that madness is health, that madness is liberation and authenticity, receives a happy welcome from a consequential part of the educated public" (171).

In finding a new value in a "rational intellect" unswayed by what seem to be the implications of literary masterworks, was Trilling moving outside the humanistic tradition and closer to the Platonic affirmation of philosophy or "mind" over literature that has been revived in another form in the postmodernist privileging of Theory over poems, plays, and novels? In answering this question, one needs to consider whether Trilling's quarrel is ultimately with the works of Eliot, Mann, Joyce, and the rest, or with the way their works have been explicated, interpreted, and used. In "On the Teaching of Modern Literature," Trilling's objection seems to be the works. It is not Norman O. Brown, R. D. Laing, or Theodore Roszak, but Trilling himself who declares that "Nothing is more characteristic of modern literature than its discovery and canonization of the primal, non-ethical energies" (17). Presumably it is the "canonization," not the "discovery," that Trilling now questions. If modern literature could be credited with discovering the self's "primal, non-ethical energies," it would be achieving the literary equivalent of Freud's psychological insights, whose profundity and importance are, in Trilling's view, undeniable. It was, however, Freud's mission to make it possible for human beings to become conscious of and thereby control those "energies," as Trilling repeatedly emphasizes. The classics of modernism, in Trilling's telling, have a very different message. Their readers are encouraged to believe that one reaches the height of spirituality by giving way entirely to one's unconscious desires, to rejecting entirely the restraints imposed by the conscience (or superego) or by the conscious self, with its concerns both about personal survival and about what people might think. The liberation of the self is thus identified with antisocial and self-destructive impulses. Trilling asserts that Clavdia Chauchat in *The Magic Mountain* is speaking not only for Thomas Mann but for "all of modern literature" when she counsels Hans Castorp about the spiritual benefits of self-destruction: "And the means of freedom which Mann prescribes (the characteristic irony notwithstanding) is the means of freedom which in effect all of modern literature prescribes. It is, in the words of Clavdia Chauchat, '*se perdre et meme ... se laisser dépérir*,'" (26). According to Trilling, "the idea of losing oneself up to the point of self-destruction, of surrendering oneself to experience without regard to self-interest or conventional morality, of escaping wholly from the societal bonds" is "the chief idea of modern literature," so much so that anyone who "is committed to an admiration of modern literature ... must also be committed to this chief idea of modern literature" (26–7).

The conclusion to "On the Teaching of Modern Literature" implies that Trilling himself is so committed; it is difficult to understand in any other way his statement that his argument should not be taken to imply an intention on his part "to question the legitimacy of the commitment" (27). It is difficult if not impossible, however, to take that statement as definitive of Trilling's overall position. The effect of the entire essay, and even more the effect of *Beyond Culture* as a whole and in particular the preface, surely is to raise questions about "the legitimacy of the commitment" to the demands of a self that recognizes no obligations and makes no commitments to family or society – to other people. Trilling's later writings, especially *Sincerity and Authenticity* and "Mind in the Modern World," leave little doubt that Trilling not only does indeed question the "legitimacy" of "the chief idea of modern literature" but sees the widespread acceptance of its "legitimacy" as a leading cause of a pervasive willingness among the cultural elite to not only tolerate but approve of "for example, disorder, violence, unreason" (*Sincerity and Authenticity* 11) as somehow inherently superior to the alternatives. But in those writings, Trilling's critique is directed not at the fiction and poetry of the modernists but at the "adversary culture" whose prestige is derived from its putative championship of modernist art and literature but which, in practice, uses that prestige to enforce a conformity more insidious than the restraints on violence and sexual conduct required by the larger culture. In his essay on "The Leavis-Snow Controversy" included in *Beyond Culture*, Trilling suggests that, whatever confusions literary intellectuals and professors may fall into, "the young" understand "quite without instruction" that great literature, if it is truly great, cannot help but promote "more energy and fineness of life," even if the author's political opinions are narrow-minded and bigoted:

They perceive that the tale is always on the side of their own generous impulses. ... They know that if a work of literature has any true artistic existence, it has value as a criticism of life; in whatever complex way it has chosen to speak, it is making a declaration about the qualities that life should have, about the qualities life does not have but should have. They feel, I think, that it is simply not possible for a work of literature that comes within the borders of greatness *not* to ask for more energy and fineness of life, and, by its own communication of awareness, bring these qualities into being. (146)

This eloquent statement reaffirming the Arnoldian view of literature as a "criticism of life" surely tells the reader more about Trilling's own feelings about literature than about the attitudes of young readers. But it is not his last word. In "The Two Environments," the last essay in *Beyond Culture*, which like the first discusses the dilemmas of the professor of literature, Trilling states flatly that "the great classic literature of modern times ... is not trivial" but warns that "there exists a trivializing force" that makes it difficult for this literature to be taken as seriously as it demands to be taken. This "trivializing force" is the adversary culture, the "second environment" (198). But if literary works are indeed to be taken as seriously as they should be, then one must reckon with the possibility that some of the implications of some of the works may be wrong-headed or misleading or dangerous to put into practice. Trilling contends that treating literature with the seriousness it demands means being willing to oppose it, to wrestle with it, and he argues that "modern criticism" has failed to meet this demand:

Modern literature ... is a literature of doctrine which, although often concealed, is very aggressive. The occasions are few when criticism has met this doctrine on its own fierce terms. Of modern criticism it can be said that it has instructed us in an intelligent passivity before the beneficent aggression of literature. Attributing to literature virtually angelic powers, it has passed the word to readers of literature that the one thing you do not do when you meet an angel is wrestle with him. (200)

It would be a mistake to suggest that the questions about modern literature Trilling raised in "On the Teaching of Modern Literature" have anything more than a superficial resemblance to the condemnation of all literature Plato mounts in the *Republic*. Nor does Trilling's statement that "art does not always tell the truth" and sometimes "might well be subject ... to the rational intellect" put him outside the humanistic tradition. Beginning with Aristotle's defense of literature against Plato, humanistic critics have refrained from making grandiose claims about the knowledge literature can provide. The notion that poetry and literature provide access to truths that are beyond criticism by the "rational intellect" is associated instead with the Neoplatonic tradition and with the claims made for literature by some partisans of Romanticism and modernism. Humanistic criticism believes literature provides insights into human life that the social sciences cannot duplicate, but its belief in the indispensability of literature does not extend to a faith in the inerrancy of even the greatest works equivalent to the faith of some adherents in the absence of error in the holy books of their religion (one reason why the notion of a "canon" of great books is source of confusion).

And even the most impressive humanistic critics can err. Trilling surely erred in assuming that Clavdia Chauchat was speaking for the author of *The Magic Mountain* when she tells Hans Castorp "It seems to us that it is more moral to lose oneself and let oneself be ruined than to save oneself" (334). Clavdia Chauchat is one of four major figures representing four alternative perspectives Hans Castorp encounters during the seven years he spends at the tuberculosis sanitarium on the "magic mountain." In the first half of the novel, Luigi Settembrini, a free-thinking intellectual who believes in "education, liberation and progress" (247), vies for influence over Hans Castorp with Clavdia Chauchat, who is no intellectual but who, in Hans Castorp's mind, stands for everything Settembrini condemns: "And what or who stood on the opposing side of patriotism, the dignity of man, and beautiful literature ... There stood ... Clavdia Chauchat – listless, worm-eaten, Kirghiz-eyed" (157). In the second half of the novel, two new figures enter: Naphta, the Jesuit priest who argues that the dictatorship of the proletariat will usher in the City of God and Mynheer Peeperkorn, who speaks incoherently but whose magnetic vitality is demonstrated when he arrives at the sanitorium with Clavdia Chauchat as a lover. Hans Castorp learns from all four, but the novel does not encourage the reader to take any one of the four as supremely authoritative.

Thomas Mann goes out of his way to make the "message" of *The Magic Mountain* clear, much clearer than one might expect from one of the masterpieces of modernism. In the chapter "Snow," Hans Castorp has a revelation, one that he himself has trouble remembering but that nevertheless stands as an explicit statement of the resolution of the contending alternatives offered in the novel. Mann even italicizes the key sentence to emphasize that this is not just Hans Castorp's thoughts but the author's as well:

I will keep faith with death in my heart, but I will clearly remember that if faithfulness to death and to what is past rules our thoughts and deed, that leads only to wickedness, dark lust, and hatred of humankind. *For the sake of goodness and love, man shall grant death no dominion over his thoughts.* (487)

To explicate the meaning of *The Magic Mountain* would, of course, require a much longer analysis, but even this short discussion should be enough to make it clear that the text of the novel does not support Trilling's claim that the work as a whole and thus Mann as the author endorses "losing oneself to the point of self-destruction." And if Trilling is mistaken about *The Magic Mountain*, the novel he chooses as the closing example to clinch his point, then his larger argument, that "losing oneself to the point of self-destruction, of surrendering oneself to experience without regard to self-interest or conventional morality, of escaping wholly from the societal bonds" is indeed the "chief idea of modern literature" seems unpersuasive. Trilling is more convincing when he argues that the "adversary culture" has made such a notion its own "chief idea" and employed the cultural prestige of art and literature, including works like *The Magic Mountain*, in furthering its advocacy.

Writing so often about what Trilling called "the dark and bloody crossroads where literature and politics meet" ("Reality in America" 10), it is no surprise that Trilling and Wilson are vulnerable to criticism for their ideas about both literature and politics. Wilson's personal life, especially his short and troubled marriage to Mary McCarthy, has sometimes been used to impugn his reputation as a judicious literary critic, as have his political opinions, which could be sympathetically characterized as deeply felt rather than judicious. In the presidential election of 1932, his candidate was the Communist William Z. Foster, while in *To the Finland Station* (1940), Lenin is presented as a heroic figure whose practical sagacity is matched by his moral probity. In *The Cold War and the Income Tax*, Wilson complains with great vehemence and moral indignation about the income tax after being taken to court by the Internal Revenue Service (IRS) for nonpayment of income tax after having failed to file returns for nine years, "unaware that failure to file had been made a serious offense" (13). In the preface to *Patriotic Gore*, Wilson refuses to find any complexity in history, explaining the cause of the opposition of the United States to the Soviet Union after World War II as nothing more than "the irrational instinct of an active power organism in the presence of another such organism, of a sea slug of vigorous voracity in the presence of another such sea slug" (xxxii).

Beyond the question these opinions raise about Wilson's moral and political awareness, they, like his sometimes chaotic personal life, raise the larger issue as to whether the study of literature really does make possible deeper insights and greater wisdom about human affairs, as the humanistic tradition affirms. Perhaps the answer may be found by way of analogy to the reply reportedly given by Evelyn Waugh when Nancy Mitford asked him how he squared "being so horrible with being a Christian." Waugh answered "were he not a Christian he would be even more horrible" (*Evelyn Waugh* 505). There seems little doubt that the political judgments Wilson expressed in his writings, foolish as these sometimes were, would have been much more foolish if he had not been determined to keep ideology from influencing his literary judgments. Wilson's essay on "Marxism and Literature" in *The Triple Thinkers*, written when Wilson was still sympathetic to Marxism if not to Stalinism, firmly rejects the Marxist demand that writers avoid merely personal issues and deal instead with the class struggle. In literature, Wilson suggests, the implications of a work go far beyond its specific content; "a sort of law of moral interchangeability prevails: we may transpose the action and the sentiments that move us into terms of whatever we do or are ourselves" (205). Even the *To the Finland Station*, written during the years when Wilson's Marxism was most ardent, retains a sense of the complexity and variety of human beings that prevents it from descending to the cheap polemics and vulgar Marxism so common among literary intellectuals of the period. And the body of *Patriotic Gore* refutes the reductivism of its preface in the most effective way possible, by bringing out, through close studies of literary works and individual lives, the inevitable failure of any historical theory, including the one offered in the preface, which claims to explain them all.

Just as Wilson remained a humanistic critic even when his faith in Marxism was strongest, so Lionel Trilling never let his lifelong faith in Freudian psychology lead him to reduce his critical response to a mere application of psychoanalytic principles. And the breadth of Trilling's literary interests seems to have been an important reason he did not, unlike so many literary intellectuals, join the "adversary culture" that claimed to base itself on what Trilling called in the preface to *Beyond Culture* "the adversary intention, the actually subversive intention that characterizes modern writing" (unpaged). Trilling revered the great modernists, and in "On the Teaching of Modern Literature," he told his readers that if one took modernist literature as seriously as it demanded, one was obligated as a matter of intellectual honesty to support the "chief idea" of that literature, the notion celebrated by the adversary culture, that one's highest goal should be "freedom from society itself," even or rather especially if this involved "losing oneself up to the point of self-destruction" (26). And yet in the preface to *Beyond Culture*, the volume in which "On the Teaching of Modern Literature" appears, and in the writings that followed, especially *Sincerity and Authenticity* and "Mind in the Modern World," Trilling does not make the case for the higher morality of self-destruction. Instead, he suggests that there are times when what seem to be the implications of a particular group of literary works, even if the works themselves are of the first rank, should be rejected: "art does not always tell the truth or the best kind of truth" (unpaged). Surely part of the reason Trilling did not commit himself for long to what seemed to him the "chief idea" of modernist literature is that he also knew and loved the literature of other times and places. Leo Tolstoy in *Anna Karenina*, Keats in his letters as well as his poems, Jane Austen in all her novels but most strikingly in *Mansfield Park*, had very different chief ideas, and Tolstoy, Keats, Austen, and their peers demanded to be taken just as seriously as the modern masters.

Lionel Trilling and Edmund Wilson were great humanistic critics not because they were always right but because they repeatedly succeeded in bringing insights gleaned from fiction, poetry, and plays to bear on moral, cultural, and political questions. Their writings are literary criticism because they begin with literature, and their literary judgments are based on the literary quality of the work under discussion, not on the moral, cultural, or political opinions it seems to promote. Both believed the critic has an obligation to present as undistorted a view of the work as possible. Wilson would have agreed with Trilling's late restatement of the creed he had affirmed in his first book: "We expect of the critic that he will make every possible effort, in Matthew Arnold's famous words, 'to see the object as in itself it really is,' and to describe it accordingly" ("What Is Criticism?" 78–9). Both Wilson and Trilling were, of course, as aware as contemporary postmodernists that complete objectivity is unattainable, but, unlike the latter, both thought the effort worth making – not only worth making but obligatory if one were to claim to be a literary critic in the tradition of Aristotle, Samuel Johnson, and Matthew Arnold.

6

Democracy, Popular Culture, and Ralph Ellison

Edmund Wilson and Lionel Trilling were both "true apostles of equality," if that distinction rightly belongs, as Matthew Arnold declared in *Culture and Anarchy*, to those "men of culture" who have succeeded in bringing "the best ideas of their time" to the general reader because they were able "to divest knowledge of all that was harsh, uncouth, difficult, abstract, professional, exclusive; to humanise it" (113). Neither patronized their readers as "the masses," as many writers were likely to do, in Arnold's opinion: "Plenty of people will try to give the masses, as they call them, an intellectual food prepared and adapted in the way they think proper for the actual condition of the masses. . . . Plenty of people will try to indoctrinate the masses with the set of ideas and judgments constituting the creed of their own profession or party" (112). The notion of "masses" is antithetical to Arnoldian "culture," which always "seeks to do away with classes, to make the best thought and known in the world current everywhere" (113).

In *The Souls of Black Folk* (1903), W. E. B. Du Bois, speaking from personal experience, eloquently confirmed the ability of high culture to provide the basis for a community in which the usual barriers to equality – class and race – are surmounted, even as they remain impassable in the world outside:

I sit with Shakespeare and he winces not. Across the color line I move arm in arm with Balzac and Dumas, where smiling men and welcoming

women glide in gilded halls. From out the caves of evening that swing
between the strong-limbed earth and the tracery of the stars, I summon
Aristotle and Aurelius and what soul I will, and they come all graciously
with no scorn nor condescension. (438)

Neither Arnold nor Du Bois expected all human beings to be
equally appreciative of high culture, but each thought it was the
obligation of those who could appreciate and understand the fine
arts and the humanities – Arnold's "men of culture" and Du Bois's
"talented tenth" – to do what they could to make art and culture
available to as large a public as possible. Du Bois, like Arnold, was
certain that great art could not but be on the side of truth and
justice. In "Criteria of Negro Art" (1926), Du Bois asserted that
"all Art is propaganda and ever must be, despite all the wailing of
the purists," but the context makes it clear that his point is almost
the opposite of what the statement taken out of context seems to
mean. In context, Du Bois is arguing that great art, Art with a
capital "A," is always "propaganda" for the truth and for justice:

The apostle of Beauty thus becomes the apostle of Truth and Right not by
choice but by inner and outer compulsion. Free he is but his freedom is
ever bounded by Truth and Justice; and slavery only dogs him when he is
denied the right to tell the Truth or recognize an ideal of Justice.
    Thus all Art is propaganda and ever must be, despite the wailing of the
purists. (1000)

Du Bois insisted that "it is, ever was and ever will be from the top
downward that culture filters," but he also insisted that the efforts
of a cultural elite are ultimately in the interests of the other nine-
tenths: "The Talented Tenth rises and pulls all that are worth the
saving up to their vantage ground" ("The Talented Tenth" 847).
Both Arnold and, to a lesser extent, Du Bois have been criticized
by contemporary proponents of cultural studies for the elitism
they displayed in stressing the importance of great works of art
and failing to appreciate the significance of works of popular
culture.
    Of course, many writers and critics, including some now clas-
sified as irremediably elitist, did not need to wait for the advent of
cultural studies to observe that popular art at its best could both

"delight and teach," in Horace's famous phrase. T. S. Eliot, for example, praised the music hall performer Marie Lloyd because her act was "all a matter of selection and concentration" ("Marie Lloyd" 406). Unlike lesser performers, she did not need to depend on "the grotesque" or "exaggeration" for humor ("Marie Lloyd" 405–6). Eliot's essay on the art of the music hall was no mere fluke; it reflected his enduring belief that a meaningful culture must involve much more than high art. *The Norton Anthology of Theory and Criticism* (NATC) implies that the notion of culture as the way of life of an entire society is a recent theoretical innovation when it comments that "Against Matthew Arnold's view of culture as the best that has been said and known, cultural studies considers culture to include the whole way of life of a people or a subset of that people" (2478). But the view of culture as a "whole way of life" was eloquently affirmed by, among others, T. S. Eliot long before the cultural studies movement got underway. In *Notes towards the Definition of Culture*, he argued that culture

includes all the characteristic activities and interests of a people: Derby Day, Henley Regatta, Cowes, the twelfth of August, a cup final, the dog races, the pin table, the dart board, Wensleydale cheese, boiled cabbage cut into sections, beetroot in vinegar, nineteenth-century Gothic churches and the music of Elgar. (104)

One can discover many thoughtful considerations of works of popular culture as art as well as data for sociology long before popular culture became a subject for academic study. George Orwell, for example, wrote about magazines for boys, off-color postcards, and crime bestsellers in essays that took account of political and economic factors but also treated the works he studied as expressions of points of view that deserved to be taken as seriously as the outlook of James Joyce or W. B. Yeats. In his 1939 study of "Boys' Weeklies" Orwell dismissed their political outlook as "that of a rather exceptionally stupid member of the Navy League in the year 1910" (109), but he nevertheless affirms their real, if limited, imaginative achievement. *Magnet* in particular "possesses a really first-rate character in the fat boy, Billy Bunter," (79) and if the papers' politics are regrettably unenlightened, "on its level the moral code of the English boys' papers is a decent one. Crime and dishonesty are never held up to admiration, there is none of the cynicism and corruption of the American gangster story" (108). And if the papers are unthinkingly patriotic, "their patriotism has nothing whatever to do with power-politics or 'ideological' warfare. It is more akin to family loyalty" (95); it is a patriotism "with no Fascist tinge" (93). In "Raffles and Miss Blandish" (1944), Orwell again draws a contrast between an outdated, class-centered outlook, here represented by E. W. Hornung's popular Raffles novels, that despite all its failings remains in some respects morally admirable, and a more up-to-date viewpoint that "takes for granted the most complete corruption and self-seeking as the norm of human behaviour" (210), represented in this essay by an American bestseller, James Hadley Chase's *No Orchids for Miss Blandish*. The Raffles stories "belong to a time when people had standards, though they happened to be foolish standards" (208). The contrast suggests an unwelcome moral: "one is driven to feel that snobbishness, like hypocrisy, is a check upon behaviour whose value from a social point of view has been underrated" (221). Orwell also wrote eloquently about the ribald postcards of Donald McGill, which gave "expression to the Sancho Panza view of life" and thus to "something enduring in our civilization" (135). McGill's postcards gave expression to a viewpoint that "can never be suppressed altogether and needs a hearing occasionally" (137). In providing that hearing, McGill was a true artist, and his postcards a kind of art.

More recently, Philip Furia has studied the lyrics of the masters of American popular song in *The Poets of Tin Pan Alley* with the kind of aesthetic judgment and close attention the New Critics devoted to John Donne. Cole Porter, Furia demonstrates, wrote songs "with witty images and allusions that keep 'topping' each other in verve and brilliance," but also "some of the worst lyrics – melodramatic, histrionic, banal – of the age" (133). Furia's praise of "Let's Do It" captures Porter's poetic achievement: "In 'Let's Do It' his listing of various creatures and their modes of copulation mirrors the very erotic universe it describes – image propagating image with an imaginative fecundity that rivals nature's own fertility" (161).

In *Hole in Our Soul,* Martha Bayles was similarly able to appreciate the best in popular music without losing the capacity to make relevant distinctions, as in this comparison between the music of the Rolling Stones and their predecessors:

Despite the boastful tone of such Chicago hits as Muddy Waters's "I Just Want to Make Love to You'" or Howlin' Wolf's "Little Red Rooster," both renditions reserve, by means of finely tuned vocal and instrumental techniques, that "mixtery" of sound and emotion that suggests a playful disinterestedness toward the boastful impulses in man. In the Stones' hyped-up covers of these same songs, there is nothing but boastfulness, in a vocal so harshly weak that it forces our attention back to the guitar, which is being played louder and faster than the original, but certainly no better. (200)

One reason such critics have been able to address works of popular culture so thoughtfully is that they did not frame their criticism around the terms that for so long dominated discussions of high and popular culture: highbrow, lowbrow, and middlebrow. Van Wyck Brooks argued in *America's Coming of Age* (1915) that American culture was characterized by a seemingly absolute division between "Highbrow" and "Lowbrow" both of which, Brooks emphasized, were intrinsically unsatisfactory:

The very accent of the words "Highbrow" and "Lowbrow" implies an instinctive perception that this is a very unsatisfactory state of affairs. For both are used in a derogatory sense. The "Highbrow" is the superior person whose virtue is admitted but felt to be an inept unpalatable virtue; while the "Lowbrow" is a good fellow one readily takes to, but with a certain scorn for him and all his works. And what is true of them as personal types is true of what they stand for. They are equally undesirable, and they are incompatible; but they divide American life between them. (18)

Brooks traces the division to the Puritans, certain that "the Puritan Theocracy is the all-influential fact in the history of the American mind" (18). The Puritans were both religious dissidents and settlers in a wilderness, but their religion provided no guidance to their urgent practical problems: "The eternal issues the Puritans felt so keenly, the practical issues they experienced so monotonously threw almost no light on one another; there was no middle ground between to mitigate, combine or harmonize them" (19). American society lacked the "genial middle ground" (18) between high culture and everyday practicalities that critics like Arnold, Du Bois, and Brooks himself were attempting to cultivate. The American writers of the nineteenth century were not Puritans, but American literature has been unable to confront or express the realities of American life because the Puritan legacy encouraged the identification of high culture with moral high-mindedness: "This is the whole story of American literature: in a more than usually difficult and sordid world, it has applied its principal energies to being uncontaminated itself. It has held aloof, as a consciously better part, like all American idealism" (78). Brooks's analysis seemed to imply that as long as Americans who attend to Arnold's "best thought and known in the world" were thought of as "Highbrows" for so doing – and, even more importantly, thought of themselves as "Highbrows" – the efforts of Arnold's "men of culture" and Du Bois's "Talented Tenth" in making high culture available to all would be wasted or at least vitiated.

Van Wyck Brooks believed that the division into "Highbrow" and "Lowbrow" was something peculiarly American, a result of the continuing influence of the Puritan heritage that did not afflict other societies. Brooks confides that "I have proposed these terms to a Russian, an Englishman and a German, asking each in turn whether in his country there was anything to correspond with the conceptions implied in them. In each case they have been returned to me as quite American, authentically our own" (17). In 1932, however, Virginia Woolf observed in "Middlebrow," an essay not published until after her death, that in England "the finest minds of our age have lately been engaged in debating, not without that passion which befits a noble cause, what a highbrow is and what a lowbrow" (196). For Woolf, however, "highbrow" and "lowbrow" have a quite different significance than they do for Brooks. In American usage, Brooks notes, both terms have "a derogatory sense." In contrast, Woolf considers both terms true honorifics. She has "always been so proud to be called highbrow" and asserts that "if I could be more of a highbrow I would" (196). Conversely, lowbrows are also worthy of respect, and they are in

fact respected by highbrows: "I honour and respect lowbrows –
and I have never known a highbrow who did not" (197).

Woolf objects, however, to "middlebrows" – "They are the
people, I confess, that I seldom regard with entire cordiality." The
closest Woolf comes to a definition of middlebrows is her description of them as "go-betweens; they are the busybodies who run
from one to the other [from highbrows to lowbrows] with their tittle
tattle and make all the mischief" (198). This sounds like an
unfriendly description of Arnold's "men of culture" and most of
Du Bois's "talented tenth" – people not among the great creators or
thinkers but critics and interpreters of the great works to the public
at large. In Woolf's view they do not occupy "a genial middle
ground" of their own, as Brooks supposed, since they are always
"betwixt and between" (198) highbrows and lowbrows. Both highbrows and lowbrows are necessary elements of any society, it
appears, but middlebrows are expendable. A highbrow, according
to Virginia Woolf, "is the man or woman of thoroughbred intelligence who rides his mind at a gallop across country in search of
an idea" (196). Representative highbrows include "Shakespeare,
Dickens, Byron, Shelley, Keats, Charlotte Brontë, Scott, Jane Austen,
Flaubert, Hardy, or Henry James" (197). Lowbrows, if they lack
intelligence, do possess vitality: "By a lowbrow is meant of course a
man or woman of thoroughbred vitality who rides his body in
pursuit of a living at a gallop across life" (197). Highbrows "depend
completely upon those who are called lowbrows" because they are
themselves "wholly incapable of dealing successfully with what is
called real life" (197). Lowbrows also need highbrows, since lowbrows urgently desire to be "shown what life looks like," and it is
only the highbrows who can create the books and films that satisfy
this desire. Middlebrows, however, do not satisfy any important
mental or physical need but only get in the way, spreading the lie
that highbrows hate lowbrows and lowbrows hate highbrows (198).
Middlebrows write, but they write poorly; they play sports, but
they do that poorly, too. A middlebrow is a "bloodless and perni-
cious pest," so much so that "highbrows and lowbrows must band
together to exterminate a pest which is the bane of all thinking and
living" (202). Woolf ends with a flourish that is also a threat,

presumably rhetorical: "If any human being, man, woman, dog, cat, or half-crushed worm dares call me 'middlebrow' I will take my pen and stab him, dead" (203).

"Middlebrow" began as a letter to the *New Statesman* that was never sent and was finally published posthumously. Woolf's *cri de coeur* is easy to criticize as an argument. Her list of "complete and representative" (197) highbrows excludes philosophers and includes writers whose interest in ideas, at least abstract ideas, seems decidedly secondary, leading one to question her description of a highbrow as someone "who rides his mind ... in pursuit of an idea" (196). Woolf's evidence that lowbrows need highbrows who can show them "what their lives look like" is based on "the crowds lining up to get into the movies" even "on a wet winter's night" (198). But very few moviemakers could be considered highbrows, at least if "Shakespeare, Dickens, Byron," and the rest of Woolf's list are supposed to exemplify the group. And very few movies, in 1932 or any other time, even pretend to dramatize the everyday lives of the kind of people Woolf designates as "lowbrows" – those who spend most of their energy working for a living. Virginia Woolf herself meanwhile wrote and published many essays during her lifetime expressly presenting the viewpoint not of a highbrow but of "the common reader." Citing Samuel Johnson, Woolf described this common reader as someone who is "worse educated" and "not [as] gifted" as the "critic and the scholar" (11) but who nevertheless has "some say in the final distribution of poetical honours" (12). Strikingly, in the light of the "Middlebrow" essay, this "common reader" is a figure that Virginia Woolf considered worthy to take as a model for her own work as a critic; her first collection of essays, including titles such as "On Not Knowing Greek," is entitled *The Common Reader*. No doubt Woolf's "common reader" differs from her "middlebrow" in a number of respects, but then her hypothetical "common reader" differs as well from her portraits of both highbrows and lowbrows. In her critical essays in the "common reader" series, Virginia Woolf is herself one of the "apostles of equality" that Matthew Arnold commended so highly – but whom she seemed to stigmatize as "middlebrows" in her unsent 1932 letter to *The New Statesman*.

Dwight Macdonald, whose clarity and wit won his essays an audience that included Virginia Woolf's common reader, who "reads for his own pleasure rather than to impart knowledge or correct the opinions of others" ("The Common Reader" 11), shared both Woolf's willingness to let lowbrows be lowbrows as long as high culture could be sustained and her distaste for middlebrow culture, which he called "Midcult." In his influential analysis *Against the American Grain: Essays on the Effects of Mass Culture* (1962), Macdonald was ready to "let the masses have their Masscult, let the few who care about good writing, painting, music, architecture, philosophy, etc., have their High Culture, and don't fuzz up the distinction with Midcult" (73). Unlike Woolf in "Middlebrow," Macdonald did not assume that the movies to which the so-called lowbrows thronged were made by highbrows. On the contrary, he believed that one "condition for success in Masscult is that the writer, artist, editor, director or entertainer must have a good deal of the mass man in himself" (32). Hollywood movies, like best-sellers and television programs, were examples of "Masscult," industrial products that were not merely "unsuccessful art" but "non-art" or "even anti-art" (4). Relying heavily on the analyses of the Frankfurt School, Macdonald argued that the products of "masscult" differed radically from even the most popular art of the past: "It is one thing to satisfy popular tastes, as Robert Burns's poetry did, and quite another to exploit them, as Hollywood does" (14). For most of his life, Macdonald was on the extreme left politically – he was unwilling to support the Allied cause in World War II because although the United States and its allies were fighting against Nazism, they were not fighting for socialist revolution, only for what then seemed to Macdonald "an opportunistic adaptation to a reactionary status quo" ("Looking at the War" 11). He was not happy, he wrote in *Against the American Grain*, to be making an argument that could be seen "as undemocratic and snobbish." Macdonald protested that "it is precisely because I do believe in the potentialities of ordinary people that I criticize Masscult" (11), but he had nevertheless come to the unpalatable but seemingly inescapable conclusion that the masses, at least in the United States, were no more likely to reject Masscult in favor of high culture than to reject capitalism in favor of socialism. Political democracy remained an undoubted good, but cultural democracy, unfortunately, seemed to involve an unwillingness to discriminate between the better and the worse in literature and the other arts. Macdonald observed that "discrimination" of any kind was "an ugly word in liberal democratic America." In contrast "Masscult is very, very democratic; it refuses to discriminate against or between anything or anybody" (12).

The greatest strength of Macdonald's argument was not his denunciation of the products of Masscult, nor his celebrations of high art, but rather his critiques of representative works of "Midcult," which was in any case the real threat to high culture. Midcult was more dangerous and confusing because, although Masscult products didn't pretend to be anything but entertainment, Midcult "pretends to respect the standards of High Culture while in fact it waters them down and vulgarizes them" (37). Works of Midcult make use of techniques associated with the modernist avant-garde in order to affirm clichés in a portentous way. Thus, Hemingway's *Old Man and the Sea* is written in "fake-biblical prose" and has "only two characters, who are not individualized because that would take away from the Universal Significance" (41). Thornton Wilder's *Our Town* offers the same "nostalgia for small-town life" as Norman Rockwell's paintings but makes use of "imaginary props and sets and the interlocutory stage manager" (43, 44) to convey an aura of avant-garde experimentation. In the course of his devastating critique of James Gould Cozzens's bestselling and critically acclaimed *By Love Possessed*, Macdonald describes a new Midcult genre, the "Novel of Resignation" whose message of conformity is utterly opposed to that of its High Culture source, a genre typified by Tolstoy's *The Death of Ivan Ilych*, in which "a successful, self-satisfied hero ... is led by experiences in 'extreme situations' to see how artificial his life has been and who then rejects the conventional world and either dies or begins a new, more meaningful life." In Midcult novels, the same plot is used, but now "the highest reach of enlightenment is to realize how awful the System is and yet to accept it *on its own terms*" [emphasis in original] (210). Macdonald lists other examples of this genre: the novels of John Marquand, Sloan Wilson's *The Man in the Gray*

Flannel Suit, and Herman Wouk's *The Caine Mutiny*, whose message seems to be that "it is better to obey a lunatic cowardly Captain Queeg, even if the result is disaster, than to follow the sensible advice of an officer of lower grade . . . and save the ship" (210–11).

More than fifty years after *Against the American Grain* was published, Macdonald's critiques of individual works remain sharp, funny, and convincing. His attempt to categorize all novels, plays, poems, and films as either Masscult, Midcult, or High Art, however, seemed unworkable from the beginning. Reducing critical judgment to the placing of any particular work in one of three pigeonholes left little room for the kind of nuanced discrimination that Macdonald claimed to champion. It turns out, furthermore, that it is more difficult to identify the real "highbrows" than one might expect. According to Virginia Woolf, Byron and Walter Scott were each "a complete and representative highbrow" ("Middlebrow" 197), whereas to Macdonald both "represented an aspect of Masscult, Scott the production line, Byron the emphasis on the artist himself" (21). The conclusion to be drawn from such disagreements is not that Woolf is to be trusted or that Macdonald knows better but rather that disputes about such crude labels for a particular artist or work are generally pointless. Macdonald himself could not help contradicting his own categorizing; in *Against the American Grain*, he characterizes virtually all Hollywood movies as Masscult, but in the reviews collected in *Dwight Macdonald on Movies*, he judged each film on its own merits, frequently finding aspects worth praising in commercial films made by the big studios.

Virginia Woolf and Dwight Macdonald considered middlebrow books, films, and programs a greater source of cultural confusion than "lowbrow" productions that had no artistic pretensions at all. Other cultural commentators, including some on both the extreme right and the extreme left – Southern Agrarians and members of the Frankfurt School, for example – saw "lowbrow" popular culture as the main enemy. Agrarians like Andrew Lytle and Donald Davidson felt that the Southern way of life was threatened almost as much by popular culture as by capitalism and technology. Lytle argued that "to maintain farming life in an

industrial imperialism," the farmer must not only become economically self-sufficient by growing his own food and even making his own clothes but also "throw out the radio" and "forsake
the movies" ("The Hind Tit" 244). Andrew Lytle and the other
Agrarians were certain that the farmers of the South were better
off without "motor-cars, picture shows, chain-store dresses for the
women-folks, and all the articles in Sears-Roebuck catalogues"
("The Hind Tit" 206). The farmers themselves clearly thought
otherwise. Another Agrarian, Donald Davidson, lamenting that
the "tradition of poetry as song survives only in our heritage of
folk song, secular and sacred, of the centuries past," found nothing
worth celebrating in the lyrics of Cole Porter, Lorenz Hart, and
Johnny Mercer and instead merely issued a wholesale condemnation of "the steady descent into vulgarization, sentimentality, and
finally outright laundry [*sic*] and obscenity that mark popular song
in our own century" ("Poetry as Tradition" 256).

The comments of Lytle and Davidson can be at least partially
justified as exaggerations made in the course of a last-ditch defense
of folk and traditional culture. The same cannot be said, however,
for the denunciations of popular culture in general and jazz in
particular issued by Theodor Adorno, a leading figure of the
Frankfurt School whose revision of Marxism as "critical theory"
was a major source of what came to be known as cultural studies.
Adorno's disquisitions on jazz stand out even among the writings of
the Frankfurt School for their union of theoretical arrogance, ignorance of subject matter, and contempt for the "masses" on whose
behalf the Frankfurt School claimed to be working. In "Perennial
Fashion – Jazz," he did not discuss any specific song, composition,
or performance by any particular singer, composer, or musician,
nor did he entertain the possibility that those who appreciated Duke
Ellington, Count Basie, or Billie Holiday might have had good
reasons for doing so. Adorno knew that "jazz fans identify with
the society they dread for having made them what they are" (126).
Adorno was certain that they had no real appreciation or understanding of the music. Instead, they were simply "intoxicated by the
fame of mass culture. . . . What is important to them is the sense of
belonging as such, identification" (128). If they seemed to be

enthusiastic about a singer or a band, it was only because "to be carried away by anything at all, to have something of their own, compensates for their impoverished and barren existence" (128). Adorno provided a more technical if equally baseless explanation by calling on psychoanalysis:

> The aim of jazz is the mechanical reproduction of a regressive moment, a castration symbolism. "Give up your masculinity, let yourself be castrated," the eunuchlike sound of the jazz band both mocks and proclaims, "and you will be rewarded, accepted into a fraternity which shares the mystery of impotence with you, a mystery revealed at the moment of the initiation rite." (129)

In the twenty-first century, the academic study of popular culture has become a part of cultural studies, a transdisciplinary approach whose attraction derives in large part from its implicit promise that adepts gain the ability to make authoritative pronouncements about all aspects of human life without going to the trouble of learning the rudiments of any particular discipline. In *Cultural Studies: A Critical Introduction*, Simon During describes the new superdiscipline as "the politically engaged study of culture, especially popular culture" (12). True enough, but it is also important to note, as Lawrence Grossberg, Cary Nelson, and Paula Treichler, in their introduction to their landmark 1992 anthology *Cultural Studies*, put it with considerable understatement, "cultural studies has not embraced all political positions" (5).

Its advocates are virtually unanimous in emphasizing that cultural studies may be pursued only by those on the political left, preferably supporters of revolution, euphemistically referred to as "social transformation." Grossberg, Nelson, and Treichler agree that

> a continuing preoccupation within cultural studies is the notion of radical social and cultural transformation ... in virtually all traditions of cultural studies, its practitioners see cultural studies not simply as a chronicle of cultural change but as an intervention in it, and see themselves not simply as scholars providing an account but as politically engaged participants. (5)

According to Douglas Kellner, "A critical cultural studies will thus overcome the boundaries of academic disciplines and will combine political economy, social theory and research, and cultural criticism in its project which aims at critique of domination and social transformation" (103). And if one is not entirely committed to revolution or even "social transformation," Simon During observes that one should at a minimum feel "a commitment to education as a tool for progressivist politics" (20).

There are some even on the left who worry that the unanimity of political opinion required in cultural studies may not be altogether a good thing. One of the pioneers of American cultural studies, James Carey, is concerned that "by putting politics outside of discussion, and insisting that intellectual work proceed within an a priori view of proper leftist belief – conveyed between the lines, parenthetically, or with knowing glances and smiles – all sorts of intellectual alliances have been foreclosed at the outset" (14). Todd Gitlin frets that cultural studies leftism may actually impede leftism outside the university: "[Cultural studies] substitutes an obsession with popular culture for coherent economic-political thought or a connection with mobilizable populations outside the academy across identity lines" (36). A serious leftist like Irving Howe worried already in 1989 that the increasing prestige of theory was vitiating the "idea of a democratic culture" that the notion of "the common reader" involved:

> What results is a conviction that the literary theorist, rid of the grubby tasks of practical criticism and not obliged to pay very much attention to literature itself, can find satisfying expression by remaining within the academy, speaking to fellow theorists, and not having to worry about that nuisance, real or imagined, known as the common reader. ("The Treason of the Critics" 30)

But even if one agrees that the obligatory leftism of contemporary cultural studies is both politically ineffective and intellectually shallow, the problem remains: is it possible to insist on high literary and cultural standards while also embracing democracy and the notion of equality – "all men are created equal" – enshrined in the Declaration of Independence? In the United States, the question of the relation between democracy and cultural standards is complicated by the issue of race. Are high art and traditional artistic criteria an instrument of racial domination, or are they, as W. E. B. Du Bois supposed in *The Souls of Black Folk*, a means of liberation from racial categorization?

The notion that high culture and democracy, especially American democracy, are incompatible is not new. Walt Whitman asserted in *Democratic Vistas* that the great poetry of the past would be "poisonous" for the democratic culture of the future (955). But although Whitman worried about the social effects of the great works, he never doubted their greatness. He called for poets "possess'd of the religious fire and abandon of Isaiah, luxuriant in the epic talent of Homer, or for proud characters as in Shakspere [sic], but consistent with the Hegelian formulas and consistent with modern science" (988). Today, the debate has proceeded a step further. Understandably giving up hope that Whitman's dubious amalgam would appear, postmodernist ideologues have decided that the very concept of artistic excellence is elitist and undemocratic. In contrast, Ralph Ellison, over a lifetime of reflection on the connections between art, race, and democracy, explored, deepened, and ultimately reaffirmed the notion that one of the glories of American democracy at its best is its ability to recognize excellence wherever it appears.

For Ralph Ellison "democracy" never meant simply the rule of the majority; like Lincoln against Stephen Douglas, Ellison repeatedly linked democracy to the freedom of individuals promised in the Declaration of Independence and guaranteed in the Bill of Rights. Over and over again, Ellison affirmed the continuing significance of the great documents of the American founding. In a 1972 commencement address at the College of William and Mary, he referred to "the 'sacred documents' of this nation – the Declaration of Independence, the Constitution, and the Bill of Rights" and affirms their significance not only for citizens but for writers in particular. Ellison does not use "sacred" as a merely conventional term of respect; he explains to the graduates that

I say "sacred" because no matter what his ideology, no matter what his racial or religious background happens to be, the writer recognizes that the underlying motives of American literature were first expressed here by those rash and dissenting young men who bore such illustrious names as

Washington and Jefferson and Madison. ("Commencement Address at
the College of William and Mary" 408)

Even if one considers the principles embodied in the Constitution
nothing but "man-made legal fictions," Ellison insists that "this
doesn't stop them from being precious or sacred" ("Perspective of
Literature" 771).

Ellison's affirmation of the importance of the "sacred documents" for writers in particular responds to Henry James's famous
lament about the difficulties that the lack of traditions and social
hierarchies in American life present for the novelist. Ellison argues
that if life in the United States lacks the continuity and social
coherence dramatized in European fiction, we have something else:

The moral imperatives of American life that are implicit in the
Declaration of Independence, the Constitution and the Bill of Rights ...
form the ground of assumptions upon which our social values rest. ...
they provide the broadest frame of reference for our most private dramas.
("Society, Morality and the Novel" 702)

Ellison's emphasis on the centrality of our "sacred principles" in no
way ignores the failure to live up to those ideals. For Ellison, indeed,
both the comedy and the tragedy of American life spring from the
gap between our ideals and our actions. Ellison emphasizes that
"*I* [emphasis in original] see Americans as motivated, even in their
failures, by the virtues embodied in the American creed" ("Address
to the Harvard College Alumni, Class of 1949" 421).

Ellison's assertion of the centrality of the "American creed" did
not prevent him from also asserting the specificity and permanent
value of African-American culture throughout his life. His 1944
review of Gunnar Myrdal's *An American Dilemma* reveals an
Ellison still very much indebted to Marxism objecting strongly to
Myrdal's neglect of "the class struggle" ("*An American Dilemma*:
A Review" 338). Ellison's most serious criticism of the book, however, is reserved for Myrdal's explanation of the attitudes of African
Americans as "secondary reactions" to "more primary pressures"
from whites (339). Ellison, later to be ostracized and condemned
for his rejection of black separatism, responds with an affirmation
that sounds one of the keynotes of his writing. Americans of African

descent, he insists, are not "simply the creation of white men" (340); African-American culture possesses "much of great value and richness," and, furthermore, "In Negro culture there is much of value for America as a whole" (340). Years later, Ellison would admonish Irving Howe in a famous exchange that there was more to African-American life than "unrelieved suffering" ("The World and the Jug," 178) and in "The Myth of the Flawed White Southerner" would register his irritation at intellectuals who objected to his 1965 defense of President Lyndon Johnson because they seemed to assume that "I and those of my background possess no interest that they, my friends and colleagues, had any need to understand or respect" (553).

Ellison believed that "You cannot have an American experience without having a black experience," for many reasons, including the historical fact that "The language of the United States is partly black people's creation. ... There is no specifically American vernacular and language which has not been touched by us and our style" ("Alain Locke" 446). Criticizing LeRoi Jones's *Blues People* in 1964 for its impoverished conception of African-American culture, just as he had criticized Gunnar Myrdal's study twenty years before, Ellison argued that Jones's "version of the blues lacks a sense of the excitement and surprise of men living in the world – of enslaved and politically weak men successfully imposing their values upon a powerful society through song and dance" (*"Blues People"* 286). Considering jazz and "American Negro choral singing" (284), as well as spirituals and gospel music, Ellison concludes that "the most authoritative rendering of America in music is that of American Negroes" (285).

Those who argue that Ralph Ellison's emphasis on the close connections between American culture as a whole and African-American culture makes him an outlier in the tradition of African-American cultural criticism in which W. E. B. Du Bois is the dominant figure must contend with the evidence that some of Ellison's most characteristic formulations were anticipated by Du Bois in his best-known work, *The Souls of Black Folk*. Du Bois, an unapologetic partisan of high culture, nevertheless asserts that "the Negro folk-song – the rhythmic cry of the slave – stands today not simply as the sole American music, but as the most beautiful expression of human experience born this side the seas" (536–7). Du Bois traces out the evidence of stages of development in which "The first is African music, the second Afro-American, while the third is a blending of Negro music with music heard in the foster land. The result is still distinctively Negro and the method of blending original, but the elements are both Negro and Caucasian." Du Bois goes on to point out a fourth stage "where the songs of white America have been distinctively influenced by the slave songs" (540). Finding what later readers might well consider an anticipation of Martin Luther King's 1963 speech at the Lincoln Memorial, Du Bois insists that the "slave songs," or, as he calls them, the "Sorrow Songs," all share a common hope: "that some-time, somewhere, men will judge men by their souls and not by their skins" (544). Du Bois insists further that the spirit of the Sorrow Songs and of African-American culture in general has not been without influence in shaping American culture as a whole, so much so that it seems impossible that America would be America "without her Negro people":

Actively we have woven ourselves with the very warp and woof of this nation,–we fought their battles, shared their sorrow, mingled our blood with theirs, and generation after generation have pleaded with a head-strong, careless people to despise not Justice, Mercy, and Truth, lest the nation be smitten with a curse. Our song, our toil, our cheer, and warning have been given to this nation in blood-brotherhood. Are not these gifts worth the giving? Is not this work and striving? Would America have been America without her Negro people? (545)

There is probably no more frequently quoted passage in African-American cultural criticism than the one in the first chapter of *The Souls of Black Folk* in which Du Bois describes the double-consciousness of African Americans:

It is a peculiar sensation, this double-consciousness, this sense of always looking at one's self through the eyes of others, of measuring one's soul by the tape of a world that looks on in amused contempt and pity. One ever feels his two-ness, – an American, a Negro; two souls, two thoughts, two unreconciled strivings; two warring ideals in one dark body, whose dogged strength alone keeps it from being torn asunder. (364–5)

What is often omitted in the countless discussions of this passage is that Du Bois does not hope for the triumph of one of the "two warring ideals" or even for a separation that would allow each to fulfill itself but instead for a reconciliation, a merger or union that will result in "a better and truer self":

The history of the American Negro is the history of this strife, – this longing to attain self-conscious manhood, to merge his double self into a better and truer self. In this merging he wishes neither of the older selves to be lost. He would not Africanize America, for America has too much to teach the world and Africa. He would not bleach his Negro soul in a flood of white Americanism, for he knows that Negro blood has a message for the world. (365).

Faced with lynchings in the South, the rise of the Ku Klux Klan in the North, and racial prejudice throughout the United States, Du Bois found it impossible to hold onto the hope of the union of blacks and whites in a shared African-American culture that he had affirmed in 1903. Always a believer in the need for leadership from an elite (the "talented tenth"), Du Bois came to feel that the Leninist concept of a vanguard party offered the only real hope for a world without racism. He broke with the National Association for the Advancement of Colored People (NAACP), became a Marxist, and, at the end of his life, a member of the Communist Party. After Stalin's death in 1953, he praised the dictator for putting "Russia on the road to conquer race prejudice," for his "calm, stern" leadership in World War II, and even commended Stalin for the Soviet take-over of Eastern Europe after the war, on the grounds that it was carried out because "the workers and peasants there must have their say" ("Joseph Stalin" 288–9).

Ralph Ellison's approach to American history is much closer to the Du Bois of *The Souls of Black Folk* than to the later Du Bois, whose praise of Joseph Stalin seems explained more convincingly as an expression of Du Bois's rejection of American society than as a serious consideration of Stalin's rule. Ellison's conception of American society and history could be dismissively categorized as a version of "American exceptionalism," but Ellison's "exceptionalism," if that is the right term, is one tempered by an awareness of the tragic quality of all human life and the congenital weaknesses of human beings. One who reads through his *Collected Essays* encounters many expressions of Ellison's often-criticized optimism about American possibility – but such affirmations are qualified throughout by eloquent reminders of the tragic dimension of human life in general and of African-American history in particular. In "Flamenco," Ellison connects the evocation of the "tragic, metaphysical elements of human life" in the "folk music of the Andalusian gypsies" with the feeling expressed in "Negro blues, early jazz, and the slave songs" (9). Ellison notes approvingly that both traditions challenge the sort of "Western optimism" that trusts entirely to "enlightenment, science, and progress" (8).

In "Perspective of Literature," Ellison observes that "the ethical implications of democratic equality were revealed as tragic" when the founding fathers, seduced by their success in war and the "tempting and virginal nature of the land," allowed themselves to believe that they could simply overlook the divisive issues of slavery and racial equality. In so doing, they "committed the sin of American racial pride." Black people became the "sacrificial victims" whose suffering was the price of independence (777). From the beginning, then, there was "a flaw in their [the founders'] hopeful project of nation building" ("Commencement Address at the College of William and Mary" 409). For some sophisticated contemporary theoreticians, the affirmations of the Declaration of Independence, like all affirmations, are mere rhetoric, and the American Revolution and the Civil War mere struggles for power, like all wars. Ellison's historical imagination, however, never descends to cynicism. If the acceptance of slavery is the tragic flaw in the national drama, it is a drama whose tragedy becomes all the more profound when measured against the still unfulfilled aspirations of the Declaration. It is an unfinished drama, and whether the sacrifices of both blacks and whites have been in vain is still in doubt. And yet, declares Ellison, the "old sacred words" have been "made luminous by human sacrifice, by the shedding of blood. ... We are not so sophisticated that we are able to throw that off" ("Commencement Address at the College of William and Mary" 412).

The involuntary sacrifice imposed on black Americans confers obligations recognized obliquely as well as explicitly in the great American novels, in which "the black American was endowed linguistically with an ambivalent power, like that vested in Elizabethan clowns, Christian martyrs, and tragic heroes" ("Perspective of Literature" 778). Ellison counts Melville, Mark Twain, and Faulkner, and, at one remove, Henry James and Ernest Hemingway among those who have probed and thus moved closer to resolving the national drama centering on equality and race. For Ellison, American history is neither a story of straightforward progress nor a narrative of power and victimization. Tragic in its structure, American history is a drama that moves slowly and crookedly toward fulfillment of the democratic faith.

The authority of Ellison's view of American history lies in his examples more than his theses. He distinguishes between "two basic versions of American history: one which is written and as neatly stylized as ancient myth, and the other unwritten and as chaotic and full of contradictions, changes of pace, and surprises as life itself" ("Going to the Territory" 594). The latter is evoked in Ellison's stories of individuals "full of contradictions, changes of pace, and surprises." One such was Inman Page, born a slave, who, after graduation from Brown University, took "the ideals of New England" to the "wild young state of Oklahoma" ("Going to the Territory" 588). In his seventies, he became the principal of Ellison's high school, Frederick Douglass. There, as a "grand, dignified elder" ("Portrait of Inman Page" 585), he conveyed to the young Ellison and his classmates that "the language of Shakespeare and the King James version of the Bible" was "as natural and as normal coming from one of our own as an inspired jazz improvisation" ("Going to the Territory" 606). Another such is James Armistead Lafayette, born a slave of the Virginian William Armistead, who enlisted in the Revolutionary Army under Marquis de Lafayette. Acting as a double agent, he "risked his life by pretending to supply [the British general] Cornwallis with information damaging to the Americans" ("James Armistead Lafayette" 402). In the last essay of *The Collected Essays*, "Address at the Whiting Foundation," Ellison describes his grandfather, "Big" Alfred Ellison. Emancipated in 1865, Alfred Ellison was elected town marshal of Abbeville, South Carolina in 1871, despite his illiteracy. He was reelected several times, even in 1876, after "white Democrats regained control" (855). Ellison himself had known his grandfather only "as a mute patriarchal figure who stared from the wall in an old photograph" (853); it was a white South Carolinian who brought his grandfather "so vividly to life in printed words on a page" (853).

These individual lives traced by Ellison are more than just fables of success. The careers of Inman Page and Alfred Ellison were limited by the end of Reconstruction, and Alfred Ellison was kept from voting in 1895. Even though James Armistead Lafayette was awarded emancipation after the American Revolution and, eventually, received a veteran's pension, he never achieved legal recognition as a citizen of the United States. The three lives demonstrate nevertheless what Ellison calls "the underground, unconscious logic of the democratic process" ("Going to the Territory" 596). Unofficial, unplanned connections are made; individuals meet, cultures overlap, and the result is something new, something American.

Although Ellison avoided theorizing, his essays connect literature and politics, high art and democracy, more persuasively than any contemporary theoreticians have yet managed to do. The first essay in *Going to the Territory*, "The Little Man at Chehaw Station," provides perhaps the fullest statement of Ellison's reflections on the cultural implications of democracy. Against both paleoconservatives and contemporary radicals who agree in linking artistic greatness to social hierarchy, Ellison insists that a truly democratic culture spurs artists to attain the highest standards possible. Hazel Harrison, his piano teacher at Tuskegee and a world-class pianist in her own right, taught him that an American artist must always play his or her best, no matter how unpretentious the setting. Even at Chehaw Station, a small train station near Tuskegee, Alabama, "the chances are that any American audience will conceal at least *one* individual whose knowledge and taste will complement, or surpass his [the artist's] own" (494). The "little man at Chehaw station" serves Ellison "as a metaphor for those individuals we sometimes meet whose refinement of sensibility is inadequately explained by family background, formal education, or social status." The expectation that the "little man at Chehaw Station" may turn up anywhere in any disguise is an article of the democratic faith precluding condescension to any audience, but especially an American audience. Characters like the little man "are products of errant but sympathetic vibrations set up by the tension between America's social mobility, its universal education, and its relative freedom of cultural information" (493). Ellison offers a hypothetical characterization of the little man suggesting that the American version of the common reader does not embrace mediocrity but instead shares an openness to art differing from traditional models while achieving its own kind of complexity:

> Possessing an American-vernacular receptivity to change, a healthy delight in creative attempts at formalizing irreverence, and a Yankee trader's respect for the experimental, he is repelled by works of art that would strip human experience, especially American experience, of its wonder and stubborn complexity. (497–8).

Democracy for Ellison promises a liberating willingness to recognize artistic excellence without regard to race, class, or anything else. It may be the case that "our most characteristic American style *is* that of the vernacular" ("Going to the Territory" 608), but that does not mean that American culture has an inherent hostility to high standards in art and literature. The manners and attitudes of a social elite are not necessary ingredients of all art that achieves excellence. American jazz is a case in point:

> In a sense jazz, which is an amalgam of past musical styles, may be seen as a rejection of a music which expressed the values of a social elite, but although jazz musicians are practitioners of a vernacular style, they are also unreconstructed elitists when it comes to maintaining the highest standards of the music which expresses their sense of the American experience. ("Going to the Territory" 609).

Ellison demonstrates the folly of confining the possibilities of individuals within sociological categories not with counter-systematizing but with images and stories. He dramatizes the folly of any "rigid ethno-cultural perspective" with a word picture of an individual sighted on "New York's Riverside Drive near

151st Street" whose appearance conveyed "status, property and authority" ("The Little Man at Chehaw Station" 507), as well as their opposites, and more than one ethnicity:

a light-skinned, blue-eyed, Afro-American featured individual ... in a shiny new blue Volkswagen Beetle decked out with a gleaming Rolls-Royce radiator ... Clad in handsome black riding boots and fawn-colored riding breeches of English tailoring, he took the curb wielding, with an ultra-pukka-sahib haughtiness, a leather riding crop. A dashy dashiki ... flowed from his broad shoulders ... while ... a black homburg hat tilted at a jaunty angle floated majestically on the crest of his huge Afro-coiffed head. (505–6)

Was he "a militant black nationalist," a member of the upper middle class, or both, or neither? Whatever his race, class, or politics, "culturally, he was an American joker." Although he rejected categorization of any kind, "his clashing of styles nevertheless sounded an improvised, vernacular note, an American compulsion to improvise upon the given (507). "Jokers" like this one are ignored by sloganeers of authenticity and avoided by sociologists seeking clear definitions, but they populate Ellison's essays and fiction.

"The Little Man at Chehaw Station" closes with an even more telling image. Ellison recalls an afternoon in the late thirties when he was going through Harlem circulating a petition. The young Ellison, already an aspiring writer who attended the Metropolitan Opera whenever possible, took for granted the gap between his own culture and that of the poor on whose behalf he was petitioning. Exploring the basement of a tenement, he hears "Afro-American voices, raised in violent argument" (515). What not merely surprises but bewilders the young Ellison is the topic of the argument: "these foul-mouthed black workingmen were locked in verbal combat over which of two celebrated Metropolitan Opera divas was the superior soprano!" (516) It turns out, finally, that these workingmen are indeed familiar with the Metropolitan Opera; as one of them explains, "we been down there wearing leopard skins and carrying spears or waving things like palm leafs and ostrich-tail fans for *years*!" (519). The incident confounds all the young Ellison's "assumptions regarding the correlation between educational levels, class, race and the possession of conscious culture" (516). These men were, undoubtedly, exceptions to the rule – but the lesson Ellison absorbed and passes on is that the artist keeps the democratic faith by recognizing the potential for such exceptions in every audience, in every individual.

Ellison has been criticized both for his political views and for his alleged lack of politics. Jerry Gafio Watts observed that "Ellison has had the rare honor of being attacked by black leftists and black nationalists" (126, ftn. 22) before himself joining the attackers, finding that Ellison was "not fundamentally democratically minded" (110) and, in fact, was a "meritocratic elitist" (117) who used "an intensified elitist individuality as a social marginality facilitator" (119). Ellison would not have worried too much about the charge of elitism, one suspects, considering his own characterization of the jazz musicians he admired so much as "unreconstructed elitists." Accusations of elitism could more plausibly be made about W. E. B. Du Bois, who began his intellectual career defending the relatively benign idea that "the masses of the Negro people" should follow the leadership of a "Talented Tenth" that would be an "aristocracy of talent and character" ("The Talented Tenth" 847) and eventually endorsed the Leninist notion that social progress could occur only under the leadership of a vanguard party, a theory that has provided the intellectual rationale for communist dictatorships in Russia, China, North Korea, and elsewhere. The more important observation about the relation between Du Bois and Ellison, however, is to note the ways in which the latter's essays (and, it could be argued, his fiction as well) provide powerful examples of ways in which the "longing" to reconcile what Du Bois calls in *The Souls of Black Folk* "two souls, two thoughts, two unreconciled strivings; two warring ideals in one dark body" (364–5) may be addressed and at least partially satisfied. In 1903, Du Bois looked to a future in which it would be possible to be "an American, a Negro" (364) without being at war with oneself. Ralph Ellison's writings drive home the human significance of slavery, segregation, and racism in the history of the United States, but those same writings also demonstrate that it is possible to be true to oneself as both "an

American, a Negro" without slighting either identity but instead reconciling, and thereby enriching, both.

The notion that the affirmation of standards in art and culture, an affirmation on which both Du Bois and Ellison insist, is intrinsically undemocratic depends on the mistaken assumption that the same standards should be applied to both politics and art. The unexceptionable idea that it is possible to arrive at generally acceptable but always debatable criteria for distinguishing between better and worse works of art and literature is confused with the truly undemocratic notion that is possible to distinguish between those who are fit to command and those who are fit only to obey on the basis of such criteria as race, sex, class, ethnicity, nationality, religion, political opinions, or indeed any criteria at all. In practice, the affirmation of independent literary and artistic standards presents a stumbling block to those who might wish to establish race, nationality, religion, politics, or anything else as the all-important marker dividing human beings from one another, as the hostility of totalitarian regimes in both the twentieth and twenty-first centuries to such independent standards amply demonstrates.

It is true that the cultural prestige of the twentieth century avant-garde has lent itself to the notion that those comparatively few capable of appreciating avant-garde art constitute an elite, culturally, spiritually, and even morally superior to the rest of the population. Although this kind of elitism does not have the disastrous consequences associated with elitisms based on race, politics, or religion, for example, it is nevertheless based on false premises. As Henry James demonstrates in discussing Flaubert, it is quite possible to appreciate the artistic achievements of modernism without condemning those, the great majority of the population, who are either less appreciative or simply uninterested. On the other hand, the notion that there are a certain number of literary and artistic works whose greatness has been firmly established over many generations is not elitist in any pejorative sense of the word. The so-called "canon" is established, evaluated, expanded, and re-established in a continuing process by the accumulated judgments of the "common reader" invoked by such diverse critics as Samuel

Johnson, Virginia Woolf, and Irving Howe. Ralph Ellison's thesis that the cultural implications of American democracy include a willingness to recognize artistic excellence wherever and whenever it appears provides a specifically American version of the traditional insistence of humanistic literary criticism that art and literature should be judged first of all by artistic standards for which criteria based on class, race, religion, or politics are irrelevant.

7

Literary Criticism, the Humanities, and Liberal Education

The place of literary criticism in American culture has been debated at least since Ralph Waldo Emerson, in the closing sentences of "The American Scholar" (1837), asserted that the practical and intellectual self-reliance he championed would transform, among other things, the "study of letters":

We will walk on our own feet; we will work with our own hands; we will speak our own minds. The study of letters shall be no longer a name for pity, for doubt, and for sensual indulgence. The dread of man and the love of man shall be a wall of defence and a wreath of joy around all. A nation of men will for the first time exist, because each believes himself inspired by the Divine Soul which also inspires all men. (71)

Ten years later, in his "Ode, Inscribed to W. H. Channing," Emerson made it clear that his hopes for the new nation had not been fulfilled. The country was prosperous enough, but "Virtue palters; Right is hence;/ Freedom praised, but hid" (62). The very economic success of the United States had allowed mere "things" to somehow control human beings: "Things are in the saddle,/And ride mankind." (63). Irving Babbitt chose as the epigraph to his *Literature and the American College* (1908) Emerson's lines decrying the apparent triumph of "law for thing" over "Law for man":

There are two laws discrete,
Not reconciled,–
Law for man, and law for thing;

The last builds town and fleet,
But it runs wild,
And doth the man unking. (63)

It was through the study of literature, Babbitt believed, that the "law for man" could best be discovered and understood, and thus the study of literature was at the core of humanistic studies. The New Humanism of Babbitt and his ally Paul Elmer More was rejected by New Critics like John Crowe Ransom and Allen Tate, but the New Criticism shared with Babbitt and More the belief that literature could provide insights into human life for which the findings of the natural and even the social sciences were no substitute. Meanwhile, critics such as Edmund Wilson and Lionel Trilling, although unsympathetic to the New Humanism and more than willing to credit new "sciences" like psychoanalysis and Marxism with seemingly groundbreaking discoveries about human life, nevertheless refused to accept that literature had been rendered obsolete. In the late twentieth and early twenty-first century, however, the rejection of traditional humanistic criticism in favor of "Theory" (to use Daphne Patai and Will Corral's apt term) and cultural studies by the most influential departments of English and literary studies gave rise to passionate critiques of the academic study of literature and the humanities in general. Titles like *The Closing of the American Mind* (Allan Bloom, 1987), *The Death of Literature* (Alvin Kernan, 1990), *Literature Lost* (John Ellis, 1997), and *Education's End* (Anthony Kronman, 2007) suggest the passion and the scope of the arguments these and similar works articulated in defense of traditional humanistic criticism and of the humanities in general. The titles also suggest, however, that the struggle is over and only catastrophe can follow. Bloom, Kronman, and the rest have indeed made cogent arguments that need to be taken into account in considering the situation of the traditional humanities in higher education, but it is time to forgo extreme rhetoric both in regard to the kind of knowledge the humanities can provide and about the supposed inevitability of cultural disaster.

Emerson himself was not averse to making extreme statements. Indeed, he rarely made any other kind. In "The American Scholar," he asserted that books "are for nothing but to inspire" (57), a thesis that seems plausible enough in regard to his own works. His oration on "The American Scholar" still inspires with its call for the true scholar to become "Man Thinking" rather than "the bookworm" (57). Since all organizations tend to become ends in themselves and thus diverted from serving the purpose they are intended to serve, Emerson's reminder that "The one thing in the world, of value, is the active soul" (57) is always in order. But Emerson offers little assistance in deciding what sort of organization might best serve the cause of scholarship when he condemns every institution just because it is an institution: "The book, the college, the school of art, the institution of any kind, stop with some past utterance of genius. This is good, say they, –let us hold by this. They pin me down. They look backward and not forward" (57–8). The particular structure of "the institution of any kind" will not matter when a society in which "each believes himself inspired by the Divine Soul which also inspires all men" comes into being.

Emerson's "Man Thinking" is equally capable of mastering the humanistic arts and disciplines – "preserving and communicating heroic sentiments, noble biographies, melodious verse, and the conclusions of history" (63–4) – and the natural sciences, since for Emerson "science is nothing but the finding of analogy, identity, in the most remote parts" (55), so that, ultimately, the study of human life and the study of nature are one: "And, in fine, the ancient precept, 'Know thyself,' and the modern precept, 'Study nature,' become at last one maxim" (56). Insight into the soul, "the one soul which animates all men" (67) takes the place of scientific observation and experiment. Although Emerson is willing to praise the astronomers Flamsteed and Herschel for carrying out "the slow, unhonored, and unpaid task of observation" (63), he is much more effusive in his praise of the eccentric theologian Emanuel Swedenborg, whom he calls a "man of genius" because "he saw and showed the connection between nature and the affections of the soul." Emerson laments that Swedenborg's "literary value has never yet been rightly estimated" (69); two centuries later, Swedenborg is remembered, if at all, only because he was once praised by writers like Emerson.

But if Emanuel Swedenborg is today unread except by academic specialists, Emerson's belief that the findings of the natural sciences about the natural world itself are trumped by intellectuals or theoreticians possessing intellectual or moral authority but lacking scientific expertise has been revived by both postmodernists and by one of postmodernism's most vehement critics, Allan Bloom in *The Closing of the American Mind*. Emerson's extreme claims were justified by his belief in a "Divine Soul," an entity to which neither Bloom nor postmodernism appeals. What secular rationale remains is unclear. Just as it is a mistake for scientists to claim any special insight into moral or political issues based on their expertise in physics or chemistry, it is surely a mistake for defenders of the humanities like Bloom to claim supervisory authority over the natural sciences.

Bloom's largely implicit hostility to modern natural science was scarcely mentioned during the controversy over *The Closing of the American Mind*, a neglect symptomatic of the failure of commentators both pro and con to recognize that the book was not so much a reassertion of the humanistic tradition as a romantic *cri de coeur*. It is now possible to see that Bloom's call for "the authentic liberation for which this essay is a plea" (48) had more in common with the '60s radicalism he excoriated than either he or his adversaries were then able to recognize. For Bloom, "the philosopher" is not someone who has written a valuable work about morality or epistemology but a romantic figure, a sort of guru who "always thinks and acts as though he were immortal, while always being fully aware that he is mortal" (290). The philosopher is unlike ordinary human beings, above all because he confronts death without illusion: "The essential difference between the philosopher and all other men is his facing of death ... He alone mixes the reality of death ... into every thought and deed and is thus able to live while honestly seeking perfect clarity" (282). In Bloom's vision, "the gulf is unbridgeable" (290) between philosophers and the rest of humanity.

Bloom hints at several points that modern science should be somehow revised under the guidance of a philosophical outlook whose appeal to Bloom is moral and cultural rather than scientific. He considers it a matter of regret that "no influential thinker has tried to return to the pre-Enlightenment understanding of nature, the so-called teleological view, in which nature is the fullness in its own kind that each of the beings strives to attain" (181) not, it appears, because such a return would provide more accurate knowledge about the natural world but because he believes such a worldview would support the moral and political ideas that are his primary concern. Bloom's deeply felt assertion of the importance of the literary and philosophical classics continues to resonate, but the humanities cannot and should not be revived on the ground that study of the classics of literature and philosophy can somehow supersede scientific research in regard to knowledge about the natural world. Defenders of the humanistic tradition should reject Bloom's call to "fight it out with triumphant natural science" (372) – unless, that is, science oversteps its own boundaries and attempts to use the prestige of natural science to make claims about morality, politics, and culture. Bloom is no doubt right to assert that "much of the classic literature claimed to be about the order of the whole of nature and man's place in it, to legislate for that whole and to tell the truth about," but he is wrong when he declares that "if such claims are denied, these writers and their books cannot be read seriously" (372). To read works of philosophy with seriousness, it is not necessary to accept all their claims – indeed, to take a philosophical work seriously includes, one would think, considering the possibility that its "claims" might be mistaken. And surely one can grant Homer and Dante the significance their works demand without believing in Zeus and Hera, or Hell, Heaven, and Purgatory. If Bloom's argument is that it is difficult if not impossible to appreciate Plato, Homer, or Dante if one regards with contempt any conception of the universe that includes a realm of the divine, then he has a point. Yet it is surely possible to read with entire seriousness a literary or philosophical work whose metaphysics one does not share, as long as the reader has the requisite intellectual humility to recognize that one can learn from those with whom one must finally disagree about important issues. The humanistic tradition, in any case, turns to works of literature for insight into human life, not for authoritative knowledge about ultimate reality.

Just as Bloom's romanticism has been largely ignored, the Romantic roots of contemporary postmodernism have also been neglected. Much more explicitly and aggressively than Bloom, influential postmodernists in the humanistic disciplines, especially philosophy and literary theory, have attempted to assert an intellectual authority over science on the basis of their skill in analyzing texts. The German philosophical Romantics, such as Fichte, Schelling, and Hegel, insisted that physicists and chemists could not have the last word about the nature of the universe because reality was ultimately mind or spirit, not matter, and thus better understood by philosophers than by natural scientists. The thesis that philosophers, not scientists, have superior access to the nature of reality is the fundamental assumption behind the culminating work of their school, the Hegelian system. Richard Rorty, himself a leading postmodernist, pointed out the parallels between the idealism of Fichte, Schelling, and Hegel and contemporary postmodernism in "Nineteenth Century Idealism and Twentieth-Century Textualism," noting that both share a typically Romantic "antagonistic position to natural science" (139).

Observing that "romanticism is what unites metaphysical idealism and literary textualism," Rorty argues that contemporary postmodernism or "strong textualism" goes beyond the Romantic idealism of the nineteenth century in rejecting entirely the notion of "truth as correspondence to reality" ("Nineteenth Century Idealism and Twentieth-Century Textualism" 151). Postmodernism derived from French theorists like Michael Foucault and Jacques Derrida thus joins hands with Deweyan pragmatism. According to Rorty, long before Foucault and Derrida, John Dewey was teaching Americans "about how to slough off our intellectual past." Fighting postmodernism's battles before postmodernism, Dewey's "chief enemy" was the great adversary of postmodernism, "the notion of Truth as accuracy of representation" ("Dewey's Metaphysics" 86). The rejection of truth as correspondence with reality opens the way to replacing science with literature, or at least a certain kind of literature, at the center of culture. Pragmatism's rejection of the correspondence theory of truth, Rorty argues in "Nineteenth

Century Idealism and Twentieth-Century Textualism," is the "third step in the process of establishing the autonomy and supremacy of the literary culture" (150). According to Rorty, postmodernism "is the philosophical counterpart of literary modernism, the kind of literature which prides itself on its autonomy and novelty rather than its truthfulness to experience or its discovery of pre-existing significance" (153). The rejection of the traditional conception of truth is what makes it possible for the claim of "the literary culture to stand apart from science, to assert its spiritual superiority to science" (149) to gain wide acceptance.

At first glance, one might think that such a displacement of science in favor of literature would be welcome news to humanistic critics. But this displacement comes at too high a price. The humanistic tradition's insistence that science is not the only source of truth has never led it to renounce the concept of truth altogether. Against Plato's belief that truth could only be found in the contemplation and analysis of unchanging Forms, Aristotle argued that the study of human life could be worthwhile even though logical certainty was not possible, observing that "we must not look for equal exactness in all departments of study, but only such as belongs to the subject matter of each, and in such a degree as is appropriate to the particular line of enquiry" (*Nichomachean Ethics* 35). In his *Poetics*, he famously asserted that "poetry is something more scientific and serious than history" because the latter only describes "particular facts" whereas the former gives us "general truths" (35). It was surely as obvious in Aristotle's time as it is today that the plot of Sophocles's *Oedipus Rex*, for example, cannot be used to provide insight into human life with the kind of simplicity and certainty that can be achieved in solving mathematical problems or working out a syllogism. Literature cannot provide the kind of absolute certainty that Plato sought, but that lack of certainty did not lead Aristotle or the humanistic tradition he founded to conclude, as Rorty seems to do, that the value of literature has nothing to do with its "truthfulness to experience." And, of course, all the scholarship indispensable to the humanities depends on a conception of "truth as correspondence to reality" in carrying on historical research, establishing texts, making accurate quotations, and providing full documentation of all factual claims. A commitment to truth as an ideal is no less important in literary criticism than in scholarship. It is notoriously difficult to arrive at unanimity in regard to the meaning of any moderately complex literary work, but the very effort to understand the meaning of another would be pointless without the assumption both that there was such a meaning and that critics should do their best to discover it.

Richard Rorty's characterization in "Nineteenth Century Idealism and Twentieth-Century Textualism" of the very different attitude of the "strong textualist" makes it clear that the postmodernism or "textualism" so influential in departments of English today has broken with the humanistic tradition: "The strong textualist simply asks himself the same question about a text which the engineer or the physicist asks himself about a puzzling physical object: how shall I describe this in order to get it to do what I want?" (153). (One might observe in passing that it is both odd that a proponent of a school of thought based on antagonism to science would approvingly characterize it as adopting the attitude of "the engineer or the physicist" and doubtful that actual engineers or physicists think this way – they might well have other questions, such "what is this?" before focusing on "what I want.")

To his credit, Rorty recognizes the seriousness of the objections to the "strong textualism" he endorses by traditional humanistic critics like Lionel Trilling and M. H. Abrams. The most important objection, in Rorty's view, is "not epistemological but moral" (156). Humanistic thought has traditionally turned to literature for moral insight, a turn that depends on a willingness to attempt to learn what another has to say rather than stopping with what one already knows – "what I want." He describes "the moral outlook which Abrams shares with Trilling" with generous accuracy: "the view that, in the end, when all the intellectuals have done all their tricks, morality remains something widely shared and available to reflection – something capable of being discovered rather than created, because already implicit in the common consciousness of everyone." Rorty calls this view a "Kantian conviction" (157), but it can be found in the founders of humanistic criticism like Aristotle and Horace, as well as in modern critics like Edmund Wilson and Lionel Trilling, none of whom is noticeably Kantian. It lies behind, for example, Wilson's observation – in an essay, "Marxism and Literature," pointing out the limitations of criticism based on orthodox Marxism – that in art and literature "a sort of law of moral interchangeability prevails: we may transpose the actions and the sentiments that move us into terms of whatever we do or are ourselves. Real genius of moral insight is a motor which will start any engine" (205–6).

Marxism and psychoanalysis are just two of the putatively scientific systems that enthusiasts once thought would obviate the need for the traditional humanistic disciplines, with their messy imprecision and tolerance for the unscientific, unenlightened, mutually contradictory ideas embodied in the works of authors like Homer, Dante, and Shakespeare. More recently, it is anti-system systematizers like Michel Foucault and Jacques Derrida who have been most influential, although there are signs that their influence is on the wane. Richard Rorty claimed that Americans didn't really need them in any case, since John Dewey's pragmatism provided all the intellectual support a "strong textualist" could need. John Dewey is undoubtedly the most influential theorist of education in American history, and any consideration of the place of the humanities should take account of his ideas. Unfortunately, his thought seems to be the impetus for two diametrically opposed misunderstandings of the place of the humanities in relation to science. Rorty himself believes that a wide acceptance of Dewey's ideas "about how to slough off our intellectual past," in particular the old-fashioned "notion of Truth as accuracy of representation" ("Dewey's Metaphysics" 86–7), would enhance the prestige of literature at the expense of the authority of science. Yet the more likely result would seem to be the end of the humanistic tradition, one of whose goals is recovery of and reflection on our artistic and intellectual past, and one of whose chief norms in that recovery and reflection is "the notion of Truth as accuracy of representation."

An alternative view of Dewey's thought, however, is possible, one based on Dewey's own words in his key philosophical statements, yet so different from the ideas imputed to him by Rorty that one cannot help but suspect the latter of acting – quite consistently – as a "strong textualist" in describing Deweyan pragmatism. Rorty argues that pragmatism leads to valuing literature over science, yet Dewey's own words in his central texts say something very different. The full implications of Dewey's pragmatism for the humanities can be grasped by turning to *Reconstruction in Philosophy*, where he outlines his central philosophical position and explains its significance for human life. In this key exposition of his philosophy, Dewey repeatedly affirms the ability of science to provide real knowledge and repeatedly suggests that science can and should replace the humanities as a source of insight about human life. In an introduction written twenty-five years after the first publication, Dewey calls for an intellectual and cultural "reconstruction" that would "carry over into any inquiry into human and moral subjects the kind of method (the method of observation, theory as hypothesis, and experimental test) by which understanding of physical nature has been brought to its present pitch" (10). Dewey attributes the delay of the hoped-for "reconstruction" to "the body of prejudices, traditions and institutional customs that consolidated and hardened in a pre-scientific age" (20). The suspicion that such "prejudices" include the humanistic belief that the literature of the "pre-scientific age" retains its significance for human life in the contemporary world is confirmed by the book's final paragraph. Dewey begins by seeming to make a generous admission about the significance of the humanities, conceding that "Poetry, art, religion are precious things" (164). It turns out, however, that the "poetry, art, religion" studied by the humanistic disciplines have been somehow "discredited," and the only "poetry, art, religion" that are truly precious are not yet here: "But while it is impossible to retain and recover by deliberate volition old sources of religion and art that have been discredited, it is possible to expedite the development of the vital sources of a religion and art that are yet to be" (164). So Dewey's concession turns out to be no concession at all, whereas his rhetoric in discussing the "poetry and religious feeling" of the future invites skepticism, given his employment of the kind of sentimental phrasing he elsewhere avoids as he assures readers that, in a future dominated by science, "Poetry and religious feeling will be the unforced flowers of life" (164).

Throughout a long career, Irving Babbitt made the case that art and literature were not merely "flowers of life" – that is to say, beautiful, surely, but scarcely to be taken into account when making important decisions for individuals and nations – but rather sources of knowledge about human life beyond the reach of the physical sciences. At the same time, however, Babbitt repeatedly emphasized that the New Humanism he championed had no quarrel with the findings of physicists, chemists, or other scientists about the natural world. Neoplatonists, Romantics, and even some modernists rest their ultimate case for the value of art and literature on the ability of the arts to make contact with a higher spiritual realm. In contrast, Babbitt adopted an agnostic position about the nature of ultimate reality. In an essay entitled "What I Believe," he described his point of view as a "positive and critical humanism" (14), a humanism that did not rely on revelation or authority but instead appealed to the critical thought of the individual. Babbitt claimed to be a "thoroughgoing modern" who differed from other moderns not in returning to religion but in working out a coherent set of standards for himself. The positive and critical humanist was different from

the man who has emancipated himself from outer authority in the name of the critical spirit (which will be found to be identical with the modern spirit), but has made use of his emancipation, not to work out standards, but to fall into sheer spiritual anarchy. Anyone, on the other hand, who worked out standards critically would be a sound individualist and at the same time a thoroughgoing modern. (9)

If Babbitt defended the value of the literary classics and supported traditional morality, he insisted that he did so because their worth could be demonstrated by an appeal to evidence available to any investigator who was willing to make a full inquiry into the facts of human life: "I may perhaps best sum up my whole point of view by saying that the only thing that finally counts in this world is a concentration, at once imaginative and discriminating, on the facts" (*Democracy and Leadership* 36).

Babbitt objected to science only when its partisans, rightly impressed with technological progress, went on to claim that science could be the source of moral and political progress as well. Babbitt objected to what he took to be Walter Lippman's claim "that if one becomes 'disinterested' after the fashion of the scientific investigator, one will have the equivalent not only of 'humanism' but of 'high religion.'" In reply, Babbitt pointed out that progress in scientific knowledge by no means guaranteed progress in human relations: "Certain scientific investigators are busy in their laboratories at this very moment devising poison gases of formidable potency. What proof is there that, as far as the scientific type of 'disinterestedness' is concerned, these gases will not be pressed into the service of the will to power?" ("What I Believe" 11). The humanistic disciplines might provide insight and guidance about human life, but only if their study proceeded along different lines than the scientific study of nature. In *Literature and the American College*, Babbitt protested that "Man himself and the products of his spirit, language, and literature, are treated not as having a law of their own, but as things; as entirely subject to the same methods that have won for science such triumphs over phenomenal nature" (86). In his view, "The humanities need to be defended today against the encroachments of physical science, as they once needed to be against the encroachments of theology" (87).

Today, departments of English gain prestige primarily as a result of the publications of their professors and the ability of their graduate program to attract students who go on to earn doctoral degrees and become professors themselves. In contrast, Babbitt was concerned above all with undergraduate education and with the ability of courses in literature to influence the lives of students who were not future professors. Himself a professor at Harvard University, in *Literature and the American College*, Babbitt eloquently made the case for the small college whose primary mission was not research but teaching. If a university like Harvard or Johns Hopkins would be dedicated to the discovery of new knowledge, "the college, if it is to have any reason at all for existing separately, must stand, not for the advancement, but for the assimilation of learning, and for the perpetuation of culture" (125–6). Babbitt carefully distinguished the "assimilation" he prized from mere passive reception or memorization. The study of literature in particular should foster the ability "to coordinate the scattered elements of knowledge and relate them not only to the intellect but to the will and character; that subtle alchemy by which more learning is transmuted into culture" (125). This could not take place as long as the study of literature was treated like a subordinate branch of philology in which the mere accumulation of facts was all-important, or, conversely, if criticism was merely a kind of "intellectual and moral impressionism" (124) in which emotional sensitivity was valued rather than intellectual rigor. Babbitt argued in "English and the Discipline of Ideas" that if the centrality of literary study to the humanities could be justified, "it must be primarily by ... the discipline of ideas" (63). English should be studied "by reference to its intellectual content" (70).

What this seems to mean for Babbitt is that literary works should be studied in the light of the principles – moral, political, or metaphysical – whose human consequences and significance are dramatized in their works. Thus, "the teacher who wishes to put ideas into his teaching" might profitably "compare the liberty of Milton, based on a conception of life that is partly humanistic and partly biblical, with the naturalistic and humanitarian liberty of Shelley" (68). Babbitt himself is best known for his study of Romantic literature in *Rousseau and Romanticism*, a work in which the critique of Rousseau's philosophy is carried out in large part by examining the evidence provided by Romantic poets, novelists, and dramatists about the human consequences of the Romantic worldview whose theoretical grounds are adumbrated in Rousseau's writings. In the chapter on "Romantic Melancholy," Babbitt calls on the works of Chateaubriand, Alfred de Vigny, and Alfred de Musset, among others, to make his case that Romantic attitudes typically result "not in happiness but in wretchedness" (307). Arguing that "the romanticist" takes perverse pride in unhappiness, Babbitt cites the eponymous hero of Chateaubriand's *René*: "'A great soul," as René says, 'must contain more grief than a small one'" (308). Babbitt cites a number of works by Vigny to support his portrait of the Romantic genius condemned to "melancholy and disillusion":

His "Chatterton" deals with the fatal misunderstanding of the original genius by other men. "Moïse" deals more specifically with the problem of his solitude. The genius is so eminent and unique, says Vigny, speaking for himself from behind the mask of the Hebrew prophet, that he is quite cut off from ordinary folk who feel that they have nothing in common with him. This forlornness of the genius is not the sign of some capital error in his philosophy. On the contrary it is the sign of his divine election, and so Moses blames God for his failure to find happiness. If the genius is cut off from communion with men he cannot hope for companionship with God because he has grown too sceptical. Heaven is empty and in any case dumb; and so in the poem to which I have already referred (*Le Mont des Oliviers*) Vigny assumes the mask of Jesus himself to express this desolateness, and concludes that the just man will oppose a haughty and Stoic disdain to the divine silence. (335–6)

Alfred de Musset, Babbitt observes, compares his relation to his readers to "the pelican who rends and lacerates his own flesh to provide nourishment for his young" and goes on to quote the lines that, as Babbitt points out in a footnote, "are inscribed on the statue of Musset in front of the Théâtre Français":

> Les plus désespérés sont les chants les plus beaux,
> Et j'en sais d'immortels qui sont de purs sanglots. (310)

It is important to note that Babbitt makes his case against the Romantic worldview by taking Romantic poets and writers at their word; far from contending that their writings display "false consciousness" or for some other reason do not deserve to be taken seriously, he relies on the Romantics themselves as witnesses whose testimony to the human consequences of their beliefs provides the key evidence for his critique of the Romantic worldview: "a movement which began by asserting the goodness of man and the loveliness of nature ended by producing the greatest literature of despair the world has ever seen" (307).

One does not need to agree entirely or at all with Babbitt's critique of Romanticism to recognize that a Babbitt-like commitment to "the discipline of ideas" in literary studies provides a much more convincing rationale for the role of literary studies in the humanities than the alternatives available in his own time – literary study as either fact-based historical and philological research or as critical impressionism. But although Babbitt thought of his own approach as a "New Humanism," there were some important ways in which his criticism could be criticized from within the humanistic tradition itself. Babbitt repeatedly argued for the importance of standards, but he was almost exclusively concerned with moral rather than aesthetic standards. *Rousseau and Romanticism* considers many Romantic poems, plays, and novels, but it rarely if ever attempts to make discriminations about the literary quality of the works it discusses. Traditionally, the humanistic tradition has insisted that the achievement of high literary quality is a signal that the testimony of the work deserves to be taken into account as an especially valuable witness to the human condition. Babbitt does indeed accept the Romantic writers as witnesses, but his failure to give the close attention to individual works that would be required for aesthetic evaluation makes it impossible for him to do justice to those works not only as works of art but also as affirmations of individual points of view whose complexities and possible insights cannot be captured by summing up the limitations of Romanticism as a movement.

In one of the programmatic essays of the New Criticism, "Criticism, Ltd.," John Crowe Ransom argued that Babbitt and the other New Humanists were not really literary critics so much as they were "moralists; more accurately, historians and advocates of a certain moral system" (332). Ransom considered it "perfectly legitimate for the moralist to attack romantic literature if he can make out his case," and Ransom for one was willing to believe that "the moral objection is probably valid" (333). From Ransom's point of view, however, New Humanists like Babbitt were no different from the "Leftists, or Proletarians" (333–4) who were determined "to ferret out class-consciousness in literature" (334) insofar as both were one-sidedly concerned with moral rather than aesthetic values. For Ransom, "Criticism is the attempt to define and enjoy the aesthetic or characteristic values of literature" (332), and in his view neither Marxists nor New Humanists were interested in making that attempt. If professors of English were not willing to focus on criticism, it was not easy to see why a department of English would be needed at all: "English might almost as well announce that it does not regard itself as entirely autonomous, but as a branch of the department of history, with the option of declaring itself occasionally a branch of the department of ethics" (335).

But if English is "entirely autonomous," what then is the special value of literary criticism and why should it be part of the humanities? At first, Ransom insists on "the autonomy of the artist as one who interests himself in the artistic object in his own right, and likewise the autonomy of the work itself as existing for its own sake" (343). Later in the same essay, however, Ransom gives "the poet" a specific purpose that certainly offers an explanation for poetry's significance for human life, at the cost, however, of making Ransom himself a moralist, or at least a proponent of a definite set of values, rather than a pure aesthetician. The best poetry, Ransom holds, conveys a view of the individual's relation with the world that is enriching and meaningful, a view to which both science and everyday practical concerns are intrinsically hostile. The role of poetry, then, is to preserve and nourish this view of our relation with the world and its objects, our relation, that is to say, with "the world's body," to use the title of the book in which "Criticism, Inc." appeared:

The poet perpetuates in his poem an order of existence which in actual life is constantly crumbling beneath his touch. His poem celebrates the object which is real, individual, and qualitatively infinite. He knows that his practical interests will reduce this living object to a mere utility, and that his sciences will disintegrate it for their convenience into their respective abstracts. The poet wishes to defend his object's existence against its enemies, and the critic wishes to know what he is doing, and how. (348)

Ransom's argument that departments of literature should focus on literary criticism was immensely influential, but his notion that the essential role of "the poet" was to convey a single attitude about the world, one which experiences objects as "real, individual, and qualitatively infinite" was not nearly so persuasive. Likewise, Ransom's thesis in the same essay that every poem was composed of both a "prose core" and its corresponding "differentia, residue or tissue" gained little support. Few agreed with Ransom that the task of "the good critic" was to analyze a poem's "way of exhibiting the residuary quality" (349) left behind after the "prose core" had been considered.

The example Cleanth Brooks provided in *The Well Wrought Urn* (1947) was much more convincing. *The Well Wrought Urn* examines ten well-known works, from Donne's "The Canonization" and Shakespeare's *Macbeth* through Pope's "The Rape of the Lock," Gray's "Elegy Written in a Country Churchyard," Keats's "Ode to a Grecian Urn," and Yeats's "Among School Children," as well as poems by Milton, Herrick, Wordsworth, and Tennyson. Brooks's goal was to read all ten works "as one has learned to read Donne and the moderns" (193) but without reducing them all to a single point of view held to be especially "poetic," even one as attractive as Ransom's notion of a world whose particulars are each "real, individual, and qualitatively infinite." Pope emerges from Brooks's reading still neoclassical, Wordsworth still Romantic, and Tennyson still a Victorian, but meanwhile those same readings have demonstrated how little such labels reveal about the ability of such poems as "The Rape of the Lock," "Ode on Intimations of Immortality from Recollections of Early Childhood," and "Tears, Idle Tears" to render permanently valuable accounts of human experience. Brooks's analyses make frequent use of terms such as "ambiguity," "paradox," and, even more common, "irony," but that is not because he is championing a philosophy that, anticipating postmodernism, rejects straightforward truth claims on principle, but because of his view of poetry. In contrast to Ransom, Brooks holds that a poem does not possess a "prose core" – paraphrases are indeed possible and sometimes useful, but they must not be mistaken for the poem itself, and certainly not for its "core."

For Brooks and for most of the New Critics, a successful literary work is characterized by an organic unity best understood as "the unification of attitudes into a hierarchy subordinated to a total and governing attitude" (207). That "governing attitude" need not be itself "ironic" at all in the usual sense of the word. Brooks insists only that the overall attitude conveyed by any significant poem is too complex to be summed up by any paraphrase. For Brooks, "irony" is used to indicate the "recognition of incongruities," (209), especially important because a large part of the importance of literature consists in its unique ability to take account of conflicting tensions and still achieve an overall perspective. The ability of the poet to achieve dramatic unity in a poem fosters the ability of the poet's readers to find unity in their own lives. As Brooks puts it, the poet's "task is finally to unify experience. He must return to us the unity of the experience itself as man knows it in his own experience" (212–13). Brooks's readings point to the ways in which literary works from diverse periods and expressing diverse opinions, including many now considered discredited, retain their human significance as examples of the ways in which discordant aspects of human experience may each be given their due and yet subsumed into an overall perspective dramatized in the specific work for which no abstract statement whatsoever can be an adequate substitute. The New Criticism at its best, as exemplified in *The Well Wrought Urn*, thus vindicates the importance of literary studies as a humanistic discipline.

The New Criticism's understanding of the humanistic grounds for literary study became widely influential in the 1940s, dominant in the 1950s, and was only seriously challenged in the late 1960s. Anthony Kronman's *Education's End: Why Our Colleges and Universities Have Given Up on the Meaning of Life* (2007) is one of the most thoughtful studies of what has changed and what has been lost since the upheavals of the '60s. Kronman's analysis stands out both because he takes seriously the arguments of those with whom he disagrees and because he is not content to lament but instead proposes his own preferred reform. He believes that it is both possible and desirable to reinvigorate literary study and the rest of the humanities by returning to the ethos of the "the age of secular humanism" (46) that lasted from shortly after the Civil

War until the 1960s. Over that near century, the natural sciences and then the social sciences (to a much lesser degree) gained prestige by accumulating vast stores of knowledge whose practical usefulness was obvious to all. The humanities meanwhile gained new importance because they were the one part of the university still willing and able to deal with the question the natural and social sciences had declared out of bounds, the question "of how best to live, of what to care about and why, the question of the meaning of life" (5).

The sciences, hard and soft, ruled out questions about the meaning of life in order to establish a methodology that could distinguish theories warranted by objective research from speculations based on subjective prejudices or intuitions. Literature and the other humanistic disciplines focused on questions about the meaning of life, the sort of questions that could not be answered by the sciences but with which all human beings are confronted. Although lacking the boundaries established to ensure responsible research in the sciences, humanistic inquiry did not become intolerably one-sided or capricious because it was carried on within a "particular framework of meaning. ... the long tradition of writing and reflection, and of artistic creation, that is still sometimes referred to as the tradition of European arts and letters" (83). Although this tradition allowed and even encouraged divergent views, it had a structure of its own that made it possible to study its "central texts and abiding themes" (85) in an organized way. Although many humanities professors envied the intellectual prestige scientists achieved by producing knowledge, others carried on "the long tradition" in their writing and in their classrooms through the first half of the twentieth century.

The conversation, however, was interrupted by the turmoil of the '60s. The radicals were much more effective in transforming the university than they were in either ending the Vietnam War or transforming American society. Student protesters could not prevent Richard Nixon from winning two terms as president, but they did force radical changes in the traditional humanities curriculum, and, when those students became tenured professors, they undermined much of what remained by replacing the ideals of the humanistic tradition with the imperatives of political correctness. Irving Howe, an early opponent of the Vietnam War and a lifelong political leftist, challenged the academic radicals in a 1991 defense of "The Canon" in *The New Republic*. The expulsion of "the canon" from the curriculum by the academic "cultural left" was, Howe observed, a break not so much with bourgeois conventions as with the left's own historic struggle to make the canonical works available to all:

> There were the Labor night schools in England bringing to industrial workers elements of the English cultural past; there was the once-famous Rand School of New York City; there were the reading circles that Jewish workers, in both Eastern Europe and American cities, formed to acquaint themselves with Tolstoy, Heine, and Zola. And in Ignazio Silone's novel *Bread and Wine* we have a poignant account of an underground cell in Rome during the Mussolini years that reads literary works as a way of holding itself together. (41)

The academic radicals might consider themselves Marxists or socialists, but Howe pointed out that "in fact the socialist and Marxist traditions have been close to traditionalist views of culture" (41). The outlook of the campus leftists, on the other hand, represented "a strange mixture of American populist sentiment and French critical theorizing. ... The populism releases antielitist rhetoric, the theorizing releases highly elitist language" (42).

Howe's defense of the canon did not mean, as *The Norton Anthology of Theory and Criticism* suggests, that Howe had "joined the establishment" (1389) and was therefore unwilling to criticize contemporary society. Quite the contrary. The canonical authors, Howe noted, have been among the sharpest critics of their own culture. He asked "Is there a more penetrating historian of selfhood than Wordsworth? A more scathing critic of society than the late Dickens? A mind more devoted to ethical seriousness than George Eliot? A sharper critic of the corrupting effects of money than Balzac or Melville?" (43). And yet great universities, urged on by self-professed radicals, had removed such works from the center of their curricula on the grounds that they stifled critical thought. Howe could only speculate on the motives of the activists: "Some of those who are now attacking 'traditionalist' humanities and social science courses do so out of sincere persuasion; some, from a political agenda (what was at first solemnly and now is half-ironically called p.c. – politically correct): and some from an all-too-human readiness to follow the academic fashion that, for the moment, is 'in'" (40–1).

Anthon Kronman's long chapter on "Political Correctness" is all the more persuasive because it begins by acknowledging that each of the three ideas whose acceptance by professors in the humanities established political correctness as a scholarly norm – diversity, multiculturalism, and constructivism – "has a core of good sense with intellectual and moral appeal" (138). Each, however, has been made into a radical slogan whose influence has diminished the intellectual authority of the humanistic tradition whose framework once enabled students to reflect seriously about the meaning of life in their literature, philosophy, or history classes. It is, of course, a good thing to have a class in which diverse points of view are expressed and debated, Kronman observes, but when, under the reign of diversity, each student is regarded as a "spokesperson" for his or her race, class, or gender, "the result is a classroom where everyone, teachers and students alike, feels compelled to tiptoe on eggshells for fear of giving offense, an intellectually and spiritually frozen classroom" (163).

Similarly, if multiculturalism is taken to mean simply that "some understanding and appreciation of non-western cultures is imperative" (165) for students in American universities, then we are all multiculturalists. Conversely, if multiculturalism is taken to mean that one should not "privilege" Western ideals such as "the ideals of individual freedom and toleration; of democratic government; of respect for the rights of minorities and for human rights generally" (172), then the multiculturalist impulse toward an enlightenment beyond liberal toleration paradoxically compels one to accept attitudes sympathetic to, and sometimes indistinguishable from, those of "a reactionary, a zealot, an obscurantist" (173). Insofar as constructivism "puts choice and freedom at the center of our moral and spiritual lives" (190) it affirms the values of the humanistic tradition, but that affirmation becomes hollow when constructivism goes on to insist that reflection on the often conflicting affirmations made by great works of literature or philosophy is pointless because "disagreements about the justice or beauty or truth of some feature of the world and what value to assign it can never in reality be anything but a declaration of or display of the disputants' interests" (182).

Why did professors in the humanities allow and often participate in the transmogrification of their disciplines demanded by political correctness? Kronman's answer is that professors in the humanities who explored questions about the meaning of life were already suffering from a lack of confidence because their work had no standing when measured against the "modern research ideal" (96) that has determined academic prestige since the leading American colleges were turned into research universities in the years after the Civil War. True scholarship, according to the "research ideal," requires specialization on topics specific enough to allow for the production of new knowledge, not open-ended conversation about questions to which no definitive answer is possible. Student radicals often found their professors almost eager to drop the claims of the traditional curriculum in favor of the politicized norms of political correctness because the classroom promotion of diversity and multiculturalism offered "an antidote to the emptiness produced by the humanities' own endorsement of the research ideal." The cure, however, turned out to be worse than the disease, since "the culture of political correctness that has grown from these ideas has not restored the self-confidence of the humanities but further weakened it instead" (135-6).

Kronman argues that the conversation undertaken by the disciplines of the humanities loses its depth, breadth, and its reason for being under the regime of political correctness. The humanities are supposed to "give young people the opportunity and encouragement to put themselves – their values and commitments – into a critical perspective" (147), yet if the notion that class, race, and gender are absolutely determinative becomes an article of faith, then the very possibility of transcending one's prejudices is ruled out. The humanistic tradition had room "for the soldier who values honor above equality, for the poet who believes that beauty is more important than justice, for the thinker who regards with disinterest or contempt the concerns of political life"(156), but would-be soldiers, poets, and thinkers find that such views are proscribed by contemporary versions of "diversity."

The regime of political correctness claims, not unreasonably in Kronman's view, that "the insights and perceptions of the victims of injustice have a greater claim to respect than those of their victimizers, that they reflect the realities of the world more accurately than the judgments of their oppressors and hence are truer in some fundamental sense" (159–60). This same claim, Kronman notes, "is a deep and recurrent theme in the sacred writings of Jews and Christians alike, and one of the cornerstones of the Western literary and philosophical tradition" (160). So far, the two outlooks are at one. The difference, however, is that the taboos imposed by political correctness make it impossible to consider another "competing and equally venerable idea ... the idea that privilege and good fortune enable sound judgment rather than compromise it – that wealth, education, and other advantages typically help the person who has them to develop his spirit and mind more fully and freely" (161).

This second idea is tacitly admitted by all those who understand that what makes poverty, for example, a morally serious issue is the recognition that it is not just an inconvenience but can be spiritually and intellectually disabling; but political correctness prevents facing its implications squarely. Kronman does not ask readers to choose one or the other but instead points out that "*both* of these ideas are deeply embedded in the tradition of Western thought, *both* have had articulate champions, *both* retain their plausibility and appeal today, and *neither* can be neglected by any son or daughter of the West who hopes to comprehend the tangled and conflicting skein of beliefs that lie at the heart of the civilization to which he or she is heir" (162).

Both Anthony Kronman's careful analysis of the key notions supplying the rationale for political correctness and his account of the limitations of the research ideal when applied to the humanities are persuasive, all the more so because he goes out of his way to bring out the strong points of the ideas he criticizes. His call for a revival of what he calls "secular humanism" in American colleges and universities is likewise compelling, except when his rhetoric on behalf of the adjective weakens his central argument for the noun. American academics need to reinvent "secular humanism," he claims because, otherwise, only "the fundamentalism of the churches" (245) will be on offer as an answer to the question of life's meaning. The answers that religion – any religion – gives to the question of life's meaning would be ruled out of court in the classrooms guided by Kronman's secular humanism, since "every religion, even the most tolerant, is fundamentalist" (199). Kronman insists, however, that he is not one of those who look down on all religion with "bemusement and scorn" and regard any belief in God as "shallow and mindless" (236). He believes there is a real "spiritual crisis" brought on by the inevitable failure of "the modern technological order" to deliver on its implicit promise "to eliminate every constraint that prevents us from doing as we please" (210). Religion, unlike technology and science, at least responds to the reality of human mortality.

According to Kronman, the classroom must nevertheless remain secular, since religion, any religion, encourages attitudes inimical to free discussion. He makes two points: all religions privilege "some attitude other than thought that has the power to carry us beyond the limits of reason" (198), and they all insist "that there is only one right answer to the question of life's meaning" (199). But the notion that "there is only one right answer" to many important questions is certainly not the monopoly of religion. Kronman doesn't exactly say that he alone is right, but he does make explicit his own belief that the humanities "offer a better response than religion does" (241) to the contemporary crisis of meaning – not better for himself or better for some people and not others, but simply "better."

As for Kronman's first point, if art and literature have the significance the humanities attribute to them, it is surely because works of the imagination, although susceptible to analysis and explication, may indeed "carry us beyond the limits of reason," making use of "some attitude other than thought." Eloquently describing representative subjects of humanistic study, Kronman mentions "Achilles' reflections on honor and memory and the fleeting beauty of youth ... Kant's struggle to put our knowledge of certain things on an unchallengeable foundation so as to place the knowledge of others forever beyond reach," and also "Caravaggio's painting of the sacrifice of Isaac, which depicts a confusion of loves that defeats all understanding" (239). One wonders if it is possible to fully respond to Caravaggio's painting if one must consider Abraham, Isaac, and Caravaggio himself in thrall to "fundamentalism" – and similar considerations apply to, for example, *The Divine Comedy*, *Paradise Lost*, and *Four Quartets*. Humanistic criticism does not look to art and literature for metaphysical knowledge; but the very understanding of religion in all its variety as an aspect of human life that literature makes possible precludes, one would have thought, the seemingly contemptuous, certainly sweeping judgment that "every religion, even the most tolerant, is fundamentalist."

Kronman's "secular humanism" bears a strong similarity to the "New Humanism" put forward by Paul Elmer More and Irving Babbitt, whom Kronman describes as "the brilliant and belligerent Harvard professor of literature" (73). Anticipating Kronman's opposition to the domination of the "research ideal" in the humanities, Babbitt observed that "it is easier to be scientific or erudite or enthusiastic than civilized" (*Literature and the American College* 144). Babbitt, however, unlike Kronman, was willing to accept religion as an ally. In confronting a situation similar to ours today – in Babbitt's words, a combination of "spiritual anarchy with an ever-increasing material efficiency" ("What I Believe" 12) – Babbitt championed a curriculum that would make possible "a reaffirmation of the truths of the inner life" that could be "traditional or critical, religious or humanistic" ("What I Believe" 18). In an uncharacteristic passage, Kronman lumps together "the fundamentalist Protestant churches in America, the jihadist wing of Islam, and the Pope" as opponents of "secular morality" (234–5). In contrast, Babbitt, surveying the state of civilization in 1924, surmounted his personal antipathy to Roman Catholicism and contemplated the possibility that "the

Catholic church may perhaps be the only institution left in the Occident that can be counted on to uphold civilized standards" (*Democracy and Leadership* 211).

Kronman is right to emphasize that the humanities are, among other things, "the record of our encounter with mortality," reminders to us of what technology's success encourages us to forget, "the fateful limits that constrain our longing for control" (238). And it surely follows that American colleges and universities would do well to recognize the special importance of literary studies and the other humanities as a source of insights unavailable to either the physical or the social sciences. Whatever reservations one might have about Kronman's view of all religions as "fundamentalisms," his central thesis about the need to renew the humanistic conversation disrupted by the twin forces of the research ideal and political correctness remains convincing. A revival of Kronman's "secular humanism" is perhaps only slightly more likely than a return to Babbitt's "New Humanism," but then the continuation and reinvigoration of the humanistic tradition of literary criticism and of the other humanistic disciplines does not require the adoption of any particular political stance or, indeed, any kind of "ism" whatsoever. What it does demand is a willingness to learn from literature and the other arts what they have to teach.

Such willingness requires an awareness that one does not already have all the answers, a Socratic awareness of ignorance very different from the dogmatic skepticism prevalent in the academy today. Those today who feel no need to learn from the insights about human life that literature and the other arts might offer rely on theoretical writings that have little in common with the Platonic dialogues. It is true that the self-professedly ignorant but inquiring Socrates of Plato's early dialogues is replaced in the *Republic* by a Socrates in possession of a theory that does supply answers to the most important questions, and this Socrates is certain that even the greatest literary works, the epics of Homer, have nothing to teach him. But many of Plato's dialogues, including the *Republic*, are not only profound philosophy but also works of great literary art that persuade not only through the

logic of the argument but also through stories like the Myth of Er
and the Allegory of the Cave, the characterizations of interlocutors like Thrasymachus and Ion, and by the depiction of Socrates
himself in dialogues such as the *Apology*, the *Crito*, and the
Phaedo. Conducting a debate with himself, in dialogues like the
Ion and the *Symposium*, Plato raises the possibility that perhaps
after all art and literature may provide access to a higher reality,
thus beginning the long and influential Neoplatonic critical tradition. Lacking both philosophical depth and literary distinction,
the dominant theorizing of the postmodernist era shares with
Plato only the belief that Theory has nothing to learn from literature and the other arts. The humanistic tradition in literary
criticism, which begins with the response of Aristotle to his
master's rejection of poetry, has already responded impressively
to the considerably smaller intellectual challenge posed by contemporary Theory's dismissal of literature. Although the task of
addressing the arguments of the dominant contemporary theories
is important, the decisive answer will come from the literary
criticism of the twenty-first century that conveys to the general
public the pleasures and insights that poems, plays, and fiction
continue to make available to all those willing to attend.

Works Cited

Adorno, Theodor. "Perennial Fashion-Jazz." In *Prisms*, trans. Samuel and Shierry Weber. Cambridge, MA: MIT Press, 1981. 119–32.

Arbery, Glenn, Ed. *The Southern Critics: An Anthology*. Wilmington, DE: ISI Books, 2010.

"Introduction." In *The Southern Critics: An Anthology*, ed. Glenn Arbery. Wilmington, DE: ISI Books, 2010. 1–11.

Aristotle. *The Nichomachean Ethics*. Trans. H. Rackham. Loeb Classical Library. Cambridge, MA: Harvard University Press, 1956.

Poetics. In *The Poetics, "Longinus" on the Sublime, Demetrius on Style*. Trans. W. Hamilton Fyfe. The Loeb Classical Library. 2nd edition. Cambridge, MA: Harvard University Press, 1932. 1–118.

Arnold, Matthew. "The Bishop and the Philosopher." In *Lectures and Essays in Criticism*, ed. R. H. Super. Vol. III of The Complete Prose Works of Matthew Arnold. Ann Arbor: University of Michigan Press, 1962. 40–55.

Culture and Anarchy: An Essay in Political and Social Criticism. Culture and Anarchy with Friendship's Garland and Some Literary Essays, ed. R. H. Super. Vol. V of The Complete Prose Works of Matthew Arnold. Ann Arbor: University of Michigan Press, 1965. 85–256.

"The French Play in London." In *English Literature, and Irish Politics*, ed. R. H. Super. Vol. IX of The Complete Prose Works of Matthew Arnold. Ann Arbor: University of Michigan Press, 1973. 64–85.

"The Function of Criticism at the Present Time." In *Essays in Criticism, First Series. Lectures and Essays in Criticism*, ed. R. H. Super. Vol. III of The Complete Prose Works of Matthew Arnold, 1960–77. Ann Arbor: University of Michigan Press, 1962. 258–85.

"George Sand." In *Philistinism in England and America*, ed. R. H. Super. Vol. X of The Complete Prose Works of Matthew Arnold. Ann Arbor: University of Michigan Press, 1974. 187–9.

"Literature and Science." In *Philistinism in England and America*, ed. R. H. Super. Vol. X of The Complete Prose Works of Matthew Arnold. Ann Arbor: University of Michigan Press, 1974. 53–73.

"The Study of Poetry." In *English Literature and Irish Politics*, ed. R. H. Super. Vol. IX of The Complete Prose Works of Matthew Arnold. Ann Arbor: University of Michigan Press, 1973. 161–88.

"Wordsworth." In *English Literature and Irish Politics*, ed. R. H. Super. Vol. IX of The Complete Prose Works of Matthew Arnold. Ann Arbor: University of Michigan Press, 1973. 36–55.

Austen, Jane. *Emma*. In Case Studies in Contemporary Criticism, ed. Alistair M. Duckworth. New York: Bedford/St. Martin's, 2002. 21–381.

Babbitt, Irving. *Democracy and Leadership*. Originally published 1924. Indianapolis, IN: Liberty Fund, 1979.

"English and the Discipline of Ideas." In *Irving Babbitt: Representative Writings*, ed. George A. Panichas. Lincoln: University of Nebraska Press, 1981. 61–70.

Literature and the American College: Essays in Defense of the Humanities. Originally published 1908. Washington, DC: National Humanities Institute, 1986.

Rousseau and Romanticism. Originally published 1919. New Brunswick, NJ: Transaction, 1991.

"What I Believe." In *Irving Babbitt: Representative Writings*, ed. George A. Panichas. Lincoln: University of Nebraska Press, 1981. 3–18.

Bayles, Martha. *Hole in Our Soul: The Loss of Beauty and Meaning in American Popular Music*. Chicago: University of Chicago Press, 1994.

Benstock, Shari. "A Critical History of *The House of Mirth*." In Edith Warton, *The House of Mirth*, ed. Shari Benstock. Case Studies in Contemporary Criticism. New York: Bedford/St. Martin's, 1994. 309–25.

Berlant, Lauren, and Michael Warner. "Sex in Public." In *The Norton Anthology of Theory and Criticism*, Vincent B. Leitch, general editor, 2nd edition. New York: Norton, 2010. 2600–15.

Bloom, Allan. *The Closing of the American Mind: How Higher Education Has Failed Democracy and Impoverished the Souls of Today's Students*. New York: Simon and Schuster, 1987.

Brooks, Cleanth. *The Well Wrought Urn: Studies in the Structure of Poetry*. New York: Harcourt, Brace, 1947.

Brooks, Van Wyck. *America's Coming-of-Age*. Originally published 1915. In *Three Essays on America*. New York: E. P. Dutton, 1934. 13–112.

Burke, Edmund. *Reflections on the Revolution in France and On the Proceedings in Certain Societies in London Relative to that Event*, ed.

Conor Cruise O'Brien. Originally published 1790. New York: Penguin, 1969.

Butler, Marilyn. "Introduction to *Emma*." In Jane Austen, *Emma*, ed. Alistair M. Duckworth. Case Studies in Contemporary Criticism. New York: Bedford/St. Martin's, 2002. 597–613.

Carey, James. "Reflections on the Project of (American) Cultural Studies." In *Cultural Studies in Question*, ed. Marjorie Ferguson and Peter Golding. London: Sage, 1997. 1–24.

Christian, Barbara. *Black Feminist Criticism: Perspectives on Black Women Writers*. New York: Pergamon Press, 1985.

——— "The Race for Theory." In *The Norton Anthology of Theory and Criticism*, Vincent B. Leitch, general editor, 2nd ed. New York: Norton, 2010. 2128–37.

Crews, Frederick. "The Partisan." *The New York Review of Books*. 25.18 (November 23, 1978): 3–10.

Coleridge, Samuel. *Biographia Literaria or Biographical Sketches of My Literary Life and Opinions*, ed. James Engell and W. Jackson Bate. Vol. 2. Princeton, NJ: Princeton University Press, 1983.

Davidson, Donald. "Poetry as Tradition." In *The Southern Critics: An Anthology*, ed. Glenn C. Arbery. Wilmington, DE: Intercollegiate Studies Institute, 2010. 241–59.

Delaney, Paul. "'A Sort of Notch in the Donwell Estate': Intersections of Status and Class in *Emma*." In *Case Studies in Contemporary Criticism*, ed. Alistair M. Duckworth. New York: Bedford/St. Martins, 2002. 508–23.

Dewey, John. *Reconstruction in Philosophy*. Originally published 1920. New York: New American Library, 1950.

Du Bois, W. E. B. "Criteria of Negro Art." In *W. E. B. Du Bois: Writings*, ed. Nathan Huggins. Originally published 1926. New York: Literary Classics of the United States, 1986. 993–1002.

——— *The Souls of Black Folk*. In *W. E. B. Du Bois: Writings*, ed. Nathan Huggins. Originally published 1903. New York: Literary Classics of the United States, 1986. 357–547.

——— "Joseph Stalin." In *The Oxford W. E. B. Du Bois Reader*, ed. Eric J. Sundquist. Originally published 1953. New York: Oxford University Press, 1996. 287–9.

——— "The Talented Tenth." In *W. E. B. Du Bois: Writings*, ed. Nathan Huggins. Originally published 1903. New York: Literary Classics of the United States, 1986. 842–61.

During, Simon. *Cultural Studies: A Critical Introduction*. New York: Routledge, 2005.

Eliot, T. S. "Arnold and Pater." In *Selected Essays of T. S. Eliot*, ed. Frank Kermode. Originally published 1932. New York: Harcourt Brace Jovanovich, 1975. 382–93.

Eliot. T. S. "From 'Henry James.'" In *Selected Prose of T. S. Eliot*, ed.
    Frank Kermode. New York: Harcourt Brace Jovanovich, 1975. 151–2.
    "The Humanism of Irving Babbitt." In *Selected Essays of T. S. Eliot*,
    ed. Frank Kermode. New York: Harcourt Brace Jovanovich, 1975.
    419–28.
    "Marie Lloyd." In *Selected Essays of T. S. Eliot*, ed. Frank Kermode.
    New York: Harcourt Brace Jovanovich, 1975. 405–8.
    *Notes Toward the Definition of Culture. Christianity and Culture: The
    Idea of a Christian Society and Notes towards the Definition of
    Culture.* New York: Harcourt Brace Jovanovich, 1968.
    "Religion and Literature." In *Selected Essays of T. S. Eliot,* ed. Frank
    Kermode. New York: Harcourt Brace Jovanovich, 1975. 343–54.
    Selected Essays of T. S. Eliot. Originally published 1932. New York:
    Harcourt, 1964.
Ellis, John M. *Literature Lost: Social Agendas and the Corruption of the
    Humanities.* New Haven, CT: Yale University Press, 1997.
Ellison, Ralph. "Address to the Harvard College Alumni, Class of 1949."
    In *The Collected Essays of Ralph Ellison*, ed. John F. Callahan. New
    York: Random House, 1995. 415–26.
    "Address at the Whiting Foundation." In *The Collected Essays of
    Ralph Ellison*, ed. John F. Callahan. New York: Random House,
    1995. 849–56.
    "Alain Locke." In *The Collected Essays of Ralph Ellison*, ed. John
    F. Callahan. New York: Random House, 1995. 439–47.
    "An American Dilemma: A Review." In *The Collected Essays of
    Ralph Ellison*, ed. John F. Callahan. New York: Random House,
    1995. 328–40.
    "Blues People." In *The Collected Essays of Ralph Ellison*, ed. John
    F. Callahan. New York: Random House, 1995. 278–87.
    "Commencement Address at the College of William and Mary." In *The
    Collected Essays of Ralph Ellison,* ed. John F. Callahan. New York:
    Random House, 1995. 405–13.
    "Flamenco." In *The Collected Essays of Ralph Ellison*, ed. John
    F. Callahan. New York: Random House, 1995. 5–11.
    "Going to the Territory." In *The Collected Essays of Ralph
    Ellison,* ed. John F. Callahan. New York: Random House,
    1995. 591–612.
    "The Little Man at Chehaw Station." In *The Collected Essays of Ralph
    Ellison*, ed. John F. Callahan. New York: Random House, 1995.
    489–519.
    "The Myth of the Flawed White Southerner." In *The Collected Essays
    of Ralph Ellison*, ed. John F. Callahan. New York: Random House,
    1995. 552–62.

"Perspective of Literature." In *The Collected Essays of Ralph Ellison*, ed. John F. Callahan. New York: Random House, 1995. 766–81.

"Portrait of Inman Page: A Dedication Speech." In *The Collected Essays of Ralph Ellison*, ed. John F. Callahan. New York: Random House, 1995. 585–90.

"Society, Morality and the Novel." In *The Collected Essays of Ralph Ellison*, ed. John F. Callahan. New York: Random House, 1995. 694–725.

"The World and the Jug." In *The Collected Essays of Ralph Ellison*, ed. John F. Callahan. New York: Random House, 1995. 155–88.

Else, Gerald. trans. *Aristotle: Poetics*. Aristotle. Cambridge, MA: Harvard University Press, 1963.

Emerson, Ralph Waldo. "The American Scholar." In *Ralph Waldo Emerson: Essays & Lectures*, ed. Joel Porte. New York: Literary Classics of the United States, Inc., 1983. 51–71.

"Ode, Inscribed to W. H. Channing." In *Ralph Waldo Emerson: Collected Poems and Translations*, ed. Harold Bloom and Paul Kane. New York: Literary Classics of the United States, Inc., 1994. 61–4.

Epstein, Joseph. "Matthew Arnold and the Resistance." In *Partial Payments: Essays on Writers and Their Lives*. New York: Norton, 1989. 17–37.

Euripides. *Iphigenia in Tauris. Alcestis/Hippolytus/Iphigenia in Tauris*. Trans. Philip Vellacott. London: Penguin, 1974. 129–178.

Ferguson, Marjorie, and Peter Golding, eds. *Cultural Studies in Question*. London: Sage, 1997.

Finch, Casey, and Peter Bowen. "'The Tittle-Tattle of Highbury': Gossip and the Free Indirect Style in *Emma*." In Jane Austen, *Emma*, Case Studies in Contemporary Criticism, ed. Alistair M. Duckworth. New York: Bedford/St. Martin's, 2002. 543–58.

Furia, Philip. *The Poets of Tin Pan Alley: A History of America's Great Lyricists*. New York: Oxford University Press, 1990.

Gitlin, Todd. "The Anti-Political Populism of Cultural Studies." In *Cultural Studies in Question*. ed. Marjorie Ferguson and Peter Golding. London: Sage, 1997. 25–38.

Graff, Gerald. "Taking Cover in Coverage." In *The Norton Anthology of Theory and Criticism*. Vincent B. Leitch, general editor, 2nd ed. New York: Norton, 2010. 1962–70.

Grossberg, Lawrence, Cary Nelson, and Paula Treichler. "Cultural Studies: An Introduction." In *Cultural Studies*, ed. Lawrence Grossberg, Cary Nelson, and Paula Treichler. New York: Routledge, 1992. 1–16.

Halberstam, Judith. "The Good, the Bad, and the Ugly: Men, Women, and Masculinity." In *The Norton Anthology of Theory and Criticism*. Vincent B. Leitch, general editor, 2nd ed. New York: Norton, 2010. 2638–53.

Hardt, Michael, and Antonio Negri. "From *Empire*." In *The Norton Anthology of Theory and Criticism*. Vincent B. Leitch, general editor, 2nd ed. New York: Norton, 2010. 2621–35.

Hastings, Selina. *Evelyn Waugh: A Biography*. Boston: Houghton Mifflin, 1994.

Hayek, Friedrich A. *The Fatal Conceit: The Errors of Socialism*, ed. W. W. Bartley III. Chicago: University of Chicago Press, 1988.

hooks, bell. "Postmodern Blackness." In *The Norton Anthology of Theory and Criticism*. Vincent B. Leitch, general editor, 2nd ed. New York: Norton, 2010. 2509–16.

Horace. "The Art of Poetry." *Horace: Satires, Epistles and Ars Poetica*. Trans. H. Rushton Fairclough. Loeb Classical Library. Cambridge, MA: Harvard University Press, 1936. 442–89.

Howe, Irving. "The Canon." *The New Republic*. 204.7 (February 18, 1991): 40–4.

——— "The Treason of the Critics." *The New Republic*. 200.24 (June 12, 1989): 28–31.

James, Henry. "The Art of Fiction." In *Literary Criticism: Essays on Literature, American Writers, English Writers*, ed. Leon Edel. The Library of America series. New York: Literary Classics of the United States, 1984. 44–65.

——— *The Bostonians*. Originally published 1886. New York: Penguin, 2000.

——— "Charles de Bernard and Gustave Flaubert." In *Literary Criticism: French Writers, Other European Writers: The Prefaces to the New York Edition*, ed. Leon Edel. The Library of America series. New York: Literary Classics of the United States, 1984. 159–83.

——— "Correspondence de Gustave Flaubert." In *Literary Criticism: French Writers, Other European Writers: The Prefaces to the New York Edition*, ed. Leon Edel. The Library of America series. New York: Literary Classics of the United States, 1984. 295–314.

——— "Elizabeth Stoddard: *Two Men. A Novel*." In *Literary Criticism: French Writers, Other European Writers: The Prefaces to the New York Edition*, ed. Leon Edel. The Library of America series. New York: Literary Classics of the United States, 1984. 614–17.

——— "Gustave Flaubert." In *Literary Criticism: French Writers, Other European Writers: The Prefaces to the New York Edition*, ed. Leon Edel. The Library of America series. New York: Literary Classics of the United States, 1984. 314–46.

——— "Harriet Elizabeth (Prescott) Spofford: *Azarian: An Episode*." In *Literary Criticism: Essays on Literature, American Writers, English Writers*, ed. Leon Edel. The Library of America series. New York: Literary Classics of the United States, 1984. 603–13.

"James Russell Lowell." In *Literary Criticism: Essays on Literature, American Writers, English Writers*, ed. Leon Edel. The Library of America series. New York: Literary Classics of the United States, 1984. 540–50.

"The New Novel." In *Literary Criticism: Essays on Literature, American Writers, English Writers*, ed. Leon Edel. The Library of America series. New York: Literary Classics of the United States, 1984. 124–59.

The Princess Casamassima. Originally published 1886. New York: Penguin, 1987.

"The Question of the Opportunities." In *Literary Criticism: Essays on Literature, American Writers, English Writers*, ed. Leon Edel. The Library of America series. New York: Literary Classics of the United States, 1984. 651–7.

"Rebecca Harding Davis: Dallas Galbraith." In *Literary Criticism: Essays on Literature, American Writers, English Writers*, ed. Leon Edel. The Library of America series. New York: Literary Classics of the United States, 1984. 222–9.

"Rebecca Harding Davis: *Waiting for the Verdict.*" In *Literary Criticism: Essays on Literature, American Writers, English Writers*, ed. Leon Edel. The Library of America series. New York: Literary Classics of the United States, 1984. 218–22.

"*The Tragic Muse.*" In *Literary Criticism: French Writers, Other European Writers, The Prefaces to the New York Edition*, ed. Leon Edel. The Library of America series. New York: Literary Classics of the United States, 1984. 1103–19.

James, William. "The Will to Believe." In *The Will to Believe and Other Essays in Popular Philosophy. William James: Writings 1878–1899*, ed. Gerald E. Myers. The Library of America. New York: Literary Classics of the United States, 1992. 457–79.

Jefferson, Thomas. *Notes on the State of Virginia. Thomas Jefferson: Writings.* New York: Literary Classics of the United States, 1984. 123–325.

Johnson, Claudia. "'Not at all what a man should be!': Remaking English Manhood in *Emma*." In Jane Austen, *Emma*, ed. Alistair M. Duckworth. Case Studies in Contemporary Criticism. New York: Bedford/St. Martin's, 2002. 441–55.

Johnson, Samuel. "Preface to Shakespeare, 1765." In *Johnson on Shakespeare*, ed. Arthur Sherbo. Vol. VII of the Yale Edition of the Works of Samuel Johnson. New Haven, CT: Yale University Press, 1968. 59–113.

Kazin, Alfred. *On Native Grounds: An Interpretation of Modern American Prose Literature*. Originally published 1942. New York: Harcourt, Brace, Jovanovich, 1982.

Kellner, Douglas. "Overcoming the Divide: Cultural Studies and Political Economy." *Cultural Studies in Question*. 102–20.

Kernan, Alvin. *The Death of Literature*. New Haven, CT: Yale University Press, 1990.

Knapp, Steven, and Walter Benn Michaels. "Against Theory." *The Norton Anthology of Theory and Criticism*. Vincent B. Leitch, general editor, 2nd ed. New York: Norton, 2010. 2491–506.

Kronman, Anthony T. *Education's End: Why Our Colleges and Universities Have Given Up on the Meaning of Life*. New Haven, CT: Yale University Press, 2007.

Kundera, Milan. *The Book of Laughter and Forgetting*. Originally published i1979.Trans. Michael Henry Heim. New York: Penguin, 1981.

Lasch, Christopher. "Modernism, Politics, and Philip Rahv." *Partisan Review* 47.2 (1980):183–94.

Leitch, Vincent B., General Editor. *The Norton Anthology of Theory and Criticism*, 2nd edition. New York: Norton, 2010.

Leavis, F. R. *New Bearings in English Poetry*. Originally published 1932. Ann Arbor: University of Michigan Press, 1960.

Lee, Harper. *To Kill a Mockingbird*. Originally published 1960. New York: Warner Books, 1982.

Looser, Devoney. "'The Duty of Woman by Woman': Reforming Feminism in *Emma*." In Jane Austen, *Emma*, ed. Alistair M. Duckworth. Case Studies in Contemporary Criticism. New York: Bedford/St. Martin's, 2002. 577–93.

Lowe, Lisa. "Work, Immigration, Gender: New Subjects of Cultural Politics." *The Norton Anthology of Theory and Criticism*. Vincent B. Leitch, general editor, 2nd ed. New York: Norton, 2010. 2519–35.

Lytle, Andrew Nelson. "The Hind Tit." In *I'll Take My Stand: The South and the Agrarian Tradition*. Originally published 1930. Baton Rouge: Louisiana State University Press, 1977. 244.

Macdonald, Dwight. *Against the American Grain: Essays on the Effects of Mass Culture*. Originally published 1962. New York: Da Capo Press, 1983.

Dwight Macdonald on Movies. Englewood Cliffs, NJ: Prentice-Hall, 1969.

"Looking at the War." In *Memoirs of a Revolutionist: Essays in Political Criticism*. Originally published 1957. New York: Meridian Books, 1958.

Mann, Thomas. *The Magic Mountain*. Trans. John Woods. Originally published 1924. New York: Random House, 1995.

Marcuse, Herbert. *One-Dimensional Man: Studies in the Ideology of Advanced Industrial Society*. Boston: Beacon Press, 1964.

McCarthy, Mary. "Philip Rahv, 1908–1973." In *Published & Perished: Memoria, Eulogies, & Remembrances of American Writers*, ed. Steven Cilbar and Dean Stewart. Boston: David Godine, 2002. 146–8.

Menand, Louis. Introduction. In *The Liberal Imagination: Essays on Literature and Society*, Lionel Trilling. Originally published 1950. New York: The New York Review of Books, 2008. vii–xiv.

Mill, John Stuart. "What Is Poetry?" In *Mill's Essays on Literature and Society*, ed. J. B. Schneewind. New York: Collier-Macmillan, 1965. 102–17.

"Writings of Alfred de Vigny." In *Mill's Essays on Literature and Society*, ed. J. B. Schneewind. New York: Collier-Macmillan, 1965. 207–39.

Murfin, Ross C. "Combining Perspectives on *Emma*." In Jane Austen, *Emma*, ed. Alistair M. Duckworth. Case Studies in Contemporary Criticism. New York: Bedford/St. Martin's, 2002. 594–7.

Narasimhaiah, C. D. "Towards the Formulation of a Common Poetic for Indian Literatures Today." In *The Norton Anthology of Theory and Criticism*. Vincent B. Leitch, general editor, 2nd ed. New York: Norton, 2010. 1382–7.

Nye, Russel. *The Unembarassed Muse: The Popular Arts in America*. New York: Dial Press, 1970.

Orwell, George. "The Art of Donald McGill. In *Dickens, Dali & Others*. New York: Harcourt Brace Jovanovich, 1946. 124–39.

"Boys' Weeklies." In *Dickens, Dali & Others*. New York: Harcourt Brace Jovanovich, 1946. 76–114.

Review of *A Coat of Many Colours: Occasional Essays by Herbert Read. I Belong to the Left: 1945*. In The Complete Works of George Orwell (20 vols.; vol. 17). London: Secker and Warburg, 1998. 402–6.

"Raffles and Miss Blandish." In *Dickens, Dali & Others*. New York: Harcourt Brace Jovanovich, 1946. 202–21.

Patai, Daphne, and Will H. Corral. "Introduction." In *Theory's Empire: An Anthology of Dissent*, ed. Daphne Patai and Will H. Corral. New York: Columbia University Press, 2005.

Plato. *Apology. Euthyphro, Apology, Crito, Phaedo, Phaedrus*. Trans. Harold North Fowler. Vol. I of Plato in Twelve Volumes. The Loeb Classical Library. Cambridge, MA: Harvard University Press, 1914. 61–145.

Ion. The Statesman, Philebus, Ion. Trans. Harold North Fowler. Vol. VIII
        of Plato in Twelve Volumes. The Loeb Classical Library. Cambridge,
        MA: Harvard University Press, 1914. 401–47.
Symposium. Lysis, Symposium, Gorgias. Trans. W. R. M. Lamb. Vol. III
        of Plato in Twelve Volumes. The Loeb Classical Library. Cambridge,
        MA: Harvard University Press, 1914. 73–245.
The Republic of Plato. Trans. Allan Bloom. New York: Basic Books,
        1968.
Plotinus. *The Divine Mind, Being the Treatises of the Fifth Ennead. Vol. 2*
        of Plotinus: The Ethical Treatises ... Forming a Conspectus of the
        Plotinian System. Trans. Stephen MacKenna and B. S. Page. 2 vols.
        Boston: Charles T. Branford Company, 1949.
Pope, Alexander. "An Essay on Criticism." In *Pastoral Poetry and An*
        Essay on Criticism, ed. E. Audra and Aubrey Williams. New Haven,
        CT: Yale University Press, 1961. 195–326.
Posner, Richard A. *Law and Literature,* 3rd ed. Cambridge, MA: Harvard
        University Press, 2009.
Ransom, John Crowe. "Criticism as Pure Speculation." 1941. In *Selected*
        Essays of John Crowe Ransom, ed. Thomas Daniel Young and
        John Hindle. Baton Rouge: Louisiana State University Press, 1984.
        128–46.
The New Criticism. Norfolk, CT: New Directions, 1941.
"Criticism, Inc." In *The World's Body.* New York: Charles Scribner's
        Sons, 1938. 327–50.
Rahv, Philip. "American Intellectuals and the Postwar Situation." 1952.
        In *Essays on Literature and Politics, 1932–1972,* ed. Arabel J. Porter
        and Andrew J. Dvosin. Boston: Houghton Mifflin, 1978. 328–34.
"On Pornography, Black Humor, Norman Mailer, Etc." In *Essays on*
        Literature and Politics, 1932–1972, ed. Arabel J. Porter and Andrew
        J. Dvosin. Boston: Houghton Mifflin, 1978. 75–8.
"Twilight of the Thirties: Passage from an Editorial." In *Essays on*
        Literature and Politics, 1932–1972, ed. Arabel J. Porter and Andrew
        J. Dvosin. Boston: Houghton Mifflin, 1978. 305–9.
Read, Sir Herbert. *Anarchy and Order: Essays in Politics.* London: Faber,
        1954.
Rorty, Richard. "Dewey's Metaphysics." In *Consequences of Pragmatism:*
        Essays 1972–1980. Minneapolis: University of Minnesota Press, 1982.
        72–89.
"Nineteenth-Century Idealism and Twentieth Century Textualism." In
        Consequences of Pragmatism: Essays 1972–1980. Minneapolis:
        University of Minnesota Press, 1982. 139–59.
Rubin, Gayle. "The Good, the Bad, and the Ugly: Men, Women, and
        Masculinity." In *The Norton Anthology of Theory and Criticism.*

Vincent B. Leitch, general editor, 2nd ed. New York: Norton, 2010. 2638–53.

Santayana, George. "The Absence of Religion in Shakespeare." In *Interpretations of Poetry and Religion*, ed. William G. Holzberger and Herman J. Saatkamp, Jr. Vol. III of The Works of George Santayana. Originally published 1900. Cambridge, MA: MIT Press, 1989. 91–101.

Scepticism and Animal Faith: Introduction to a System of Philosophy. In The Works of George Santayana. Triton Edition. Vol. XIII. Originally published 1923. New York: Charles Scribner's Sons, 1937. 1–275.

Shelley, Percy Bysshe. *A Defence of Poetry. Prose: The Complete Works of Percy Bysshe Shelley*, vol. VII, ed. Roger Ingpen and Walter E. Peck. New York: Gordian Press, 1965. 109–40.

Sidney, Sir Philip. *The Defence of Poetry.* In *Sidney's "The Defence of Poetry" and Selected Renaissance Literary Criticism*, ed. Gavin Alexander. London: Penguin, 2004. 1–54.

Tate, Allen. *Essays of Four Decades.* Wilmington, DE: ISI Books, 1999

"The Function of the Critical Quarterly." In *Essays of Four Decades.* Wilmington, DE: ISI Books, 1999. 45–55.

"The Man of Letters in the Modern World." In *Essays of Four Decades.* Wilmington, DE: ISI Books, 1999. 3–16.

"Modern Poetry." In *Essays of Four Decades.* Wilmington, DE: ISI Books, 1999. 211–221.

"Poetry Modern and Unmodern." In *Essays of Four Decades.* Wilmington, DE: ISI Books, 1999. 222–36.

"The Present Function of Criticism." In *Essays of Four Decades.* Wilmington, DE: ISI Books, 1999. 197–210.

"Remarks on the Southern Religion." In *I'll Take My Stand: The South and the Agrarian Tradition.* Originally published 1930. Baton Rouge: Louisiana State University Press, 1977. 155–75.

"What Is a Traditional Society?" In *The Southern Critics: An Anthology*, ed. Glenn C. Arbery. Wilmington, DE: ISI Books, 2010. 61–70.

"Emma and the Legend of Jane Austen." In *Beyond Culture: Essays on Literature and Learning*, ed. Lionel Trilling. Originally published 1965. New York: Harcourt Brace Jovanovich, 1978. 28–49.

"In Defense of Zola." In *A Gathering of Fugitives*, ed. Lionel Trilling. Originally published 1956. New York: HBJ, 1978. 14–22.

"Freud and Literature." In *The Liberal Imagination: Essays on Literature and Society*, ed. Lionel Trilling. Originally published 1950. New York: HBJ, 1979. 33–55.

"Freud: Within and Beyond Culture." In *Beyond Culture: Essays on Literature and Learning,* ed. Lionel Trilling. Originally published 1965. New York: Harcourt Brace Jovanovich, 1978. 77–102.

"The Function of the Little Magazine." In *The Liberal Imagination: Essays on Literature and Society,* ed. Lionel Trilling. Originally published 1950. New York: HBJ, 1979. 89–99.

"The Hunter Gracchus." In *Prefaces to the Experience of Literature.* New York: HBJ, 1979. 118–22.

"The Leavis-Snow Controversy." In *Beyond Culture: Essays on Literature and Learning,* ed. Lionel Trilling. Originally published 1965. New York: Harcourt Brace Jovanovich, 1978. 126–54.

The Liberal Imagination: Essays on Literature and Society. Originally published 1950. Introduction by Louis Menand. New York: New York Review of Books, 2008.

"Mansfield Park." In *The Opposing Self: Nine Essays in Criticism,* ed. Lionel Trilling. Originally published 1955. New York: Harcourt Brace Jovanovich, 1978. 181–202.

"The Meaning of a Literary Idea." In *The Liberal Imagination: Essays on Literature and Society,* ed. Lionel Trilling. Originally published 1950. New York: New York Review of Books, 2008. 264–84.

"Mind in the Modern World." In *The Last Decade: Essays and Reviews, 1965–75,* ed. Diana Trilling. New York: Harcourt Brace Jovanovich, 1977. 100–28.

Preface. In *Beyond Culture: Essays on Literature and Learning,* ed. Lionel Trilling. 1965. New York: Harcourt Brace Jovanovich, 1978. Unpaged.

Preface. In *The Opposing Self: Nine Essays in Criticism,* ed. Lionel Trilling. Originally published 1955. New York: Harcourt Brace Jovanovich, 1978. Unpaged.

"The Princess Casamassima." In *The Liberal Imagination: Essays on Literature and Society.* 56–88.

"Preface." In *The Opposing Self: Nine Essays in Criticism,* ed. Lionel Trilling. Originally published 1955. New York: Harcourt Brace Jovanovich, 1978. Unpaged.

"A Ramble on Graves." In *A Gathering of Fugitives,* ed. Lionel Trilling. Originally published 1956. New York: HBJ, 1978. 23–33.

"Reality in America." *The Liberal Imagination: Essays on Literature and Society.* 3–21.

Sincerity and Authenticity. Cambridge, MA: Harvard UP, 1972.

"On the Teaching of Modern Literature." 1965. *Beyond Culture: Essays on Literature and Learning.* 3–27.

"That Smile of Parmenides Made Me Think." In *A Gathering of Fugitives*, ed. Lionel Trilling. Originally published 1956. New York: HBJ, 1978. 164–79.

"The Two Environments: Reflections on the Study of English." In *Beyond Culture: Essays on Literature and Learning*, ed. Lionel Trilling. 1965. New York: Harcourt Brace Jovanovich, 1978. 181–202.

"Two Notes on David Riesman." In *A Gathering of Fugitives*, ed. Lionel Trilling. Originally published 1956. New York: HBJ, 1978. 91–107.

"The Uncertain Future of the Humanistic Educational Ideal." In *The Last Decade: Essays and Reviews, 1965–75*, ed. Diana Trilling. New York: Harcourt Brace Jovanovich, 1979. 160–76.

"William Dean Howells and the Roots of Modern Taste." In *The Opposing Self: Nine Essays in Criticism*, ed. Lionel Trilling. Originally published 1955. New York: Harcourt Brace Jovanovich, 1978. 67–91.

Tobin, Beth Fowkes. "Aiding Impoverished Gentlewomen: Power and Class in *Emma*." In Jane Austen *Emma*, ed. Alistair M. Duckworth. Case Studies in Contemporary Criticism. New York: Bedford/St. Martin's, 2002. 473–87.

Warren, Robert Penn. "The Briar Patch." In *I'll Take My Stand: The South and the Agrarian Tradition*. Originally published 1930. Baton Rouge: Louisiana State University Press, 1977. 246–64.

The Legacy of the Civil War: Meditations on the Centennial. New York: Random House, 1961.

Segregation: The Inner Conflict in the South. New York: Random House, 1956.

Who Speaks for the Negro? New York: Random House 1965.

Watts, Jerry Gafio. *Heroism and the Black Intellectual: Ralph Ellison, Politics, and Afro-American Intellectual Life*. Chapel Hill: University of North Carolina Press, 1994.

Wellek, René. *The Attack on Literature and Other Essays*. Chapel Hill: University of North Carolina Press, 1982.

"Destroying Literary Studies." In *Theory's Empire: An Anthology of Dissent*, ed. Daphne Patai and Will H. Corral. New York: Columbia University Press, 2005. 41–51.

Wheatland, Thomas. *The Frankfurt School in Exile*. Minneapolis: University of Minnesota Press, 2009.

White, Hayden. "Northrop Frye's Place in Contemporary Cultural Studies." In *The Fiction of Narrative: Essays on History, Literature and Theory 1957–2007*, ed. Robert Doran. Baltimore, MD: Johns Hopkins University Press, 2010.

Whitman, Walt. *Democratic Vistas. Complete Poetry and Collected Prose.* New York: Literary Classics of the United States, Inc., 1982. 929–94.

Wilson, Edmund. "Archibald MacLeish and the Word." In *Classics and Commercials: A Literary Chronicle of the Forties. Literary Essays and Reviews of the 1930s & 40s,* ed. Lewis M. Dabney. New York: Literary Classics of the United States, 2007. 479–84.

"The Author at Sixty." In *A Piece of My Mind: Reflections at Sixty.* New York: Farrar, Straus and Cudahy, 1956. 208–39.

"Axel's Castle: A Study in the Imaginative Literature of 1870–1930." In *Literary Essays and Reviews of the 1920s & 30s.* Originally published 1930. New York: Literary Classics of the United States. 641–854.

The Bit Between My Teeth: A Literary Chronicle of 1950–1965. New York: Farrar, Straus and Giroux, 1965.

"C. L. Dodgson: Poet and Logician," In *The Shores of Light: A Literary Chronicle of the Twenties and Thirties. Literary Essays and Reviews of the 1920s & 30s,* ed. Lewis M. Dabney. New York: Literary Classics of the United States, 2007. 439–47.

The Cold War and the Income Tax: A Protest. New York: Farrar, Straus and Giroux, 1963.

"A Dissenting Opinion on Kafka." In *Classics and Commercials: A Literary Chronicle of the Forties. Literary Essays and Reviews of the 1930s & 40s,* ed. Lewis M. Dabney. New York: Literary Classics of the United States, 2007. 776–83.

"The Documents on the Marquis de Sade." In *The Bit Between My Teeth: A Literary Chronicle of 1950–1965,* ed. Edmund Wilson. New York: Farrar, Straus and Giroux, 1965. 174–227.

"Epilogue 1952: Edna St. Vincent Millay." In *The Shores of Light: A Literary Chronicle of the Twenties and Thirties. Literary Essays and Reviews of the 1920s & 30s,* ed. Lewis M. Dabney. New York: Literary Classics of the United States, 2007. 601–40.

"George Saintsbury's Centenary." In *Classics and Commercials: A Literary Chronicle of the Forties. Literary Essays and Reviews of the 1930s & 40s,* ed. Lewis M. Dabney. New York: Literary Classics of the United States, 2007. 715–18.

"George Saintsbury: Gourmet and Glutton." In *Classics and Commercials: A Literary Chronicle of the Forties. Literary Essays and Reviews of the 1930s & 40s,* ed. Lewis M. Dabney. New York: Literary Classics of the United States, 2007. 763–6.

"The Historical Interpretation of Literature." In *Literary Essays Reviews of the 1930s & 40s.* New York: Literary Classics of the United States, 2007. 256–69.

"Kay Boyle and the Saturday Evening Post." In *Classics and Commercials: A Literary Chronicle of the Forties. Literary Essays and Reviews of the 1930s & 40s*, ed. Lewis M. Dabney. New York: Literary Classics of the United States, 2007. 575–8.

"Leonid Leonov: The Sophistication of a Formula." In *Classics and Commercials: A Literary Chronicle of the Forties. Literary Essays and Reviews of the 1930s & 40s*, ed. Lewis M. Dabney. New York: Literary Classics of the United States, 2007. 672–6.

"Marxism and Literature." In *The Triple Thinkers: Twelve Essays on Literary Subjects. Literary Essays and Reviews of the 1930s & 40s*, ed. Lewis M. Dabney. New York: Literary Classics of the United States, 2007. 197–212.

"'Mr. Rolfe.'" In *The Triple Thinkers: Twelve Essays on Literary Subjects. Literary Essays and Reviews of the 1930s & 40s*, ed. Lewis M. Dabney. New York: Literary Classics of the United States, 2007. 233–55.

"The Musical Glasses of Peacock." In *Classics and Commercials: A Literary Chronicle of the Forties. Literary Essays and Reviews of the 1930s & 40s*, ed. Lewis M. Dabney. New York: Literary Classics of the United States, 2007. 793–8.

"The Nietzschean Line." In *The Shores of Light: A Literary Chronicle of the Twenties and Thirties. Literary Essays and Reviews of the 1920s & 30s*, ed. Lewis M. Dabney. New York: Literary Classics of the United States, 2007.396–99.

Patriotic Gore: Studies in the Literature of the American Civil War. Originally published 1962. New York: Oxford University Press, 1966.

"Paul Rosenfeld: Three Phases." In *Classics and Commercials: A Literary Chronicle of the Forties. Literary Essays and Reviews of the 1930s & 40s*, ed. Lewis M. Dabney. New York: Literary Classics of the United States, 2007. 869–82.

"The Poetry of Drouth: T. S. Eliot." In *The Shores of Light: A Literary Chronicle of the Twenties and Thirties. Literary Essays and Reviews of the 1920s & 30s*, ed. Lewis M. Dabney. New York: Literary Classics of the United States, 2007. 865–71.

The Shores of Light: A Literary Chronicle of the Twenties and Thirties. Originally published 1952 in *Literary Essays and Reviews of the 1920s & 30s*. New York: Literary Classics of the United States, 2007. 1–640.

"The Vogue of the Marquis de Sade." In *The Bit Between My Teeth: A Literary Chronicle of 1950–1965*. New York: Farrar, Straus and Giroux, 1965. 158–173.

"'You Can't Do This to Me!' Shrilled Celia." In *Classics and Commercials: A Literary Chronicle of the Forties. Literary Essays* and *Reviews of the 1930s & 40s*, ed. Lewis M. Dabney. New York: Literary Classics of the United States, 2007. 636–9.

Woolf, Virginia. "The Common Reader." In *The Common Reader*. New York: Harcourt, Brace and Company, 1925. 11–12.

"Middlebrow." In *Collected Essays*. Vol. 2. Originally published 1942. London: Hogarth Press, 1966. 196–203.

Wordsworth, William. "Preface to Lyrical Ballads, 1800." In *Lyrical Ballads and Other Poems, 1797–1800*, ed. James Butler and Karen Green. Ithaca, NY: Cornell University Press, 1992. 740–60.

Index

Abrams, M. H., 179
"Absence of Religion in Shakespeare, The" (Santayana 1900), 79–80
Adorno, Theodor, 51, 52, 156–7
African-Americans: Du Bois and tradition of cultural criticism, 161–3; Ellison on centrality of "American creed" in culture of 160–1. *See also* racism; segregation
Against the American Grain: Essays on the Effects of Mass Culture (Macdonald 1962), 153, 155
Agrarians: and modernism, 47, 48, 49; and New Criticism, 105; and popular culture, 155–6. *See also I'll Take My Stand*; South
Alice in Wonderland (Carroll 1865), 120
Althusser, Louis, 111
Ambassadors, The (James 1903), 28, 56
American Dilemma, An (Myrdal 1944), 160
"American Scholar, The" (Emerson 1937), 172, 173–4
America's Coming of Age (Brooks 1915), 149
anarchism, and modernism, 41
Anarchy and Order (Read 1954), 41
Anna Karenina (Tolstoy 1873–1877), 92–3, 143

anthropological perspective, in Menand's critique of Trilling, 116
"antitheory," in *The Norton Anthology of Theory and Criticism*, 56, 57–9, 61
Apology (Plato), 11, 15–16, 17, 18, 21, 198
Arbery, Glenn, 48, 105
"Archibald MacLeish and the World" (Wilson 1940), 117
Aristophanes, 20, 21
Aristotle, and Aristotelian tradition: Arnold's paraphrase of text on poetry, 37; and humanistic tradition, 73–109; and overview of history of literary criticism, 2; and science, 178; Trilling on, 139; and view of poetry, 37, 73, 75–9, 82
Arnold, Matthew: Aristotle and humanistic tradition in works of, 89–93; on Burke, 131; and concept of "men of culture," 145–6, 151; and cultural studies, 7, 9; and humanistic tradition, 3, 144; and Neoplatonic tradition, 5; and Romantic claims for poetry, 35–9; and science, 75; and Trilling's concept of "culture," 133; and view of literature as "criticism of life," 138–9; views of similar to those of Wilson and Trilling, 112, 145

CPSIA information can be obtained
at www.ICGtesting.com
Printed in the USA
LVHW011748121119
637142LV00013B/415